Young Liszt

U.S. DISTRIBUTOR
DUFOUR EDITIONS
CHESTER SPRINGS
PA 19425-0007
(610) 458-5005

Franz Liszt's Paris 1823 – 1835

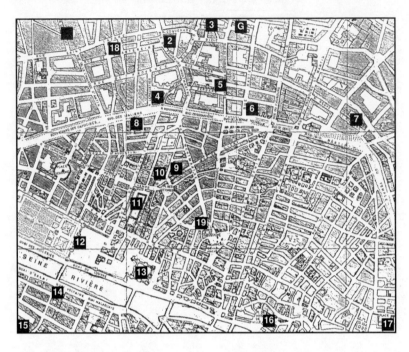

1 Mme Alix's School
2 Church of Notre Dame de Lorette
3 Church of St Vincent de Paul
4 Opéra (Académie Royale de Musique)
5 Conservatoire
6 Gymnase
7 Wauxhall
8 Théâtre des Italiens (Bouffons)
9 Erard Showrooms
10 Church of les Petits Pères
11 Palais Royale
12 Palais des Tuileries
13 Palais du Louvre
14 D'Agoult residence
15 Apponyi residence
16 Hotel de Ville
17 Hugo residence
18 Salle Chantereine
19 Church of St Eustache
G Garrison

Young Liszt

IWO AND PAMELA ZAŁUSKI

U.S. DISTRIBUTOR
DUFOUR EDITIONS
CHESTER SPRINGS
PA 19425-0007
(610) 458-5005

Peter Owen Publishers
London & Chester Springs

PETER OWEN PUBLISHERS
73 Kenway Road London SW5 0RE
Peter Owen books are distributed in the USA by
Dufour Editions Inc. Chester Springs PA 19425–0007

First published in Great Britain 1997
© Iwo and Pamela Załuski 1997

ISBN 0–7206–1003–6

A catalogue record for this book is available from
the British Library

Printed and bound in Great Britain by
Biddles of Guildford and King's Lynn

*The authors should like to acknowledge the help in the
preparation of this book of*

Jan Hoare, Michael Short (Liszt Society, London),
Maria Eckhardt (Budapest),
Dr Emese Duka-Zólyomi, Mária Žišková (Bratislava),
Gunther Fischer (Bayreuth),
Dr Fred Büttner (Munich)
Dr Gerhard Winkler (Eisenstadt),
Bruno Desoutter, Marie Caruel, Irène Bentami (Bernay),
Philippe Autexier, Nadine Massias, Francine de Bellaigue, (Bordeaux),
Yves Castel (Dinan),
Marie Solange Vincent (Dijon),
Philippe Durey (Lyon),
Martine Nougarède, Raphaële Mouren, Pascal Trarieux (Nîmes),
Christiane Weissenbacher (Strasbourg) and
Robert Gillis (Toulouse).

Contents

Illustrations between pages 118 and 119

Western Hungary (Burgenland)
in 1811

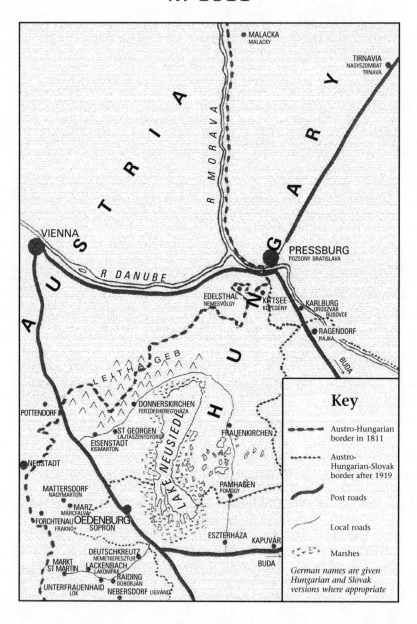

MALACKA
MALACKY

TIRNAVIA
NAGYSZOMBAT
TRNAVA

A U S T R I A

R MORAVA

H U N G A R Y

VIENNA

PRESSBURG
POZSONY BRATISLAVA

R DANUBE

EDELSTHAL
NEMESVÖLGY

KITSEE
KOPCSÉNY

KARLBURG
OROSZVAR
RUSOVCE

RAGENDORF
RAJKA

BUDA

LEITHA GEB

POTTENDORF

DONNERSKIRCHEN
FERTŐFEHEREGYHÁZA

ST GEORGEN
LAJTASZENTGYÖRGY

EISENSTADT
KISMARTON

FRAUENKIRCHEN

NEUSTADT

LAKE NEUSIED

PAMHAGEN
POMOGY

MATTERSDORF
NAGYMARTON

MARZ
MARCFALVA

FORCHTENAU
FRAKNO

OEDENBURG
SOPRON

ESZTERHÁZA

KAPUVÁR

DEUTSCHKREUTZ
NEMETKERESZTUR

MARKT
ST MARTIN

LACKENBACH
LAKOMPAK

RAIDING
DOBORJÁN

BUDA

UNTERFRAUENHAID
LÖK

NEBERSDORF LIGVÁND

Key

- - - Austro-Hungarian
border in 1811

· · · Austro-
Hungarian-Slovak
border after 1919

Post roads

Local roads

Marshes

*German names are given
Hungarian and Slovak
versions where appropriate*

ONE

Adam Liszt's Burgenland

THE EASTERN Austrian province of Burgenland is a sliver
of land stretching from a point just short of the River Danube
at Bratislava in the north to a short, Alpine frontier with Slovenia
to the south. Until it was ceded to Austria after World War I the
province had always been part of the ancient kingdom of Hungary. In the latter part of the eighteenth century, this region of
western Hungary was peopled by a mix of Hungarians, Austrians,
Croats, Slovenes, Slovaks and gipsies, all living in varying states
of apartheid or integration – a true microcosm of the multi-ethnic
Austro-Hungarian Habsburg Empire. Despite its proximity to Vienna,
the administrative hub of the northern part of the region was
Bratislava, then known by its official German name, Pressburg
(Pozsony in Hungarian). A fine city whose imposing tenth-cen-
tury castle still stands sentinel on the Danube from its perch above
the river, Pressburg was situated at a point where three major
European ethnic groups met. To the north-east lay the Slav lands,
to the west the Germans and to the south-east the Hungarians.
The result was a cosmopolitan city where, apart from the official
German, many different languages and dialects were heard in the
streets and markets, as merchants, peasants and travellers from all
over the region mixed. Music, from the classical European tradition, through Slavonic folk-dances to the exotic virtuosity of the
gipsy Csárdás, played a vital part in the city's cultural life. Every
musician worth his salt made a point of being heard there, including the six-year-old Mozart, who, accompanied by his sister and
parents, took time off from entertaining the Empress Maria Theresa
and her numerous children at Schönbrunn and braved the freezing

winter of 1762–3 to play for the very appreciative Hungarian aristocracy.

This cabal of nobles was centred round Pressburg, the castle being the venue of the convention of the Hungarian States, which took place every two years. Despite adhering to Magyar traditions, music and dress, they saw themselves as Hungarians within the multi-ethnic framework of the Empire and thus were loyal Austrians in the same way as Scots and Welsh are loyal Britons. They spoke German as their first – sometimes only – language. By far the most important of these were the Princes Esterházy, whose palace at Eisenstadt – Kismarton in Hungarian – was one of the most magnificent in the Empire. If Pressburg was the administrative hub of the region, then Eisenstadt was the cultural heart and soul, whose influence spread far beyond its confines.

The Palace of Eisenstadt was built between 1663 and 1672 by Prince Paul Esterházy, the first of the dynasty to hold the title. It was situated fifty kilometres from Vienna in the Leithagebirge hills overlooking the Hungarian plains and the marshy Lake Neusiedl, through which today's Austro-Hungarian border passes. The marshes were rich in wildfowl, and many roofs in the area boasted a stork's nest. The big but shallow and stagnant lake, and the swamps around its edges, were a haven for mosquitoes, which accounted for a high incidence of malaria in the region. Eisenstadt was originally intended as a summer residence but very soon became the principal Esterházy castle, for there were many others in north-western Hungary, in addition to the family's official residence in Vienna.

Prince Paul Anton Esterházy inherited the title in 1721. A talented violinist and cellist, he established a strong musical ethos at Eisenstadt with the help of his Kapellmeister, Gregor Werner. In 1761, in anticipation of the aged Werner's death, the Prince offered the post of assistant Kapellmeister to the up-and-coming Joseph Haydn, then not yet thirty. The following year Prince Paul Anton died, and the successor to the title was his 48-year-old younger brother, Nicolaus. Prince Nicolaus I, nicknamed 'The Magnificent', was a soldier, musician and art connoisseur who lived in the hunting lodge – humble by Esterházy standards – of Süttör, near Fertőd, to the south of his beloved Lake Neusiedl.

Prince Nicolaus moved to Eisenstadt and promptly began rebuilding Süttör as a palace intended to rival Versailles. In the meantime he kept Haydn on and advanced further the musical ethos established by his brother. He was also passionately interested in the theatre, which he developed in parallel with the music. When old Gregor Werner died, Prince Nicolaus appointed Haydn as Kapellmeister and moved most of his court bodily to the newly finished Eszterháza. Unlike in most courts of the Habsburg Empire, the Esterházy orchestra was part-time, made up of musical employees of the enormous family estates and commercial concerns – mostly clerks, estate managers and timber-mill operatives – who were appointed to their jobs as much for their musical background as for their professional qualification. They would be on call to take part in whatever was being produced, be it an intimate soirée or a large-scale religious work. Not everyone was happy about moving to Eszterháza, not least on account of the mosquitoes. Despite the enormity of the palace – there were 126 rooms, richly decorated and furnished in rococo style – the servants' quarters were small and cramped and could not accommodate the families of the staff. The musicians among them longed to return to Eisenstadt.

One of the numerous villages in thrall to the Esterházys was Edelstal – Nemesvölgy in Hungarian. It was situated ten kilometres to the south of Pressburg, at the northern tip of today's Burgenland. In 1775 the local school welcomed as its new schoolmaster 20-year-old Georg List and his 22-year-old wife, Barbara. They had just married at Barbara's home village of Rusovce, on the Danube a few kilometres downstream from Pressburg, in today's Slovakia. Barbara's parents, the Schlesaks, were poor tenant farmers. Georg's family originated in Lower Austria and had migrated to the Esterházy lands in search of work. His appointment, like all appointments in the village, was made through the Esterházy administration, which was impressed by his ability to play the violin, piano and organ. From the start Georg proved himself to be an efficient if unstable teacher who in turn terrified his pupils with his aggressive manner and inspired them with his musicianship. He was a passionate choirmaster and a strict disciplinarian to whom corporal punishment was very much the norm.

In the September of that same year the Lists produced their first child, Michael. The following year, on 16 December, Barbara presented her husband with a brother for Michael. The boy was baptised Adam. Two years later Magdalena was born, and when she was only one year old Michael died, the first in a tragic line of infant deaths in the List family. Of their thirteen children at least five died in infancy. Adam was taught at the local school by his father and proved to be a very bright pupil and a devout member of the Roman Catholic Church. From his father Adam inherited a passion for music; Georg was pleased with this and formally taught him the basic skills. Soon Adam, apart from singing in his father's choir, was also showing promise as a pianist and cellist. Georg watched his son grow into a strong, spiritual and highly intelligent boy.

In 1786 Georg List was transferred – possibly because of complaints about his teaching methods – to Kittsee, the next village to the east, which was dominated by the Esterházy castle used by Prince Nicolaus during the conference of the Hungarian States. The List family now consisted of ten-year-old Adam, with Magdalena, Rosalie, Anna Maria, Barbara – and another on the way.

Adam's musical talents were noted by Prince Nicolaus. Like all musical employees, Georg was required to stand by with his violin at Eisenstadt or Eszterháza, and he often brought Adam along too. On one such occasion young Adam List, not yet into his teens, found himself by chance playing the cello in the orchestra. Haydn took to the boy enough to play a game of cards with him afterwards. This event marked the beginning of a hot and cold relationship between the Esterházys and the Lists. Adam was overwhelmed by the splendour of Eisenstadt and by the romance of playing in an orchestra under the great Haydn. He dreamt that one day he, too, would be a professional musician.

On 9 May 1788, while twelve-year-old Adam List was dreaming of fame and fortune and agonizing over ways of escaping the humdrum poverty of life in Kittsee, a hundred kilometres away upstream on the Danube, in Krems, Maria Anna was born in House No. 314 to the 73-year-old baker Matthias Lager and his 38-year-old wife Franziska, the daughter of a Bavarian watchmaker. The Lagers were a large family, and Anna's childhood was hard, not least because of the unrest in Europe at the time.

Emperor Joseph II of Austria considered himself an enlightened ruler, and many of his ideas on land and social reform owed some passing allegiance to the prevalent ideas on human rights. A decade had passed since the American War of Independence curtailed British imperialism in America. Closer to home, Anna was just over a year old when the Bastille was stormed in Paris in 1789, marking the beginning of the end of absolute monarchy in France. These events sent shivers down the spines of the remaining European monarchs, including that of Emperor Joseph, who in that year saw not only the arrest of his sister, Queen Marie-Antoinette, wife of the equally ill-fated King Louis XVI of France, but also the revolt and secession of the Austrian Netherlands (broadly today's Belgium) from Habsburg rule. His empire was the most multi-ethnic in Europe. Apart from the German-speaking Austrian heartlands, it included Hungary, Bohemia, Moravia, Slovakia, the southern Polish province of Galicia, western Ukraine, northwestern Romania, most of Croatia, the Italian states of Milan, Parma and Tuscany, parts of southern Bavaria and the Black Forest, and the Austrian Netherlands, all speaking a dozen different languages, not counting dialects. The desire for democracy and independence, which led to the rise of the Jacobins – possibly the first modern democratic agitators of history – was a serious threat to Imperial power in Europe. Added to this was the growing philosophy of nationalism, then still very much in its infancy. The Habsburg Empire lacked any united national sense of purpose, which made it all the more vulnerable to nationalist movements within its borders.

In 1790 both Emperor Joseph II and Prince Nicolaus Esterházy died. The former was succeeded by his brother Leopold II and the latter by Prince Anton, who disbanded the orchestra and thereby brought to a close the golden age of music at the court of Esterházy. He retained Haydn, who had been awarded a pension for life by Prince Nicolaus, although by then he had virtually no duties. Also retained were the great violinist Luigi Tomasini, a small wind band and a small string band. That year also saw the beginnings of major renovations at Eisenstadt.

The same year Georg List was transferred to Pottendorf, and fourteen-year-old Adam, supported by the Catholic Church, left home to enrol at the Roman Catholic Gymnasium in Pressburg, where he was to remain for five years. Adam studied philosophy, geography, history – and Hungarian, which he never mastered. He also studied music with the former concert keyboard player Franz Paul Riegler. Under his tutelage Adam learnt to play the guitar, the flute and the violin, in addition to the cello. But his greatest advances were in piano technique: in this and other areas of his musical development he was fortunate that Pressburg was among the first cities to benefit from the latest music fashions and publications to come from Vienna. His mother often used to visit him at the Gymnasium, bringing news from home, encouragement and bread and *speck* (fatty smoked bacon).

The Emperor Leopold II died in 1792, after only two years on the Imperial throne, and was succeeded by his son, Franz II. Two years later Prince Anton Esterházy died and was succeeded by his son, 29-year-old Prince Nicolaus II. Nicolaus disliked Eszterháza, moved back to Vienna and used Eisenstadt as his summer palace. He was not a practising musician, although he had a penchant for church music. He had inherited Haydn, but the two men did not get on, and there was some acrimony between them. The Prince's taste in music was also suspect – he preferred Michael Haydn's Masses to those of Joseph, and he had little regard for Beethoven. He did re-establish the orchestra, but lacked the inspiration and dedication of his grandfather, and the musical life of Eisenstadt was a shadow of its former glory. His artistic tastes lay rather in painting, drama, architecture, sculpture and literature – he spoke and read several languages. He collected artefacts and enlarged the picture gallery, which his recent predecessors had neglected. He enriched the Esterházy library and built the sumptuous theatre for which he regularly engaged strolling players, marionette troupes and gipsy dance bands. He generously entertained and patronized many leading artists. He was also an avid womanizer, whose conquests included Luigi Tomasini's daughter – won with the dubious collusion of Tomasini himself.

As Anna Lager grew up in Krems, her parents witnessed the rise to power in France of Napoleon Bonaparte – the embodiment of all that was anathema to Imperial Europe. Emperor Franz, fearing the dangers, joined a coalition with Prussia, Holland, Great Britain and Spain, as a barrier against him. This was to little avail, as in 1795, to Emperor Franz's consternation, Napoleon invaded Italy, seized and plundered Milan and Florence and overthrew the Doges of Venice.

That year Adam List graduated from the Gymnasium in Pressburg, and on 21 September he entered the Franciscan Monastery in Malacky, thirty kilometres to the north of Pressburg, as a novice for one year. He was registered as: 'Adamus Matthäus Liszt, natio et locus natalis Germanus, Edelsthal, aetas 22'. In fact he was aged nineteen. The spelling of the surname was probably magyarized by his father: 'List' was pronounced 'Lisht' in Hungarian, so Georg substituted 'sz' to obtain the ordinary 's' sound. Adam adopted this now definitive spelling, thus ensuring the correct pronunciation of his name. When he had completed his year's novitiate, he joined the Monastery at Tyrnavia (Trnava in Slovak),

forty kilometres north-east of Pressburg. Adam Liszt had forsaken
a musical career and chosen the religious life.

In the meantime Georg was moved again, this time to the village school at St Georgen (in Hungarian Lajtaszentgyörgy) in the
Leithagebirge hills just to the east of Eisenstadt. In 1796 Matthias
Lager died in Krems, aged eighty-one, followed six months later
by his widow. The house was sold and the inheritance divided
among the children, most of whom were by now independent.
Nine-year-old Anna and her brother Franz, two years older, found
temporary refuge with older siblings in Krems. To make matters
worse, the war with Napoleon was getting closer. Young men were
conscripted as reinforcements to be sent over the Brenner Pass
into Italy to confront the French invaders. This army was defeated by Napoleon at Rivoli, on Lake Garda, leaving Austria's
southern flank guarded only by the Alps. In 1797 Napoleon crossed
these into the Austrian heartland at Villach and Klagenfurt and
marched on towards Vienna. At Leoben the Austrians negotiated
a peace, whereby they relinquished their claims to their Italian
possessions to Napoleon's Cisalpine Republic, and Austria breathed
a sigh of relief. By way of compensation, Napoleon awarded Austria the Republic of Venice.

It was time for Franz and Anna Lager to move on and build
their own lives. Franz found his way to Mattersdorf (in Hungarian
Nagymarton) to the south of Eisenstadt, where he manufactured
soap. Anna, not even in her teens, went to seek her fortune in
Vienna. Pretty and charming, she was resourceful enough to find
employment as a housemaid, first in the Kärntnerstrasse, then in
the Tiefer Graben. Vienna was a hive of military activity, its narrow,
cobbled streets constantly echoing to the sound of horses as officers,
soldiers and Imperial officials went briskly about the business of
preparing for war. Gone, for the time being, were the foppish,
superficial attitudes of the pleasure-seeking Viennese; it was time
to confront the real world. As unkempt soldiers press-ganged from
the poverty-stricken villages of Ruthenia, Transylvania and the
Balkans watched the carriages of the rich clattering to the Opera,
their eyes filled with incomprehension. Anna's job enabled her to
observe, listen and learn about the ways of the world. She watched
closely who came and went and picked up street wisdom. Conversation among the people she served revolved largely around Napoleon
and his campaigns, and she feared from what she gleaned that it
would be only a matter of time before Vienna fell to the French.

Meanwhile, Adam was having second thoughts about the priest-hood and requested permission to leave. This was granted on 29 July 1797. According to the Church, he had been dismissed for 'unsteady and inconsistent behaviour'. With a sense of failure mixed with relief, he returned to Pressburg and enrolled at the University to study philosophy. After one term he was forced to scrap the idea, as he had no money. The Church was no longer interested in investing in a failed priest, and his father certainly could not afford it; especially as his mother was pregnant – for the thirteenth and last time – with Friderika, who would survive only a few months. Adam had no alternative but to abandon his studies and find a job. Fortunately his early connection with the Esterházys paid off, and he found employment as a clerk on their estate at Forchtenau – in Hungarian Frakno – twenty kilometres from Eisenstadt. It was only a few kilometres from St Georgen, where his father was teaching. The appointment was from 1 January 1798. Prince Nicolaus had gained not only a clerk but a musician, and Adam looked forward to taking part in the concerts at Eisenstadt, as well as being near his parents once more.

No sooner had Adam settled in to his job than his mother died of dropsy on 31 March. On 29 April, after what was felt to be an indecent interval, Georg remarried. Adam's new stepmother, Barbara Weninger, of St Georgen, was a year younger than him. In April 1799 his first half-brother, Anton, was born.

An army under the Archduke Karl, Emperor Franz's younger brother, set off up the Danube to rout the French under General Jourdan in Germany, while an allied Austrian and Russian army under General Suvarov marched back into northern Italy, recaptured Milan and pressed on to take Genoa. The victory was short-lived, because the following year Napoleon moved back into northern Italy with lightning speed and defeated the Austrians at Marengo, to the north of Genoa. At the same time, General Moreau defeated the Austrians at Hohenlinden, just to the east of Munich, and advanced on Vienna. Emperor Franz called for an armistice, and once more Austria could celebrate the easing of pressure on its territories.

In June 1800 Adam was promoted to a managerial post at Kapuvár, a town on the way to Győr. Kapuvár was deep in Hungary proper, and few people spoke German. As Adam's Hungarian was virtually non-existent, he found himself unable to function, and four months later returned to Forchtenau to news of trouble with his father. Once again his teaching methods had been the subject of a number of complaints, and there were moves to get rid of him. Adam did what he could to reason with his father, who had grown even more aggressive and irascible than ever. His corporal punishments had regularly overstepped the abuse line, even for those times, and the following year he was sacked.

Adam, out of a mixture of filial concern and the possibility of having to support his father and his still growing family (at this time Adam's second half-brother, Andreas, had died at two months and his step-mother was pregnant with Barbara), tried to intercede with Prince Nicolaus to give his father back his job. The Prince was adamant that Georg was not a fit person to be in charge of children, but, because of his past loyalty – and presumably his musicianship – he agreed to re-employ him as bookkeeper at his timber yards at Marz, three kilometres from Forchtenau. Adam was relieved that his father still had a job and somewhere to live.

Eisenstadt was well within riding distance from Forchtenau, and over the ensuing years Adam frequently visited the Palace on business. While there he involved himself in the musical ethos of the place. He met Haydn again, as well as Haydn's eventual successor, Johann Nepomuk Fuchs, who had been his deputy since 1802. By now Old Papa Haydn was virtually retired and living in Vienna, but he still liked to keep an eye and an ear on what was going on, the early enmity with Prince Nicolaus now largely forgotten. Adam also met the violinist Luigi Tomasini and the Pressburg-born pianist and composer, Johann Nepomuk Hummel, who had been at Eisenstadt since 1804. In 1805 he met the Italian-born but Paris-based opera composer, Luigi Cherubini, who was visiting Eisenstadt. Adam always looked forward eagerly to these visits. Fired by what he had seen and heard at Eisenstadt, and aware of Prince Nicolaus's love of church music, he wrote a Te Deum for mixed choir and orchestra with organ, which he humbly dedicated to the Prince. He gave the score to Fuchs, who had it performed with the choir and orchestra, pronounced it good and recommended it to Prince Nicolaus. As a result, in February 1805, the Prince transferred Adam to Eisenstadt, where his duties as a clerk alternated with playing in the eighty-piece orchestra and singing bass in the choir. During public concerts and theatrical productions, his additional brief was to sell tickets.

After two years of relative peace and quiet, Napoleon was on the move again, initially in the North Atlantic and the New World, but his adventures grew to involve the whole of Europe. In 1804 he crowned himself Emperor of the French and set in motion a maritime campaign against Great Britain, which had joined a Third Coalition to block his ambitions. Adam Liszt was already installed at Eisenstadt when Napoleon's plans were dashed in the waters off Cape Trafalgar in October 1805, when Admiral Villeneuve's Franco-Spanish navy was destroyed by Lord Nelson. But the new French Emperor refused to fall back and rest on his laurels, shelved the idea of invading England and embarked on a definitive drive eastwards with the destruction of the other Third Coalition nations in mind. Again Austria quaked in fear, and Adam was consternated by the news. The monumental changes taking place in Europe were getting very close to home.

Autumn had already given way to winter when seventeen-year-old Anna Lager watched as Napoleon's army, having defeated the Austrians at Ulm, continued unopposed along the Danube and entered, victorious, into Vienna, having negotiated the safety of the citizens and the buildings with the city magistrates. But Emperor Franz, although down, was not yet out. The Russians, having marched from the east, joined forces with a fresh Austrian army to confront Napoleon at Austerlitz. Napoleon was not only victorious but the Russian army was utterly destroyed. Its remnants fled eastwards and with them Russian ambitions in central and western Europe – for the time being. Pressburg was the venue of the subsequent Peace Treaty in which Emperor Franz was forced to cede the historic Habsburg lands of the Tyrol and Voralberg, as well as all of Italy and Austrian Dalmatia, today Croatia's Adriatic coast. Anna Lager saw nothing but despondency and humiliation on the faces of the Viennese.

In 1806 Georg was in trouble again. His bookkeeping at the timber yards at Marz was suspect, and had to be investigated. Accusations of embezzlement were found to be false, but his accounts were inefficiently done, and he was again moved to nearby Mattersdorf and given the job of head shepherd. In December his second wife died, having borne five children, of whom at least two survived into adulthood. In February the following year, Georg married 26-year-old Magdalena Richter – without Prince Nicolaus's permission, thus causing further hassle with his master. In October she gave birth to Johanna, who lived for seven months. The newly-weds began to visit Vienna – under the false pretence of Esterházy estates business. For this they clandestinely borrowed estate carriages and horses, which always returned lame or exhausted. Despite his father's antics, Adam was getting involved in the Eisenstadt music scene. On 13 September 1807 he played in the orchestra in the first performance of Beethoven's Mass in C, which the composer himself conducted at the Bergkirche and which Prince Nicolaus had commissioned and subsequently dismissed as 'unbearably ridiculous and detestable'. He also took part in an official sailing outing on Lake Neusiedl as a crew member and applied to the estate to have his soaked clothing replaced.

In 1808 the vacancy arose of estate manager at the Esterházy sheep farm at Raiding – in Hungarian Doborján – fifty kilometres south of Eisenstadt. As the job was a promotion, well paid, and included a house, Adam applied for it and was duly appointed, as from 3 October. The village of Raiding consisted of sixty-four peasant cottages, built of sun-dried brick plastered with lime-washed mortar, and thatched straw roofs, on the poplar-lined eastern bank of the Raidingbach. Arriving in the village along the sandy track, Adam crossed the little bridge over the stream and passed under the arched, stone gate – which still bore the coat-of-arms of the original owners, the Császár family – and into the courtyard of his new home, a T-shaped, single-storey stone building, with a tiled roof. It was originally a manor, built in 1587, which had been recently acquired by Prince Nicolaus. There were three outhouses – and a well – set among casually planted fruit trees. To the east of the village, the woods had been felled for timber and fuel and vineyards planted; to the west was forest. A sandy track linked Raiding with Unterfrauenhaid (where the main church was) and Markt St Martin to the west and the road to Oedenburg – today Sopron in Hungarian – and Eisenstadt to the north.

Like all Esterházy employees, Adam was paid both in cash – 130 gulden per annum – and in kind. Apart from the free house, his further entitlement included 24 pecks of wheat, 48 pecks of corn, 10 barrels of wine, 10 fathoms of firewood and 20 hundredweight of hay.

His duties carried some large-scale responsibilities. He was in overall charge of the estate, including the staff, the sheepmasters, shepherds and farmhands, and their wages, and he had powers of dismissal wherever he saw fit. In winter he would be responsible for fodder, and in springtime for the shearing and subsequent selling of the wool to the merchant Ruben Hirschler in nearby Lackenbach. Fleeces were also to be delivered to Oedenburg, the

main town in the area. Animal carcasses were to be disposed of to
the knacker in Markt St Martin or to Franz Lager's soap factory
in Mattersdorf – the town where Adam's father now worked. The
estate ran to 50,000 fat, shaggy-fleeced sheep, 100 goats and an
unknown number of working Hungarian black-coated dogs (Prince
Nicolaus once bet an English noble that he had more sheepdogs
than the Englishman had sheep – he won his bet). Adam was allotted
a landau in which to get around the estate and to drive to Eisenstadt
to fetch a doctor in an emergency. The population of Raiding consisted of about 650 German speakers, of mixed ethnic groups.

In the woods beyond the village lived an encampment of gipsies, whose involvement with the world at large was peripheral. As
fortune-tellers they claimed to read signs and stars, and they were
often consulted in matters of fortune by the villagers, in much the
same way as horoscopes are read in papers today. But it was as
musicians that they were really admired and regularly booked to
perform. No Hungarian wedding or celebration was complete without
the distinctive sound of the Csárdás.

In the spring of 1809, while Adam was supervising his first
sheep-shearing, war was again in the air. Napoleon had embarked
on his Spanish campaigns and was having enough problems for
Austria to take advantage of his weakness and declare war on
France. This time the Austrian army, having learned new skills
and tactics on the battlefields of Europe, was honed into a veritable fighting machine. Napoleon, now accustomed to waging war
on a number of fronts simultaneously, managed to defeat the new-
look Austrians and again marched on Vienna. The aristocracy
fled, and on 11 May Anna Lager, like every inhabitant of the city,
learned the meaning of modern warfare the hard way. Instead of
two armies confronting each other on a field of battle, the French
cannons opened up and began the bombardment of the city, its
buildings and its civilians. The effect on the population was devastating, and many became crazed with terror. In the basement of
his brother's house, Beethoven cowered in fear and pain; the noise
of the cannons physically hurt his damaged hearing. Clutching
pillows to his head he tried to sublimate his agony by continuing
with his Piano Concerto in E flat – ironically dubbed by histori-
ans 'The Emperor'. In his house 77-year-old Papa Haydn tried to
calm his panic-stricken servants and was struck by blind panic
himself. The bombardment made him ill, and he had to be put to
bed. The next day the Vienna elders surrendered, and Napoleon

marched in triumph into the city. He placed a guard of honour at Haydn's house. One of the officers, Clément Sulémy by name, called on the old maestro and sang 'In native worth' from his oratorio *The Creation* with such feeling that tears came to Haydn's eyes. Haydn never recovered from the shock of the bombardment and died on 31 May, wondering what kind of a world he was leaving, in which a conqueror first bombards you into submission before saluting and honouring you.

Anna Lager decided to leave Vienna and join her brother Franz in Mattersdorf, where she met Adam Liszt. She saw a good-looking, tall, slim, well-built 32-year-old with blond hair which he wore to his shoulders; in his eyes she saw intelligence, prudence and a decisive nature. He was well-dressed, as befitting a man with responsibilities. He saw a strikingly pretty girl of twenty-one, tall and slim, with a serene expression and enormous eyes. She had a luxuriant mane of black hair piled high on her head; she was lively, intelligent and well-read, and as their friendship developed, they found they had a great deal in common. Both were religious, and both loved music; Anna had a lovely voice, and Adam often accompanied her on guitar.

In July, after the fall of Vienna and the final defeat of the Austrian army at the battle of Wagram – to the west of Pressburg and thus very close to home – Adam watched the arrival of French soldiers in Raiding. He had hoped that the war would not reach this rural outback of the Empire, but these hopes were ill-founded. Veterans of the wars, many crippled, scarred or limbless, were to be seen all over the Empire, returning home or just passing through. A garrison of Napoleonic troops was installed at Raiding in forty-two specially built 'mercenary' houses. As an army of occupation they constituted a nuisance rather than a force for oppression, and apart from ravaging the forests for timber they did no real harm.

Despite these reminders of the horrors of war, there was romance in the air. It was obvious to everyone in Raiding and its environs that their well-liked manager and the pretty young girl from Krems were in love, and it was no surprise when Adam wrote to Eisenstadt requesting permission to marry. Prince Nicolaus eventually gave it, for some reason taking a year to get round to it. Perhaps he wrily recalled Adam's irresponsible father, who had failed to observe this regulation courtesy three years previously.

Adam and Anna were married on 11 January 1811. The date would perhaps have been significant to the gipsy soothsayers had they known that the date was a perfect, invertible palindrome – surely the most auspicious of signs to the superstitious. The wedding took place at the thirteenth-century Parish and Pilgrimage Church in Unterfrauenhaid, a village three kilometres from Raiding. As both were devout Roman Catholics, it was a full ceremony, with a dean, a priest and deacons officiating. The witnesses were the Raiding schoolmaster Johann Rohrer and Anton Illéssy, whose family owned the estate until 1810. Afterwards the young couple returned to the little manor at Raiding, to a feast beside the blazing stove to keep the white, Hungarian winter at bay.

Anna's dowry, between 1,200 and 3,000 gulden (the figure varies), was invested for the family's future. She became a working wife and took on her share of her husband's responsibilities. She supervised the servants in the everyday running of the house and the garden and kept an eye on the care of the hens, geese and ducks that roamed freely on either side of the stream.

During the lambing season Anna announced that she was pregnant. On 26 March, a French astronomer from Viviers by the name of Flaugèrgues announced the arrival of a comet in the solar system.

Anna regularly drew water from the well in the courtyard, and one day in early summer she slipped and fell in. Fortunately, the well was not very deep, and her clothes inflated enough to prevent her from drowning. Her cries for help were heard by a farmhand, who rushed to the rescue and hauled her out.

Meanwhile, talk revolved everywhere around the comet. As the year progressed, it increasingly lit up the night sky, and stargazers everywhere watched its progress in fascination. Fortune-tellers were having a field day, and the gipsies in the woods spoke of little else. Even Napoleon consulted astrologers about the comet's significance – he had Russia on his mind. By the middle of October it was so bright that some contemporary chroniclers wrote of night turning into day.

Adam frequently travelled to Oedenburg on business. On the night of Monday 21 October he was there and followed the schoolboys carrying candles, incense and holy pictures, joining in the traditional procession to the four monasteries outside the town. The ceremony lasted all night, into the early hours of the following morning.

In the early hours of Tuesday 22 October 1811, in the manor at Raiding, Anna Liszt gave birth to Franz.

TWO

The Raiding Years
1811–22

IN ANNA's own words, Franz was an ugly child for the first few days of his life. He was sickly and may have been premature, otherwise Adam would not have gone to Oedenburg at that time. Looking in consternation at her frail baby, Anna thought of the string of infant mortalities of her fecund father-in-law. When he heard the news, Adam returned from Oedenburg on Wednesday 23 October, accompanied by Franz Zambothy, who was to be the baby's godfather. He collected Julianna Frankenberg, née Szalay, of Deutschkreutz (Németkeresztúr in Hungarian), which was on the way. As soon as he saw his new-born son, Adam feared he would not live and decided on his immediate baptism. Anna stayed at home while he and the godparents took the fragile infant to the Pilgrimage Church at Unterfrauenhaid (in Hungarian Lók). The parish priest, Father Georg Mersitz, was called to the stone font. The baby was baptised Franciscus, after St Francis di Paula, the founder of the Order of Minims, Franz Zambothy and Anna's mother and grandmother, who were both named Franciska. The details are recorded in the baptism certificate:

[October] 23	Franciscus	List [*sic*] Adamus ovium Rationista [sheep accountant] Principis Esterházy et Lager Maria Anna	Reiding [*sic*]	Patrini: Zambothy Franciscus et Szalay Julianna	Mersitz Georgius capellanus Lookiensis

Word of Franz's birth reached Eisenstadt, and Prince Nicolaus sent Anna a congratulatory brooch – which is now lost. It also reached the humbler surroundings of the gipsy encampment in the woods outside Raiding, where the birth during the spectacular

prime of the comet evinced great excitement, and the unasham-
edly Messianic utterances of the soothsayers were being quoted
all over Raiding. The child, they said, would return to the village
one day, a great man, rich, honoured and in a glass house – meaning
a coach with glass windows, a luxury few could afford at the time.
Even the midwife who attended the birth predicted the 'glass
coach', which suggested that the prophecy was doing the rounds
that month and applied to all babies born at around the time. For
Franz Liszt, born on the actual night of the comet's apex, the
prophecy came true in 1840, unlike for any other local October
babies of that year.

Adam entertained his own very personal prophecies for his son,
in whom he saw a realization of his own one-time dreams of fame
and fortune. In later years he confided these thoughts to his diary:
'My son, you are destined by Fate. You will become that ideal
artiste, that I hoped vainly in my youth to become. In you my
hopes will be realized. My genius, born at the wrong time in me,
will bear fruit in you. In you will I be rejuvenated and reproduced.'

Adam was already thirty-five years old. His boyhood dreams of
a career in music, which germinated when he played under Haydn
in Eisenstadt even before his teen years, had worn thin. The years
had gone by and his talent had not been picked up beyond a
peripheral involvement in Eisenstadt's musical activities. His Te
Deum, although pronounced good by Fuchs, did not stand the
test of time and is now lost. At this stage, although in a well-paid
and respectable job, he would have been living in a cultural wil-
derness had he not kept up his musical contacts, including Fuchs
and Tomasini. Hummel had left Eisenstadt, and his closest friend
in the town was councillor Ludwig Hofer. Adam called on him at
his official apartment at 39 Esterhazystrasse, opposite the Bergkirche,
every time he was there, and Hofer, with some of the musicians,
visited the Liszts at Raiding, when the talk would be about music
and the spinet would be played. Adam had bought the spinet shortly
after his arrival; the villagers thought it was a waste of money, but
Adam saw it as a musical lifeline. As an Esterházy employee he
had access to all the latest music for the piano from Vienna.

Apart from the traditional classical repertoire of Haydn, Mozart
and the numerous works of the very popular Bohemian composers, there was the radical Ludwig van Beethoven, whose ex-
pansion of form and sonorities was considered unacceptably 'modern'
for many listeners – including Prince Nicolaus. Adam was particularly

fond of Beethoven and had a portrait of the composer hanging on the wall in the house. Then there was the growing trend of Romanticism, specifically in the field of piano music. Piano manufacture was a fast-growing industry, and names like Graf and Stein were synonymous in Vienna with fine, sensitive instruments which in turn created a generation of players anxious to make the most of them. Composer-performers such as Johann Nepomuk Hummel, Ignaz Moscheles, Ferdinand Ries and John Field took up the gauntlet, and the nineteenth century opened to the arrival – in a blaze of musical fireworks – of the Romantic piano concerto. The art of improvisation, rare in the days of Mozart, was a growing trend and overturned established composition techniques. Instead of crafting a work on manuscript paper before playing it, pianists created instant tone poems at the keyboard, which they then wrote down. Adam decided that Hummel and Beethoven did not sound good on the spinet – and anyway the damp caused it to go out of tune. He threw financial caution to the winds and bought himself a piano – a luxury for someone in his position.

Apart from his own piano playing, there was also the music of the gipsies, which Haydn had loved and frequently reworked in a more classical setting, as in the String Quartet Op. 54 No. 2. For a man of Adam Liszt's musical mentality, gipsy music and the odd sessions with friends in his home was not enough. He desperately missed the grand musical extravaganzas at Eisenstadt, and the occasional visits, on estate business, afforded him only a tantalizing glimpse of what might have been: he often reflected that promotion came at a price.

The following March, Georg List was sacked again, this time, it seemed, for good. His regular, unscheduled visits to the Prater in Vienna with his third wife, Magdalena, had been discovered. He was further accused of maltreating the estate horses which he 'borrowed' for the purpose. Added to this were accusations of careless bookkeeping and irregularities with the corn. In despair, for the family were now destitute, Georg went to Raiding to try to persuade Adam to intercede to get his dismissal annulled. Adam tried, but failed. In July Georg, in desperation, walked by night to Raiding to beg his son to accommodate him and his family. Adam had no option but to go to Mattersdorf with an ox-cart, load it with his father's meagre belongings and bring his whole family back to Raiding – much to Anna's annoyance. By then Georg had fathered twenty-two children, but he brought with him between four and eight; some would already have left home, and the fate of others is not known.

Franzi – as he was called in the home – lived on a tightrope between life and death, and his infancy was marked by nervous disorders and fevers. The region was dominated by the malarial swamps of Lake Neusiedl, mainly in the hot summer months. Those able to afford it kept malaria at bay by taking quinine, but the mosquitoes still claimed many lives, and infant mortality was exceptionally high. Franzi was a sickly child anyway, and his early years caused great concern. In keeping with custom, he was vaccinated against smallpox. Vaccination was still in its infancy and was often fatal, especially for a sickly child, but Adam and Anna decided, on balance, that it had to be done. It was an anxious time for the Liszts, and Anna asked her younger sister Therese, who lived in Graz, to come to stay and help her look after Franzi. Aunt Therese, whom Franzi grew to know and love dearly, was a godsend to the Liszts.

The Napoleonic campaigns continued unabated. In 1807, after the defeat of Prussia, Napoleon created the puppet Duchy of Warsaw out of the Prussian sector of partitioned Poland. In Napoleon the Poles saw hopes of a restored Poland which would include the Austrian sector, Galicia. In 1809 Austria invaded the Duchy and took Warsaw, but the victory was short-lived, and the Austrians were driven out. In the summer of 1812, as Georg List was moving in with his son, and Franzi had begun to crawl, Napoleon was in Warsaw, building up his multi-national Grande Armée of half a million men for his invasion of Russia. The French soldiers stationed in Raiding left and marched north to join their Emperor. Before the year was out, to Austria's relief, the campaign was over. Napoleon, the greatest general in history, was defeated by Russia, as a result of a scorched earth policy and a particularly severe winter.

The Asiatic winter encroaches well into central Europe, and that of 1812–13 was strongly felt in Raiding. Snow lay thick on the ground, and temperatures were well below average. Adam was forced to give the excuse of his father and his family staying with him, when he was accused by the Esterházy administration of using more than his official quota of firewood, as specified in Prince Nicolaus's 'Thirty-five Rules for Employees'.

The following year Georg managed to find the first of a series of temporary jobs, as steward with Count Niczky in Nebersdorf.

At the same time, Adam's duties included temporary postings, in turn to Pamhagen (Pomogy), in the marshlands to the south-east of Lake Neusiedl, Frauenkirchen sixteen kilometres to the north, and then to Donnerskirchen (Fertőfehéregyháza), fifteen kilometres north of Eisenstadt, before returning to Raiding. The family went with him.

Franzi was well into toddlerhood when his precarious health deteriorated dramatically. His parents expected the worst and had a little coffin prepared. Miraculously, largely through Aunt Therese's tireless ministrations, he survived, but the next four years continued with a never-ending series of crises. By 1815 Adam and Anna saw Franzi's health start to improve, and they were reasonably confident that any immediate danger was now past and that he would survive beyond infancy. News from Vienna also gave rise to cautious optimism. The Austrian capital was awash with diplomats and politicians, all assembled under the aegis of a great Congress, convened to redraw the map of Europe in the wake of the final defeat of Napoleon on the field of Waterloo. The Austrian Government under Foreign Minister Prince Clemens Metternich played host to the Alliance leaders, including Tsar Alexander, Charles Talleyrand, Lord Castlereagh and the Duke of Wellington. With Napoleon banished to St Helena, every indication pointed to peace in Europe, and Vienna expressed its relief in a bout of unbridled celebration that often verged on debauchery. There were concerts, banquets and events of every kind, and wine, beer and brandy flowed in abundance. One of the great musical attractions was the famous Vienna Musikkapelle, a five-piece gipsy band under the direction of Johann Bihari, the son of a gipsy musician from Pressburg. His virtuosity dominated musical conversation that year. After nearly two decades of sober apprehension Vienna returned to the hedonistic flippancy to which it had been accustomed. The Liszts looked forward to the future with renewed hope.

Franzi's mental and intellectual development told a different story to that of his health. His warm personality, charm and wit won him many friends. He had a clear, inquiring mind that liked order, and he showed a depth of interest and understanding for everything about him that was unusual in a boy so young. He was easygoing, liked to be helpful and enjoyed working at things and getting them right. Although he was physically delicate he was an exceptionally good-looking child and had about him a certain air of confidence which suggested a high rather than peasant birth.

He was a religious boy who loved music above all else. He enjoyed listening to his father playing the piano and accompanying his mother on the guitar while she sang.

Among Adam and Anna's friends were the Frankenbergs of Deutschkreutz – Julianna Frankenberg was Franzi's godmother and her husband was manager of the Esterházy estate there. On one such visit there was a get-together of some local families, among them the Liszts. While the adults stayed indoors all the children trooped off to the garden to play. Four-year-old Franzi, being the most delicate, was 'persuaded' to stand against a wall while the other children pelted him with mud. Franzi was not enamoured of this game, and his howls brought the grown-ups to the rescue, and the game was summarily suspended. The game Franzi enjoyed most was messing about at the piano. One of the children at the reunion was Maria, the little daughter of a Captain Niesner. Some months later, Franzi and Maria were vamping about at the Niesners' piano when Franzi fell into a sudden fit. He shivered uncontrollably and had to be taken home, where he stayed in bed for a week. Fits had now become one of the features of his early childhood.

Franzi was brought up in the bosom of the Roman Catholic Church. He was instructed by Father Mersitz, either at the Pilgrimage Church at Unterfrauenhaid or at home. Father Mersitz featured prominently in the Liszt household and became very fond of the bright and attentive boy. He was an organist and often played while Franzi sang songs and hymns. Franzi's general education was initially left in the hands of Johann Rohrer from Donnerskirchen, the Austrian schoolmaster at the Raiding village school who had been a witness at the Liszts' wedding; he also acted as the village scribe. Franzi joined sixty-six other children in the school hall, measuring six by four metres, which was situated beside the Raidingbach between the Liszts' home and the village church. Herr Rohrer's basic course, in German, did not stretch the intelligent boy beyond reading, writing, counting and singing in the choir. Herr Rohrer was not an educated man of the world, and his teaching reflected the sum total of his disciplines. Franzi, completely unmotivated, became bored and was not a good pupil. He had little interest in writing and sums, and his work was messy and covered in ink blots.

Adam was an educated man, yet did not condemn this deficiency. Had he taken more interest in Franzi's mental processes he would have found a mind receptive to history, geography and the study of nature. The only stimulus he recognized was Franzi's obvious love of music. He allowed him to play on the floor in the room while he practised the spinet or the piano to encourage the boy to listen. Franzi responded, and as he grew up he often begged his father to teach him to play, but Adam considered Franzi too young. There were two major factors that shaped Franzi's formative musicianship. The first happened when he was six years old and laid the foundation of his pianistic virtuosity. His father had been practising Ries's Piano Concerto in C sharp minor. It was the first Romantic piano concerto that Franzi had heard, and he was entranced by its glitter and excitement. As if in a dream, he leaned against the piano and stayed there, motionless, for a full hour, listening. When his father had finished, he went out into the garden to play. Later that evening he came back indoors and sang the complete theme from the concerto, which had been churning round and round in his head. Adam, amazed, asked him to repeat it – which he did. The sparkling theme is by no means easily hummable, and he began to suspect that he had a very talented musician – possibly even a genius – on his hands and decided that the time had come to give him lessons.

These got off to a bad start. Father and son would sit at the piano, side by side, and Adam would guide Franzi's fingers onto the keys. Adam may have been a more than adequate pianist, but he was not a particularly good teacher. He was short-tempered, lacked patience and thumped Franzi when he played something in his own way or hit wrong notes – but, as Franz Liszt pointed out in later life, severe corporal punishment as an aid to upbringing was the norm at the time. The lessons stopped abruptly after three days, when Franzi got into a nervous state, had a fit and became feverish. After an interval in which Adam took stock of his son and decided that nothing was to stop Franzi from learning to play the piano, the lessons started up again. The boy was obviously destined to be a great musician who did not need a wider education, just extensive cramming and lots of practice, and he would be beaten if he slacked. Fortunately, Franzi, now recovered, needed neither threats nor encouragement. He spent every available moment practising, until even Anna wondered if it was good for such a young boy to spend so much time at the piano. Adam suddenly maintained that one can never start too young.

Franzi learned quickly, even though Adam's lessons lacked any system. He allowed Franzi to get into bad habits, such as slapdash fingering and playing with his nose if he could not stretch the span of a chord. Despite everything, Franzi learned to read music and played Beethoven's 'Hammerklavier' Sonata before he was nine. He loved it very much and went at it hammer and tongs; his undisciplined interpretation used to irritate his father, who thumped him for his pains. Nevertheless, inspired by this sonata, which he practised when his father was out at work, Franzi composed many of his own, having largely taught himself to write them out. By the time he was ten, he recalled in later life that he had 'filled not a few sheets with notes'. His numerous childhood sonatas are now lost.

Despite his father's erratic music lessons and Herr Rohrer's uninspiring teaching, Franzi grew up to understand his heritage, his roots and the finer points of his Hungarianness. The Liszts considered themselves German-speaking Hungarians, and Franzi was formally called Franz Liszt, and not Liszt Ferenc, the Hungarian form, in which the Christian name comes after the surname. Thus, by a mix of genes and circumstances, Franz Liszt was born with a built-in dual nationality. This curious quirk has produced a number of 'nationalist' musicians, notably Franzi's almost exact contemporary in Poland, Frederick Chopin. Franzi's ancestry on both sides was German, as was his mother tongue, and he was born in a region of Hungary that was half a day's ride from Vienna, the cultural centre of the German-speaking world at the time. Accounts of his boyhood described his German looks. Like his father, he never learned to speak Hungarian, a language with Asiatic roots that bore no relationship to any other European language – save a tenuous one with Finnish. Despite these factors Franz Liszt always considered himself Hungarian, with an empathy for the very soul of Hungarianness, notably in music, that was equal to that of any ethnic Magyar of Asiatic, European or gipsy extraction.

It was the distinctive sound of the music of the gipsies that was the second major factor in Franzi's musical development and laid the foundation for the Hungarian compositions of his later life. Nineteen Hungarian Rhapsodies, the Hungarian Fantasia, the little known Concerto in the Hungarian style and the symphonic poem, *Hungaria*, all had their roots in the music of the gipsies, which became deeply etched on Franzi's psyche from his earliest years.

Gipsy music originated in northern India, and some aspects of the form and tonality of Raga can still be found in today's evolved form. Gipsy bands have not changed significantly since the days of Franz Liszt's childhood. Then, as today, they varied in style. Those of western Hungary, where European instruments were easier to come by, were more sophisticated than those of Transylvania and Romania, where home-made instruments such as pan-pipes and shepherd pipes were common.

Over the centuries, gipsy music has evolved into a fusion of ancient Indian derivative forms and the European classical and folk traditions. A typical Hungarian gipsy band consists of two violins, a viola and a double bass. The first violin leads, the second fills in the harmonies with the viola, and the double bass, always bowed, drives the beat. The comparatively new clarinet, as popularized by Mozart some twenty years previously, was also enthusiastically adopted. The cymbalom's roots lay in the ancient Greek kithara and the Viennese zither, with its strings struck with little hammers instead of being plucked. As Indian classical music is based on Raga, so gipsy music is based on Csárdás.

Like its ancestor, the Csárdás is in binary form. The first section, known as Lassan, is a slow, often rhythmless, introduction. It is always highly charged emotionally and consists of a broad, rhapsodic melody played by the leading instrument – usually a violin – while the other instruments fill in the harmonies. The melody is improvised at the soloist's whim in rubato and decoration. Franz Liszt recorded in later life that no two performances were ever the same. The other members of the band follow and change the harmonies accordingly. As these often go beyond the usual tonic, dominant and subdominant and go through series of key-changes, a high degree of musical empathy exists between the players. While the accompanying strings sustain long notes, the cymbalom player gives a tremolando effect.

The second part is the Friska, when the Csárdás breaks into a rhythm, at first slow, but gathering in speed and excitement. In this it resembles Raga, where the rhythm pattern of the tabla drives the piece to its frenzied conclusion. The Friska is a vehicle to show off the skill of the leading performer on violin or alternatively the cymbalom and clarinet – both evolved into highly virtuosic instruments in their own right. The music builds up to a frenzy of excitement and invariably ends with the distinctive three-chord cadence – subdominant, dominant, tonic – often with a flourish on the last chord.

The ancient eastern modes had been largely abandoned in favour of the European major and minor scales. However, some modes are frequently used, such as the Lydian, with the sharpened fourth, the Mixolydian, with the flattened seventh, or a combination of both. Quarter-tones are often found, either to give an 'out of tune' effect – a device used by Bartók in his String Quartet No. 5 – or to bend a note a quarter-tone flat before 'lifting' it to its resolution. Some gipsy rhythms are specifically ambiguous. Phrases often come in sets of three bars rather than the usual four – a device used by Brahms in his Hungarian Dances. There is virtually no gipsy music in three-four time, although gipsy bands frequently played Viennese waltzes.

In many ways the technique of the gipsy fiddler surpasses that of a trained musician, for it goes beyond the widely accepted European tradition of violin playing. The gipsy plays by instinct and recognizes no rule book except tradition. He is at one with his instrument and has an extensive repertoire of tricks and techniques that have been passed down the centuries. There is more to his performance than just music; it is a total expression of self: virtuosity, machismo, theatre and ecstasy. Many hold their violin in unusual positions, such as against the shoulder instead of under the chin, and theatrical posturing includes playing above the head, lying down or like a cello – all designed to whip up high excitement in both performer and audience alike. Harmonics are used extensively to imitate the sounds of nature, especially birdsong. 'A Pacsirta' (The Lark), perhaps the most well-known display piece, is the ultimate vehicle for the virtuoso fiddler, who will use glissandi and trills on harmonics to convey birdsong in a way not generally taught in music conservatories. The greatest fiddlers can play solos entirely on harmonics. Notes are bent for emotional effect, and the same note repeated on different strings in different positions can give a sense of turbulence. Violins may be tuned in many ways, and it is not uncommon to retune a violin in mid solo, with the retuning process subtly incorporated into the music.

All gipsy musicians know their traditional melodies and a scratch band should be able to 'busk' the established repertoire, but a good 'empathetic' band will always come up with a complex, modulating collective improvisation, with spectacular solos, at any time.

Apart from the case of Johann Bihari of the Vienna Musikkapelle, most attempts to bring gipsy fiddlers into the European classical mainstream have been doomed to failure – as Franz Liszt discovered twenty-five years later, in Paris, when he received the brilliant but untameable gipsy fiddler, Jozi Sárai, into his care. Jozi, a vain, egocentric thief, had been bought from his gipsy family by Count Sándor Teleky, and sent to Liszt for social and musical instruction. Liszt failed on all counts except friendship. Jozi remained a vain, egocentric thief and a brilliant gipsy fiddler who never forgot his master's kindness and understanding.

Franzi assimilated all aspects of this music. He took it for granted as the music of his country, rather than of the gipsies. To him gipsy music was Hungarian music, part of his Hungarian heritage as he saw it. His Hungarian Rhapsodies were Csárdás in all but name. Like the Hungarian Fantasia for piano and orchestra, they are all divided into Lassan and Friska sections. The rhapsody principle was featured largely in the heavily rubato Lassan sections, while in the sparkling Friska some of his tremolando pianistic effects owe a debt to the jangling cymbalom. He sought to achieve the same emotional effect through music as expressed by the gipsies, who were in total control of their instruments, creating music through ecstasy as if it were the most natural thing in the world. Franzi learned to improvise, like the gipsies, by instinct and, like the gipsies, he became a law unto himself. Despite being regularly thumped for it by his father, he never really lost this attitude. He set about mastering the piano inspired by an amalgam of Ries's Piano Concerto and the sound of Csárdás. He sought to achieve complete control so that the piano would become part of his being. In later life Franz Liszt analysed the gipsy psyche in his book, *The Gipsies and Their Music*.

On his seventh birthday Adam and Franzi made a business call on Ruben Hirschler, a Jewish merchant in Lackenbach, a few kilometres from Raiding. As the two men were discussing the price of wool, Franzi heard the sound of piano music from an upstairs floor. Intrigued, he followed the sounds till he came upon the daughter of the house, Fanni, playing. Franzi was entranced, not only by her playing but also by the quality of the instrument. He stood there, motionless, listening and did not hear the sound of his father coming up quietly behind him.

It was a singularly good piano, so Adam offered to buy it for Franzi to replace the one at Raiding, which was now in a bad state. Herr Hirschler agreed, and the price was settled at 400 florins. Seeing that Franzi was exceptionally musical, he further offered to pay for music lessons from Fanni's teacher. According to legend, this was the young Oedenburg virtuoso Franz Kurzweil; his piano, on which he reputedly taught Franzi, is today at the town's Liszt Museum.

By 1819 Franzi was already playing Bach fugues and transposing them. Adam had become aware of a serious responsibility and feared that his strained circumstances would deprive Franzi of the chance of fame and fortune. He was also not unaware that Franzi could eventually be earning a very good living from music, which would lead to support in old age. So heavy investment in Franzi became Adam's first priority.

Aiming for the best, he contacted Hummel, who had been Hofkapellmeister at Weimar since 1 January of that year, inquiring after lessons for Franzi and hoping for a fee that would reflect their friendship. Hummel quoted an exorbitant one louis d'or per lesson, so the idea was put on hold while Adam wrote to Prince Nicolaus asking for patronage and funds for his son. While waiting for a reply he began to take Franzi with him on his trips to Eisenstadt and to get him heard on the music circuit. They stayed at his friend Ludwig Hofer's apartment next to the Bergkirche. Adam also took Franzi to meet various friends and acquaintances at the Engels Gasthof, the local tavern and Eisenstadt's meeting-place and watering hole, where Franzi played the piano. They also regularly called on Father Stanislaus Albach at the Franciscan Monastery – which is still there, in what is today Haydngasse. Father Stanislaus was a friend and spiritual confidant of Adam's and took a great interest in Franzi, who in later life dedicated a Mass for male voices and a Pater Noster to him. Franzi was also shown the Bergkirche, Eisenstadt's main church, where his father first played the cello under Haydn when he was not much older than his son.

At the end of July Adam took Franzi to Vienna and called on pianist and teacher Carl Czerny. 'The child was pale and sickly-looking and swayed on the chair while he played as if he were drunk,' wrote Czerny in his *Memoirs*, 'so that I was afraid he might fall off at any moment. Also his playing was irregular, faulty and confused. He had very little idea of fingering, that he just threw his fingers all over the keyboard as the fancy took him.' Franzi then played several pieces that Czerny put before him at sight and improvised on a given theme. 'In spite of everything,' continued Czerny, 'I was astounded at the gifts with which Nature had endowed him.' Czerny told Adam that he would be very happy to take Franzi on as a pupil.

Adam reckoned that the prospects of a good musical education for Franzi, if the funds could be found, had taken a turn for the better. On 4 August 1819 Johann von Szentgály passed on a report to his employer, Prince Nicolaus Esterházy: 'His [Adam Liszt's] supplication concerns the education of his seven-and-a-half-year-old son, who has a great talent and musical ability.' The request was either for board and lodging and tuition fees for music and languages, or a transfer to Vienna, in which case only tuition fees would be required. Adam's application listed detailed figures and estimated costings. Prince Nicolaus had heard rumours about Franzi Liszt and expressed a wish to hear this amazing seven-year-old for himself. He had organized a hunting party at Eisenstadt for 21 September and instructed Adam to bring his boy along to give a little divertissement. The guests were invited to the Wild Boar Room at the Palace to be entertained by the son of the Rentmeister of Raiding. The concert was a spectacular success, and everyone was delighted.

However, Adam noted ruefully, there was no follow-up offer of funds or patronage, but Prince Nicolaus gave Adam leave of absence to look around for further possibilities. In common with his employer, Adam Liszt was a hunting enthusiast and usually took Franzi with him on his expeditions, even though he found him a hindrance to the enjoyment of his sport. But he did make some attempts to teach him to shoot. Franzi was not a good shot, which made Adam lose patience with him, until one day, in the swamps beside Lake Neusiedl, by luck rather than skill, Franzi downed a duck. Franzi was fascinated by gunpowder and liked the loud bangs it made when the gun was fired. He watched, fascinated, as his father poured measured amounts of the powder from little tubes in his hunting bag into the barrel of the gun. On one occasion Franzi wondered whether igniting all the powder in the hunting bag in one go would produce an even bigger bang. 'Obviously,' Franz Liszt recalled in later years, 'I already had a penchant for spectacular effects.' In the room there was a green-tiled burning stove, into which he threw the whole hunting bag. There was a tremendous explosion, part of the stove was shorn off and Franzi was hurled across the room by the force of the blast. 'There was a gloriously noisy effect,' continued Franz Liszt in reminiscence, 'but unfortunately it was immediately followed by a less attractive, striking effect, that of my father giving me a glorious thrashing.'

In December the soundboard and screwplate of Adam's piano,

damaged by damp, became unusable and had to be replaced at a cost of 550 florins. To raise the money he had to sell his gold watch and a cow. As spring advanced, Adam became very depressed about his financial situation, and on 13 April 1820 he again petitioned Prince Nicolaus for funds. This time he listed the sacrifices he had already made for Franzi's benefit, which had brought great financial hardship to the family. The tone of Adam's petition was deferential to the point of grovelling.

The following month there was a Whitsun fair at Nyék – today Neckenmarkt – just beyond Unterfrauenhaid, to which Anna took Franzi. Along with some other people, including J. Berlakovics, an elderly cleric, they called on Herr Haller, the local schoolmaster, and his family. Herr Haller had an old piano, and Franzi was asked to play. He was in the middle of a game with a pretty little girl, rolling her red painted egg around, and despite all entreaties Franzi refused – the egg, or possibly the little girl, being of greater importance to him. Eventually he agreed, on condition that he could have the egg. This was out of character, as he had an essentially generous nature. But the girl refused to be parted from her egg. The impasse was broken by Herr Haller, who offered to buy it from her to pay Franzi's performing fee. The girl agreed, and the price was settled: a piece of cake, ten cherries and a copper kreutzer. Franzi sat at the piano and delighted everyone all evening with his playing. By now his repertoire consisted of works by Bach, Mozart, Beethoven, Clementi, Hummel and Cramer. His playing was note perfect, and he could sight-read without mistakes. But when the recital came to an end, Franzi found that the girl had re-taken her egg. 'The little minx hoodwinked me even then,' he recalled.

That year Joseph Haydn's remains were brought to the Bergkirche in Eisenstadt for reburial, at the instigation of Prince Nicolaus, eleven years after his death and burial at the Hundsthurmer cemetery in Vienna. To everyone's horror, the head was missing. The body had been secretly exhumed and the head hacked off by Haydn's friend and secretary, Joseph Rosenbaum, with accomplices, the night after the burial. This was in keeping with the sometime custom of removing the heads and brains of people of genius, among them Schiller and Mozart, for phrenological study. Haydn's skull was passed on to the Society of Friends of Music in Vienna, who refused to release it. Only in 1954 was it finally reunited with the body in the Mausoleum at the Bergkirche.

At long last Adam received an answer to his petition from Prince

Nicolaus. After the sheep-shearing, he could have a year off and 200 gulden towards his expenses. Adam saw this as a refusal and unacceptable. He returned the 200 gulden but took up the offer of leave, in a polite but underlyingly sarcastic letter to Prince Nicolaus. 'In deep respect,' the letter concluded, 'I kiss your High Honour's gown for the undeserved high favour . . . and regret with tears in my eyes and the full heart of a father that I can make no use of this and a young genius will have to travel in poverty.'

Franzi's reputation was spreading, and in the autumn of 1820 his career as a concert pianist took off in earnest. In October he was invited to take part in a charity concert organized by the blind nineteen-year-old flautist Baron Sigismund von Braun at the Music Academy, later the Casino, in Oedenburg. The Baron's agent welcomed Adam and Franzi at the Hotel Posthorn and saw them settled in. The concert was attended by the cream of local Hungarian society: Prince Nicolaus was there with his younger brother, Count Michael Esterházy; Count Miháli Viczay, who discussed with Count Michael a fund for Franzi's education; Count Zichy of Pressburg and his family, who were involved with the later Franz Liszt story; Count Niczky of Nebersdorf, who had for a time employed Georg List as steward, was there, along with Counts Szapáry and Széchenyi, the hero after whom the Casino Square outside the concert venue came to be named. Also present were doctors, notaries, professors and high officials. Seated in a box, Adam and Anna Liszt watched their son perform in his first public concert.

Franzi, wearing a ceremonial Hungarian court dress, climbed onto the platform, past the conductor and the orchestra. He played the Piano Concerto in E flat by Ries, and, as was the trend among the new Romantic pianists, he improvised on themes suggested by the audience. His confident and flawless performance earned him much applause. After the concert he was laid up at home with a fever, and a deputation that arrived from Oedenburg to request a repeat of the concert was initially disappointed. A week later Franzi recovered and gave a second performance, after which Count Michael asked Franzi to play at his Pressburg palace in November. Oedenburg is today Sopron, and the Casino square area has been redeveloped since Liszt's day. The square is now called Széchenyi Tér, and on the site of the Casino stands a school, on the corner of Liszt Ferenc utca and Petőfi Tér. A plaque commemorates the concert.

Pressburg Castle, high on its hill overlooking the north bank of the Danube, was visible from afar; it was the first glimpse that Adam and Franzi had of the great Hungarian city as they approached it from the south. They crossed the Danube over the pontoon bridge and almost immediately came to Count Michael's palace, situated at the foot of the hill just below the Castle and connected to it by a pathway. In the surprisingly small garden there was a summer pavilion, where Count Michael gave musical entertainments, which on fine, warm days spilled onto the terrace outside. On 26 November, when Franzi played to a glittering and highly appreciative Hungarian audience, the doors and windows were firmly shut against the cold.

The *Pressburger Zeitung* reviewed the occasion:

> At noon last Sunday the nine-year-old virtuoso Franz Liszt had the honour of exhibiting his talents before a large gathering of the local nobility and music lovers at the residence of Count Michael Esterházy. The young artist's extraordinary skill, and his rapid grasp of the most difficult pieces when playing at sight anything placed before him, excited general admiration and justified the highest expectations.

After the concert, Count Michael, along with Counts d'Amadé, Apponyi, Szapáry, Erdödy and Viczay, decided, on the strength of what they had seen and heard, to initiate a fund for Franzi's education. The Liszts had been granted a year off, leaving only the question of money for tuition fees, board and lodgings in Vienna. An annual grant of 600 florins over a period of six years was agreed and a very dazed Adam notified.

Pressburg is now the capital of Slovakia, and the Castle, a prestigious concert venue, still dominates the landscape. Count Michael's palace is today the University Library, situated in Jiráskova Michalska Street, which retains many old and historic buildings. A plaque commemorates Franzi's concert. The summer pavilion is still there, its exterior unchanged, although its interior has been altered through the decades to accommodate a factory and a school. It is now part of the library complex. The garden, which includes an open-air café, is now the Liszt Garden and open to the public.

Back at Raiding, an excited family conference was held to discuss this very tempting offer from the Pressburg Six. Anna's dowry, which had been hitherto stubbornly untouched, was now called into play. Vienna had become a reality, but their initial joy was tempered with fear: fear of unemployment and poverty; fear for Franzi's health, as he was still subject to fits and fevers; and fear of what would become of them all when the six years were up or, more immediately, when the year's leave was up. Would Adam – as well as Franzi, who would be sixteen by then – be in a position to make a living? Franzi himself made the family's mind up. 'What God wills,' he said confidently.

Over the next year preparations were made, Adam settled his duties and affairs and sold up. His cattle fetched 600 gulden, which would contribute towards the start to their new life in the capital. Goodbyes were said, as friends from all over the region came to wish the Liszts good luck for the future. Before their departure in the spring of 1822, the family, accompanied by the whole community, went to the church at Raiding – rebuilt in 1924 – for a service of blessing. Eleven-year-old Franzi knelt, his hands together and his head bowed, praying hard throughout the service.

On 8 May the head shepherd took the Liszts and their possessions in his wagon to the post station at Horitschon. The coach set off towards Lake Neusiedl. Franzi gazed at the flat plain of Oedenburg county and noticed its unspoilt roughness and peaceful air of prosperity. Where the road came to the marshes of the southern reaches of the lake it joined the main post route from Körmend to Oedenburg, then continued across the Leithagebirge hills along what is today Route 16 all the way to Vienna. They put up at the 'Green Hedgehog' guest-house near the Mariahilfstrasse end of Stiftsgasse.

THREE

Czerny's Vienna
1822–23

C ARL CZERNY's apartment was full of cats. Evidence of
their dominance was everywhere: threadbare patches on the
furnishings, kittens, some awaiting adoption, running wild over
carpet and curtain, mothers suckling their still blind offspring in
boxes, and the inevitable smells. Czerny and his cats shared the
modest but tasteful apartment, on the second floor of 1047
Krugerstrasse – today Number 3 – with his parents.

Czerny's roots were in Bohemia. Piano teacher Václav Černý
and his wife had migrated in 1786 from Nymburk to Vienna,
where their son Karel was born in 1791. The Černýs were insu-
lar and chose to socialize with fellow Bohemians, and for the first
few years of his life Karel only spoke Czech. By the age of three
he was picking out tunes on the piano, so Václav gave him his
first musical grounding and found he had a prodigious talent on
his hands. When Karel was eleven, Václav Krumpholtz, violinist
at the Opera and a fellow Bohemian, introduced the Černýs to
Beethoven. Karel played him Mozart's Piano Concerto in C major
and, diplomatically, the Master's recently published 'Pathétique'
Sonata. As a result, Beethoven took the boy on as his pupil. Three
years later he wrote that Carl Czerny, who had by now learned
German and had germanicized his names, had made such progress
as to be musically way beyond his fourteen years, with every
prospect of a future as a virtuoso pianist. Carl's theories on piano
teaching methods took over, and he evolved into one of the
most sought-after piano teachers in Vienna. He also became one
of the leading interpreters of Beethoven's piano music and was
a torchbearer at his master's funeral. Czerny died in 1857.

Czerny accepted Franzi as a pupil, at a fee of two gulden per hour (compared to one louis d'or, approximately ten gulden, charged by Hummel), knowing he had a veritable task ahead of him. Franzi's genius was out of control. He was tense and nervous, the obvious victim of bad teaching, lack of method and an unhealthy regard for his father, whom he was anxious to please from fear rather than love. His fingering had scarcely improved since their first interview three years previously, and his timing was still irregular. Czerny put a block on any further concert performances until the boy had unlearned his bad habits and undertaken a strict regime of exercises, scales and arpeggios. Instead of piano concertos, he had to work out on Clementi sonatas, which Czerny regarded as the best school of pianism.

It took nearly half an hour to walk from the 'Green Hedgehog' in the suburb of Mariahilf to Czerny's apartment, a journey that Adam and Franzi undertook every evening, after the language lessons that Franzi attended during the day. Patiently, Czerny put Franzi through the mill, instilling in him discipline and method. Franzi responded, and a strong bond based on mutual respect and admiration developed between teacher and pupil. Under the chaotic morass of nervous energy Czerny perceived a raw genius struggling to get out, while Putzi – Franzi's nickname – saw in his master a guru who taught him how to make the best of his musical genius in an atmosphere of affection, kindness and reward. 'Never', wrote Czerny in his *Memoirs*, 'have I had so eager, talented and hard-working a pupil.' He also introduced Franzi to one of music's most enduring teaching aids – the metronome – invented by Johann Nepomuk Mälzel in 1816. Franzi's tensions eased up and he learned to relax and not fear constant censure. Old Václav Černý and his wife also took to 'Putzi' and treated him like a late son, thoroughly spoiling him. 'I loved him like a brother,' wrote Czerny.

Franzi observed, fascinated, his master's composition methods and marvelled at the sheer quantity of his output. Czerny was a workaholic who would sometimes have up to five compositions on the go simultaneously and would run from one to the other, his skull-cap on his head and his spectacles on his nose, writing one while the ink was drying on the other. And all the while he would hold a conversation with whoever happened to be present.

It has been said that Czerny was the greatest pianist who never performed. He loathed playing in public, and his agoraphobia precluded travel; he spent nearly all his life in Vienna. Except for some early performances, such as the première of Beethoven's E flat Concerto on 12 February 1812, he preferred to stay at home with his parents, his cats and his reams of music paper, giving lessons and composing. He had over a thousand opus numbers published and many more works that remained in manuscript. His output included compositions for up to sixteen hands on eight pianos – he ignored the logistics of arranging a performance. His compositions have been all but neglected, though some, such as the Variations on 'La Ricordanza' and the Sonata d'Étude, Op. 268, have earned high praise. It is his piano method that has assured him his place in history, and his volumes of Exercises have undoubtedly contributed to pianistic virtuosity to this day. His rules were logical and familiar to today's piano students: the thumb must never be placed on a black note; two or more keys one after the other must not be struck with the same finger; the little finger must never be placed on black keys during runs. That is not to say that he did not allow these rules to be broken, as some written music could not be played any other way; Czerny's rules were guidelines.

A month later Adam realized that his son was in the best possible hands. Franzi's technique had improved beyond recognition, and his posture at the piano showed a composure that had been absent in his early childhood. Adam proffered Czerny's first fee of sixty gulden, but Czerny declined. 'For Putzi,' he said in his Czech-accented German, 'I take no fee.' Adam was very touched and grateful for Czerny's generosity. There was money available, but Vienna was expensive, and Adam had to count the kreuzers carefully. He had foolishly declined Prince Nicolaus's 200 gulden in disgust, and he was aware that he was on a year's unpaid leave; he still had Anna's dowry as well as the first year's grant of 600 florins (about 300 gulden) from the Pressburg Six. He supplemented this capital by teaching. The 'Green Hedgehog' was modest but cheap, and Czerny's generosity was an added relief.

For composition lessons Adam approached Antonio Salieri, whose list of past pupils, friends and associates during his thirty-six years as Imperial Kapellmeister read like a musicians' *Who's Who* of the time. He was born in Legnano, Italy, in 1750 and brought up by an older brother in Padua. He was discovered in Venice by Florian Gassmann, the Kapellmeister to the Imperial Court, who brought him to Vienna in 1766 and arranged his musical education. Prior to 1788, when he succeeded Gassmann to the most prestigious

musical post in Europe, he was appointed the Court's official composer, with numerous operas, orchestral and chamber works to
his credit. A widower since 1807, when his wife Theresia died, he
lived at his father-in-law's house in the Seilergasse near the
Gottweiher Hof. His only son Alois had died in 1805 aged twenty-
three and, of his seven daughters, two, Francisca and Anna, were
still living at home. Now seventy-two and suffering from gout, an
eye infection and the beginnings of mental decline, Salieri had
steadfastly refused them permission to marry, so that they would
stay and look after him in his old age. The house, once a shrine
of glittering elegance, heady conversation and fine music, was
degenerating into decay and bitterness. He suffered from depression – as did his spinster daughters. His world of music was now
yesterday's world, for history had passed and new fashions had
taken over, many of which were beyond his understanding. He
was still venerated as the Grand Old Man of the Viennese music
scene, and many musicians who had passed through his world
and had benefited from his generous spirit still came to pay their
respects at his feet.

Salieri numbered Beethoven, Schubert, Hummel, Franz Xaver
Mozart, Franz Süssmayr, the opera composer Peter von Winter,
Meyerbeer, Moscheles and Czerny among his pupils. He rarely
charged a fee, except from the wealthy. His own output was
craftsmanlike and of its time, and survives more because of its
historical significance than the work of genius; but his tried and
tested method was to compose by the book. He knew the rules of
harmony governing consecutive fifths and doubled thirds, as established by Classical tradition, abided by them and ensured his
pupils did so too. Classicism was giving way to the new Romanticism, but Salieri, like Czerny, maintained that ground rules had
to be thoroughly learned before they could be broken; all his pupils
were ultimately beneficiaries of Salieri's philosophy and training.

He was still composing, mostly religious canons. Gioacchino
Rossini was in Vienna that summer, basking in the enormous
popularity of his operas, eight of which had recently played in the
Austrian capital. *Zelmira* was playing there at the time. Salieri visited him in his lodgings for some after-dinner dessert and music
talk. He brought his canons with him, and along with Rossini's
wife Isabella, Giovanni David and Andrea Nozzari, they sang their
way through them well into the night, for Salieri had worked up a
head of steam and would not let go. 'We constituted quite a passable

vocal quartet,' wrote Rossini, 'but those never-ending canons made us quite dizzy, and we asked him to restrain himself a little.'

Salieri listened in amazement as Franzi improvised to him, a skill that was expected as a matter of course from the new generation of pianists but had been comparatively rare in the days of his prime and one that he himself lacked. Through Franzi's 'free fantasia', as an improvisation was called, he discerned a true composer dormant and agreed to take him on as a composition pupil. Franzi began lessons with Salieri in the middle of July, three times a week at eleven o'clock in the morning. Typically, the fee was waived, another relief for Adam. Salieri did not presume to teach Franzi to compose; that, Franz Liszt wrote later, is something that cannot be taught. The lessons were theoretical and included singing – part-writing for voices in harmony and counterpoint rather than voice training, working from a figured bass, reading scores, both mentally and at the piano, and understanding all the different clefs. Writing out music, which Franzi had largely taught himself, also needed tightening up, and a number of bad habits had to be eradicated. Franzi responded and never forgot Salieri's lessons. 'He still has my deep gratitude,' wrote Franz Liszt later.

By the middle of August, Salieri began to worry about the exhausted state in which Franzi, who was still very delicate, arrived at his house. He discussed his concern with Adam and suggested that the family should move closer to the centre; an ideal solution, were it not financially unviable, as rents in the city centre were far higher. Salieri took it upon himself to write 'humbly' to Prince Nicolaus, requesting additional funds so that the Liszts could move closer to the venues of Franzi's lessons. He signed his letter Antonio Salieri, writing in his capacity as Kapellmeister to the Imperial and Royal Court of Vienna – thus hinting that a refusal on the Prince's part might be discussed in the halls and corridors of the Hofburg and Schönbrunn and beyond. The implied threat paid off, because in October the Liszts moved to an apartment on the second floor of 1014 Krugerstrasse, virtually next door to Czerny and within five minutes of Salieri.

By midsummer Czerny decided that Franzi could try his hand on Vienna's soirée circuit – playing only the Classical repertoire and no Romantics until further notice. This was good news for Adam, as the family's financial situation was, at times, critical. The first soirée was at the residence of Councillor Raphael Georg Kiesewetter, who, as a director of an army education department and a music researcher, organized musical events. The private concert brought in Franzi's first Viennese fee. This was followed by a soirée at the home of Josef Hohenadel, the military assistant book-keeper, who also gave soirées. Among his regular artistes were young opera stars Wilhelmina Schröder, Karoline Unger, Beethoven's favourite and protégée, and Henrietta Sontag, regarded as the best soprano of her day. The three divas were utterly seduced by Franzi, whom they pampered mercilessly, showered with presents, took to their opera performances, rehearsals, buggy rides round the city and smothered with hugs and kisses. Franzi had his first real ex-periences of female adulation.

Rossini was asked to the Palffy residence, a noble Hungarian house, for a grand all-night ball. Also booked was Franzi, who immediately took to the renowned opera composer, still only thirty years old; the occasion was the start of a lifelong friend-ship. 'It was in Vienna in 1822 that I began to love and admire you,' wrote Franz Liszt long afterwards. 'The years that have passed since then have only served to increase the affection that I feel for you.' Rossini left Vienna for Italy in July to continue his tour.

That night Franzi heard for the first time Johann Bihari's gipsy band, the Vienna Musikkapelle, who were booked to play. This spectacular outfit ensured that the party went with a swing. No one enjoyed the music more than Franzi, who had never heard violin playing like that of this legendary bandleader from Pesth. Bihari's playing reinforced Franzi's musical Hungarianness and stayed with him for the rest of his life.

Johann – János in Hungarian – Bihari was born in 1769 in Nagyabony (today Velki Abon in Slovakia, near Pressburg), the son of a gipsy musician. He learned the violin the traditional gipsy way, by ear and without reading music. At eighteen he married Eva Banyak, the beautiful daughter of a renowned cymbalom player, in whose band he played. After his father-in-law's death he went to Pesth, where he formed his own band. This consisted of three violins, cello and cymbalom. All five players were superb performers. For a quarter of a century the Bihari band went from success to success and played at major functions all over the Habsburg Empire, dressed in their costume of dark blue trousers, embroidered with black cord and buttoned up the sides in the Hungarian manner, and a red cape, also ornamented with galloon and lace of black and dark blue and, in Bihari's case, gold. Each wore an otter-fur

kolpak hat with a white feather. In addition Bihari sported gold
and diamond rings on his fingers, for he was a profligate spender.
The costume had a military dash: it was designed by a Colonel
Károly Kubinyi.

Bihari's most famous work, the Rákóczi March, was attributed
to Nicolas Scholl, who wrote it out and had it published under
his own name, since the composer could not. It was based on a
Hungarian folk-melody: Ferenc Rákóczi, one of Hungary's greatest heroes, led the insurrection of 1703–11. The Rákóczi March
gained prominence as the marching song of the Hungarian legions
fighting Napoleon.

In 1815 Bihari was the toast of the Vienna Congress, and his
band's reputation was thus carried all over Europe. He was a great
favourite with the Imperial Family and adored by the Hungarian
aristocracy. He had a penchant for beautiful aristocratic women,
and not a few princesses came close to swooning to his music, his
dusky good looks and his roving eyes. In 1825 he broke his left
arm in a coach accident near Pesth, which severely impaired his
performance. He carried on as best he could, but his health deteriorated, and he died in poverty, aged fifty-eight, of gout, dropsy
and black depression two years later.

'We were just beginning to grow up,' wrote Franz Liszt in his
The Gipsies and Their Music,

> when, in 1822, we heard this great man amongst other Bohe-
> mian [Liszt's word for gipsy] musicians. . . . Bihari was particu-
> larly distinguished by the virtuosity with which he executed the
> national music. It was so freshly delivered as to produce an
> effect of improvisation. His style, although full of that drive without
> which no Hungarian audience can be carried away, was not
> loaded with passages of showy display. There were melodies
> whose beautiful and expressive rendering touched all hearts. His
> Friska was full of intoxicating enthusiasm, and his Lassan of a
> heartbreaking and elegiac melancholy. . . . Whatever theme he
> played, he at once gave an accentuation which changed its
> nature . . . and seemed to infuse it with another soul. . . . If it
> were a lively dance he would make it mad with joy and drunk
> with pleasure; he would turn a sentimental operatic air into a
> passionate scene calculated to draw tears from his listeners, and
> an already melancholy theme immediately became a funeral scene.
> When he thought he had caused enough emotion, he would
> break into a march tune to bring the company back to the re-
> quired mood for dancing.

It was a difficult act to follow. Franzi, excited from his meeting with the great Rossini and riding high on his own adrenalin, provided the finale to the night's musical entertainment and came away with a 'present' of ten ducats (forty-five gulden). The Theresianum was Vienna's most prestigious school, where all the Austro-Hungarian nobility sent their boys for the highest standards of education found anywhere in Europe. The Hungarian Prefect of the Theresianum, Professor Johann Karl Unger, father of singer Karoline, entertained lavishly at his house in Herrengasse. The Liszts were asked to one such evening. The Professor was looking forward to conversing with them in Hungarian and was disappointed to find they only spoke German. Among the entertainers were Schubert's friend, the singer Johann Michael Vogl, Léon de Saint-Lubin, one of Vienna's leading violinists – and Franzi. Also present was Anton Schindler, Beethoven's secretary. He went up to Franzi after his performance, congratulated him warmly, shook his hand, hugged him, and promised to introduce him to the Master. The evening was deemed a great success, and a second, similar evening took place, at which again Saint-Lubin played the violin, Franzi played the piano and nineteen-year-old Karoline sang.

The Liszts were also asked to the Hackelberg-Landau residence for a lavish soirée for 300 of Vienna's most fashionable glitterati, including the Chancellor and his wife, Prince and Princess Metternich. While a disgruntled Adam had to sit and wait in an anteroom, a thousand candles lit the room where Franzi entertained an adoring audience with a programme of Czerny, Mozart and Beethoven. During the thunderous applause Franzi, already aware of his effect on women, forgot courtly etiquette, ran up to Princess Metternich and asked her if she liked his performance. The Princess, perhaps recalling a precedent, when Empress Maria-Theresa hugged six-year-old Mozart on her knee exactly sixty years previously in similar circumstances, also eschewed courtly procedure and did the same. As the Liszts went home that night, Adam swallowed his humiliation as he pocketed the 'present' of five ducats – about twenty-two gulden.

Adam took advantage of Czerny and Salieri, who knew the right people, to push Franzi's career, with some very satisfactory results. He agitated for a public concert, but Czerny would not hear of it until Franzi's technique had improved to his satisfaction and he had cut his teeth on some soirées. Adam busied himself contacting the rich and influential, including Count Fürstenberg, President of the newly formed Society of Austrian Friends of Music, university Professor Johann Zizius, in whose house the Society was formed, and the famous Hungarian violinist Joseph Boehm.

'Salieri was very satisfied with the work of his pupil,' wrote one of Liszt's biographers, Lina Ramann, 'and was delighted with a Tantum Ergo [S 702] which Franz had lovingly composed and which he singled out for special praise.' This was effectively Franzi's first composition, now lost. At this time Anton Diabelli, a music publisher with a shop in the Graben, was canvassing composers, including Franzi, to write a variation on a waltz tune that he had written, with a view to publishing a grand, multiple opus. The tune, never intended otherwise, was trite, but the idea was eagerly taken up. Schubert, Czerny, Hummel, Kalkbrenner, Stadler, Winkhler and Tomášek accepted in the spirit in which it was intended, and each contributed a variation. Beethoven took the request seriously but found the theme wanting and declined to contribute. 'Schusterfleck' (cobbler's patch) was how he described it. To Franzi it was his first commission for a composition, and he jumped at the opportunity. He wrote a sixteen-bar Allegro of semi-quaver arpeggio figures, in C minor and in regular 2/4 time. The altered time signature and the minor were undoubtedly Czerny's idea, and the evenness and logic of the writing certainly testified to Czerny's tuition. The crossed hands device and a flight up to the top end of the keyboard pointed to a composition style already germinated. Franzi's variation [S 147] was inscribed 'Franz Liszt (boy of 11 years) born in Hungary'.

Franzi also contributed a Waltz in A (S 126bis) for violin and piano to a collaborative ballet by the director of the Kärntnertor Theatre, Count Wenzel von Gallenberg, entitled *Die Amazonen*, cobbled together from a variety of sources.

Franzi was there when Adalbert Gyrowetz, sixty-year-old composer and director of the Court Opera, was at Diabelli's for lunch. The talk turned to the difficulties of Hummel's Piano Concerto in A minor, and the score was produced, perused and discussed. Franzi inspected it, said, 'I can read that', went to the piano in the next room and proved his claim to the astonished professionals. Diabelli then decided that the time was ripe for Franzi's first formal concert. He consulted Czerny, who conceded that Franzi was ready to perform to the greater public. So Diabelli organized a concert for 1 December in the Landständischen Saal of the Town Hall – today the Altes Rathaus, at 8 Wipplingerstrasse. Franzi shared the bill with two familiar faces, Karoline Unger and Léon de Saint-Lubin. The programme opened with an Overture by Clementi, after which Franzi played Hummel's Piano Concerto in A minor. Léon de Saint-Lubin followed with the Variations in E by Jacques Rode, a French violinist and friend of Beethoven, and Karoline Unger sang an aria from Rossini's *Demetrio e Polybio*. The concert finished with Franzi's free fantasia based on the slow movement of Beethoven's Seventh Symphony and the cantilena from Rossini's *Zelmira*.

'A young virtuoso has fallen from the clouds, and compels us to the highest admiration,' wrote a critic in the *Allgemeine Musikalische Zeitung* on 22 January the following year.

The performance of this boy, for his age, borders on the incredible, and one is tempted to doubt any physical impossibility when one hears the young giant, with unabated force, thunder out Hummel's composition, so difficult and fatiguing, especially in the last movement. . . . It was fine to see the little Hercules unite Beethoven's Andante from the Symphony in A and the theme from the cantilena from Rossini's *Zelmira*, and knead them into one paste. Est deus in nobis.

On 9 December Franzi took part in a short concert at the Kärntnertor Theatre which acted as a prologue to a ballet entitled *Margarethe von Catanea*. The concert opened with an improvisation by an Italian guitarist, Luigi Legnani, followed by a Danish cellist, Frederik Christian Funcke, with a performance of the Divertissement for cello and orchestra by Bernhard Romberg, the cellist much admired by Beethoven. Franzi rounded off the opening set with the Rondo from Ries's Piano Concerto in E flat.

The *Allgemeine Musikalische Zeitung* of 14 December, having praised Legnani as a truly great master, went on to praise the eleven-year-old Liszt as 'a little David [who] laudably overcame his giant, and with such artistic skill, can take on many more Goliaths-of-the-keyboard. He is a model of distinctness, expression and feeling, and in days to come will surely take his place among the greatest artists.' A further review appeared on Christmas Day. Legnani's great bravura was praised, as was Funcke's tone and shading, which had never sounded better. 'The conclusion of the concert was by the interesting young Liszt,' it continued. 'He definitely shows great talent as a virtuoso. The manner and style with which he tackles the most difficult compositions are remarkable.' The Kärntnertor, one of Vienna's premier concert venues, is no longer there. Its site is at 4 Philharmonikerstrasse, behind the Opera, approximately where the Hotel Sacher now stands.

On 18 December Franzi was in Pressburg again, to play at painter Baron Ferdinand Lütgendorf-Leinburg's house. The occasion was marked by a fight in the garden with the Baron's sons, with Franzi ending up at the bottom of the heap. At supper, to Franzi's delight, Székelyer káposzta, a popular Hungarian goulash with diced cabbage, was served. Afterwards, when the grown-ups had withdrawn to the smoking room, Franzi withdrew to the kitchen. He found the pot with the goulash, sat on the floor with it nestling between his knees and finished it all with his fingers.

On 18 January 1823, and a few days later, Franzi gave two more concerts in Vienna, but neither the programmes nor the venues are known. 'Eleven-year-old Liszt', wrote the *Allgemeine Musikalische Zeitung* in its end-of-year report, 'amazed every listener with a delicacy of touch unusual for one so young; and a few days later he gave another concert to yet another numerous audience.'

Beethoven had changed his mind about Diabelli's variations. He had written not one but thirty-three, in a massive work lasting almost an hour and imbued with the pianistic creativity of his late sonatas. Diabelli published Beethoven's Variations separately that year as Book I. Franzi was included in Book II, along with the forty-nine other composers, the following year.

At the beginning of April Czerny took Adam and Franzi to see Beethoven at his apartment in Pfarrgasse, where he lived with his nephew Carl, and to invite him to Franzi's forthcoming concert. It was not an easy meeting to arrange, as Beethoven had become a distrustful and cantankerous recluse who disliked concerts and child prodigies. Czerny, Adam and Franzi climbed the ramshackle staircase leading to Beethoven's apartment on the top floor. The door opened into a dingy dwelling in a state of total chaos. Cracks in the ceiling, which was directly under the roof, revealed the open sky. The piano and the table were strewn with music and music paper. Adam and Franzi looked at the legendary composer of the 'Hammerklavier' Sonata who stood before them and noted that his portrait back at Raiding did not show the bleak melancholy of his features, the heavy eyebrows and the sunken eyes that looked piercingly at his visitors. His speech was soft and slurred. On the table lay a notebook; the only way that Beethoven, now completely deaf, was able to communicate was writing down questions and answers. There seemed little point in playing to him, but Franzi sat down at the piano and asked Beethoven for a theme. Franzi improvised, transposed and finally played Beethoven's own C major Piano Concerto. Beethoven's skills at hearing music with his mind's ear had developed to a high degree. He composed in his head and read scores like a book – not as a study exercise but for enjoyment. When Rossini visited him during his Vienna stay, Beethoven said of his *Barber of Seville*, 'I congratulate you; it is an excellent opera buffa. I read it with pleasure and it delights me.' Now he listened to Franzi with his eyes, watching his fingers on the keyboard. He so 'enjoyed' Franzi's performance of his Concerto that afterwards he gave him a hug and kissed him on the forehead. His visit made a deep impression on Franzi, who venerated Beethoven all his life.

Franzi's concert was set for the afternoon of Sunday 13 April at the small Redoutensaal in the Hofburg, but Beethoven's attendance is not verified. Herr Hildebrand, the assistant director of the Hoftheater, conducted the orchestra, which played the first movement of Mozart's 'Jupiter' Symphony as an overture. Then Franzi played Hummel's Piano Concerto in B minor, which was followed by Amalie Schütz with a Rossini aria. Franzi then played the Variations by Moscheles, which were followed by an item by Konradin Kreutzer from a male vocal quartet. Franzi finished the concert with an improvisation on a Rondo theme, which delighted the audience with its humour and whimsy. The *Allgemeine Musikalische Zeitung* wrote of the ease and elegance of his performance, even though he lacked the sheer physical strength needed in parts of the Concerto. 'About the theme given for improvisation,' continued the review, 'one required not only talent but years of musical study to achieve what this eleven-year-old wizard achieved when given a very difficult twenty-four-bar Rondo theme. Risum teneatis [Hold your laughter].' Tickets cost three gulden and Adam made a handsome profit at the end of the day.

With the coming of spring, Salieri's condition worsened. He took the waters at Baden, but to no avail. He injured his head in a fall and became frequently confused as a result. The sessions with Franzi were less frequent and were often merely visits from a concerned boy rather than lessons.

Franzi's reputation was spreading, and, to Adam's satisfaction, the gulden were beginning to come in. Anna's dowry had now gone, as had the grant from the Pressburg Six. Adam's teaching was bringing in a subsistence income, which was supplemented by Franzi's 'presents'. This was a euphemism for the fee paid to unestablished performers – established artists commanded real, often astronomical fees. By tradition 'presents' were open-ended and varied according to the quality of performance or the philanthropy of the giver. 'From the age of twelve,' recalled Franz Liszt, 'I was obliged to earn my living and support my parents. This specifically necessitated music studies which absorbed all my time.' He was now on the threshold of a glittering career as a concert pianist, but Adam's year's leave of absence from Raiding was up. Needing a little more time, he applied to Prince Nicolaus for just two months longer, to give Franzi the opportunity to play in Pesth, where music publisher Karl Miller wanted him to give a concert, and then to tour Paris and London. Prince Nicolaus granted two weeks.

Two weeks later, a resolute Adam and an excited Franzi were on their way to Pesth. The post road left Vienna along the south bank of the Danube, on what is now Route 9. It bypassed Pressburg, which was on the north bank, veered away from the river and continued to Győr and Komárom and to the historic hill city of Offen Bude. The diligence stopped at the Bomben Platz, on the banks of the Danube underneath Castle Hill. From here the Liszts found local transport to take them over the pontoon bridge across the Danube and into Pesth.

The Inn of the Seven Electors was Pesth's premier concert venue. At the end of April posters appeared on the walls of the city:

> High Gracious Nobility Estimable Officers of the Royal and Imperial Army Esteemed Public

> I am a Hungarian and do not know of any greater happiness that to respectfully offer the fruits of my education and studies to my beloved Fatherland, as the first offering of my devotion before my journey to France and England. What is missing in maturity, I intend to acquire through persistent diligence and I may perhaps in days to come be fortunate enough to become one small branch in the adornment of my country.

The notification for the concert, which was held on 1 May, got the date wrong:

With high permission will the eleven-year-old Liszt Franz Liszt born in the Oedenburger County have the high honour on Thursday March 12 [*sic*] in the afternoon at four in the Salon at the Seven Electors give a musical entertainment.
Pieces to be played:
1. Overture by Friedrich Schneider.
2. Concerto for pianoforte by Ries with orchestral accompaniment, given by the concertgiver.
3. Duet from the opera 'Elisabeth' (by Rossini) sung by Demoiselle Teyber and Herr Bübbnig.
4. Concerto for pianoforte with orchestral accompaniment by Moscheles, played by the concertgiver.
5. Aria from the opera 'Libussa' by Konradin Kreutzer, sung by Demoiselle Teyber.
6. A fantasia on the pianoforte by the concertgiver.

The thunderous applause and very favourable press reports ensured that he would not be leaving Pesth just yet; sure enough, a second concert was arranged for 10 May. This was a short recital which took place in the German Theatre. Franzi, whose performances were interspersed with songs and arias from Fräulein Keyser, was loudly applauded, and he was recalled for encores. He played twice more at the German Theatre, on 17 (or 18) May and on Whit Sunday 24 May, which was his farewell appearance in the Hungarian capital. On 19 May he also played at a soirée; among the pieces were the Rákóczi March – which he heard Bihari play at Count Palffy's and later fashioned into his Fifteenth Hungarian Rhapsody – and Weber's *Momento Capriccioso*.

The *Wiener Zeitschrift für Kunst* of 26 June 1823 summed up Franzi's Pesth appearances:

His first performance was on 1 May at the Inn of the Seven Electors and the numerous audience found no lack of charm. . . . On 10 May the eleven-year-old boy Liszt gave a concert with the same applause in the theatre in a short musical recital. . . . On the first day of Whitsun the eleven-year-old boy had the further honour to give a farewell concert by public demand, of which no more can be said than that the concertgiver played excellently and received great applause.

Before leaving Pesth, Adam took Franzi to see the Fathers at the Franciscan Monastery in the Alte-Stadt and introduced him to some old friends and fellow novices from his student days. Franzi gladly played for the monks, who were amazed at his talent,

while he, in turn, was deeply moved by their discipline and god-
liness. Fr Capistran Wagner particularly exerted a profound influence on him; Franzi's singular spiritual bond with St Francis of
Assisi, which he later expressed in his music and religious convic-
tion, dates from this time. He later recalled all the fathers by name
and expressed a wish to be buried there.

Today the two cities of Offen Bude and Pesth are united as the
Hungarian capital of Budapest. The post stage at Bomben Platz,
today Batthyány Tér, is still a transport terminus; the pontoon
bridge linking the two cities was about 200 metres downstream
from the Széchenyi chain bridge. The Inn of the Seven Electors was
demolished in 1840. On its site, at 9 Váci utca, stands the Pest
Theatre. The Franciscan Monastery no longer exists, but the church,
consecrated in 1743, is still there, on the corner of Kossuth utca and
M. Károlyi utca. The German Theatre was burned down in 1847.

After the Whitsunday concert Adam and Franzi left Pesth and
made for Eisenstadt, where Adam looked up old friends and reported on his son's successes in Pesth. They revisited Pressburg,
where Franzi gave a concert on 27 May, before returning to
Vienna and to trouble.

Adam had already begun planning a trip to France and England. Franzi's fame had now reached London with a review in the
June issue of the *Harmonicon*, a London music journal, of his 13
April concert at Vienna's Redoutensaal: 'Liszt played with so much
precision, correctness and execution, united to such taste and
elegance, that he is already placed by the side of the greatest
piano players of the present day. As to physical powers of hand,
he leaves nothing to wish for; and he indeed seems destined to
attain the highest rank in art.'

Adam, keen to capitalize on Franzi's successes, was loath to
drop the momentum but was strongly reminded that his time was
now definitely up, that he 'had overstretched the favour of the
Prince' and was to return to his post at Raiding or else he would
be replaced. Adam's reply verged on desperation, as he pointed
out all the sacrifices that he had made for the sake of his son and
begged the Prince to reconsider his stance and permit a tour of
France and England. Prince Nicolaus did not reply, and Adam,
taking it for granted that he had been sacked, continued throughout the summer to make positive arrangements for the further-
ance of Franzi's career. In May Adam commissioned Baron
Ferdinand Lütgendorf-Leinburg, the artist at whose Pressburg house

Franzi had performed the previous winter, to draw a portrait of the young pianist, dressed in his Hungarian finery, for publicity purposes. The portrait now hangs in the Franz Liszt Museum, Budapest. By midsummer a new rentmeister was appointed at Raiding. Prince Nicolaus's role in the financing of Franzi Liszt's musical education consisted of a series of barely adequate hand-outs. As a last gracious favour, Prince Nicolaus issued a travel pass to the Liszts. On 4 August Adam wrote to Prince Clemens Metternich, requesting a passport and letters of introduction to the ambassadors of Paris, Munich and London:

Gracious Sir,

After the high graciousness which your Serene Highness has shown to me and my son, I ask with the deepest respect that in order to forward the musical talent of my son and develop his creativity and originality it is my ardent wish, and is also the counsel of experts, to pursue his further education abroad and little by little to bring the young talent to Parnassus. To this end I would like to travel, at the end of next month, by way of Munich (where I plan to arrange a concert to meet the travelling costs) to Paris, to continue his studies in composition at the Conservatory of Music there, to stay there for a year, and then to journey on to London or Italy, to stay away in all for at least two years. To achieve this I will gladly undertake every hardship, and I need the grace and protection of your Serene Highness. I have no recommendation to Munich, Paris or London, yet I have highly placed acquaintances who assure me that this step is absolutely necessary. In deepest respect and esteem I consequently venture to the throne of your Serene Highness to seek help and to humbly request that you, moved with pity towards my poor but gifted boy, would graciously condescend to grant me the necessary recommendation that your judgement and insight would see fit to bestow and to issue me with a passport to grant your protection.
    In deepest respect and esteem,
        the humble request is repeated,
            Your Serene Highness' humble pleading servant,
                Adam Liszt
                official of Prince Esterházy.

The reply came from Franz Joseph von Bretfeld, the rector of the University, writing on the Prince's behalf. It was addressed to the Royal Ambassadors to Paris and London and to the Embassy in Munich:

... The musical talent of this boy is a really unusual, momentous phenomenon, and in every respect deserves encouragement in order not be frustrated in the development of its originality. So I have no hesitation in agreeing to his [Adam Liszt's] request, and I recommend this promising young artist to your Excellency for your kind acceptance and ask that you confer on him your patronage necessary for the fulfilment of his originality. I also ask you to arrange for those further dispositions which, in the case of famous and recognized artistry, every talented countryman of ours has, up to now, enjoyed on his journey to Paris, London and Munich, even when he has not been invited.

The Liszts could only look forward. The Esterházy boat was burned, and Europe now beckoned. Vienna, the music capital of Europe, was a fickle city that took its artists for granted. Mozart, Beethoven and Schubert flourished there only tentatively, and Adam knew that the time had come to move on.

Adam and Franzi said their goodbyes. Salieri was now a very sick man, his legs were paralysed and he was often confused. Francisca and Anna found themselves unable to cope with their father, and Adam saw that the situation was becoming hopeless. To make matters worse, rumours had begun to circulate about Salieri during that summer and culminated in a campaign of character assassination during that autumn: he was accused of having poisoned Mozart. The allegations hurt him very badly and accelerated his mental decline.

Czerny was deeply upset by the Liszts' plans to move on, for he did not believe that Franzi was ready yet for the open world and believed that travelling at his age would not be good for him. Like all music teachers who have found a rare talent in their care, he was loath to give up his pupil at just the time when he was beginning to be master of his art. But, as Adam pointed out, he was now unemployed, and the family had no income. Franzi's 'presents' had been good, as were now the prospects of a living. Supporting the family was about to fall on the shoulders of a twelve-year-old boy, which, according to Czerny, was immoral. Despite the exchanges of harsh words between him and Adam, the two men remained friends for life.

The Liszts left Vienna by post coach on 20 September 1823.

FOUR

The Road to Paris
1823

TRAVEL WAS largely controlled by the Thurn und Taxis organization. The English music traveller, Edward Holmes, described the Vienna to Munich run in his *A Summer Among Music and Musical Professors in Germany*, published in 1828:

> As [the traveller] mounts into an ordinary and lumbering diligence ... he deeply laments that no other illustrious potentate [than Prince Thurn und Taxis] will undertake for his more speedy consignment from one city to another, than in six days' time, the sad term of imprisonment which the people of the post office promise. ... As there is no great communication between the capitals of Bavaria and Austria, the road is barren of inns, other than cabarets and beer houses, at which is to be found but lenten entertainment, and the forlorn voyageur must be content to appease his hunger with a crust, and allay his thirst with a draught of poor liquid, as all ideas of dinners and suppers (those celestial respites to the tedium of ever rolling onwards) would be the dreams of a distempered fancy.

Diligences travelled all day and all night. Post stages, in towns or villages, were halts for rest and refreshment and to change horses – or drivers – every forty kilometres or so. In charge of each coach was a team of two: the driver and the postilion, who usually worked in pairs. Staging posts had stables, rooms for hire, food and drink; the facilities ranged from comfortable to squalid. Journeys were fraught with danger. Overturns and armed robbery by highwaymen were a constant hazard, and the possibility of the postilion – or the driver – being struck by lightning was not to be dismissed. On a flat plain their exposed position was as attractive to lightning as a solitary figure on a golf course today. The Liszts braved these hazards as they set off out of Vienna, through the hilly woodland of the now golden Wienerwald, and on through St Pölten, along what is today Route 1. The post road joined the south bank of the Danube at Melk, where they could glimpse the magnificent Benedictine monastery perched on its hill overlooking the river. The road left the Danube at Linz to head for Salzburg, the city of Mozart, passing another Benedictine monastery at Lambach.

After Salzburg was the frontier with the Kingdom of Bavaria, where the German border is today. 'In Bavaria,' wrote Holmes,

> the livery, or rather uniform of the postilion (which varies in every state) mounts to an extravagance of absurdity; he here indues black breeches, a yellow fringed jacket, a cocked hat and green feather, and looks half priest, half mountebank.... The fresh air gives him elastic and unvarying spirits; he is ever carrolling and gay, cracking his whip and his jokes, till some entanglement of the harness dashes his merriment; he stops, groans as he hoists his ponderous boot over the horse's side, and while remedying the accident is melancholy for two minutes, adjuring by the 'heilige sacrament' these calamities of existence.

The post road, today Route 304, continued through virgin forest, picturesque hills and past friendly Bavarian farm villages. The Liszts took it all in. Vincent and Mary Novello were there during this period. 'The costume of the Bavarian peasants is very peculiar and picturesque,' wrote Vincent Novello in their joint diaries of 1829, *A Mozart Pilgrimage*, 'it seems not to have changed for the last 500 years. They wear a kind of plush or velvet breeches of dark green, waistcoats of a bright colour, single-breasted jackets with rows of bright buttons, short thick curly hair, and steeple crowned hats like the Cavaliers of England in the time of Charles the 1st.'

After six harrowing days on the road, the Liszts crossed the River Isar and drove into Munich on the evening of 26 September.

The Kingdom of Bavaria, an Electorate of the Holy Roman Empire until its abolition by Napoleon, was established in 1806, with the Elector, Maximilian IV Joseph, on the throne as King Maximilian I. His capital was seen as a city of culture and gaiety, full of inns and taverns serving good food and fine beers, much patronized by the citizens, who enjoyed dining out. Music was largely dominated by old Peter von Winter, the cantankerous but talented Grand Old Man of Munich's music scene. He was born in the Palatinate city of Mannheim in 1754, during the heady days of the famous Mannheim Orchestra, which he joined at the age of ten as a violinist. In 1778 the Elector of the Palatinate, the musically enlightened Karl Teodor, inherited the Electorship of Bavaria, and the whole Mannheim court, including the musicians, moved to Munich, where von Winter was appointed vice-Kapellmeister. He went to Vienna and worked with Salieri. On his return to Munich he was appointed court music director and spent the rest of his life there. He was not a charismatic person, and many people, including Mozart, whom he slandered, had cause to dislike him. Edward Holmes found 'his manners were what the Germans expressively term *grob* (something between surly and deficient in politesse)'. Despite all this, his influence on Munich's strong musical ethos was never in doubt. He composed operas, chamber and orchestral works, all of their time and now passed into oblivion but which enjoyed some modicum of success in Europe. Von Winter died in 1825 and with him Munich's Mannheim pedigree of excellence.

Adam presented his credentials to the Austrian ambassador, and doors opened for Franzi's Bavarian début. Two problems precluded a concert in the immediate future. First, the 29-year-old Moscheles was in town doing a concert tour, so competition would have been counter-productive. Secondly, the annual Beer Festival, the Oktoberfest, was about to take place, and with it at least a temporary lowering of cultural standards, even though Munich would fill with provincial visitors. The Liszts had no option but to bide their time, wait until Moscheles had finished, join in the fun, witness some bawdier-than-usual behaviour from a city renowned for its friendly sociability and do some sightseeing.

There was much to see in Munich: the brick, late-Gothic Cathedral, or Frauenkirche, the Nymphenburg Palace on the north-western outskirts and the royal Residenz complex in the city centre. Munich's wide reputation as a city of art was due to the famous art gallery, situated on the north side, which was full of Old Dutch Masters – a passion of the King's. It looked out onto the Hofgarten and was open to the public. Beyond it lay the open English Gardens, the creation of Count Rumford, now in the golden splendour of autumn. Here there were pleasant walks along the banks of the swiftly-flowing Schwabingerbach and Eisbach streams, tributaries of the Isar, that cut across it. The park was a favourite haunt of students from the University, many of whom, to any visitor's bemusement, made striking sartorial statements in their often eccentric dress. 'So unfettered by custom or prejudice in the mode of wearing their habiliments', wrote Holmes, 'that no possible extravagance in that respect would excite remark.' They gathered in groups to converse, smoke, drink beer or just to desport themselves. Street entertainments were a feature of Munich, and street musicians ranged from military bands to instrumental groups playing anything from folk-tunes to arrangements of arias from whatever opera happened to be playing in town. Their qualities varied from excellent to awful.

The Liszts also met Moscheles socially and found him to be a charming, kind man with a sweet nature and generous spirit. Ignaz Moscheles was born in Prague in 1794 and spent his early years in Vienna, where he studied under Salieri. He soon became a rival of Hummel, who was sixteen years his senior, with his Alexander's March Variations of 1815. These were one of his set pieces, which he always had to play and grew to loathe. The 14 October issue of Munich's 'what's on' magazine, *Flora*, commented that 'Fortunate indeed is the artist, who, with the skill of his hands and a regularly repeated little piece, can always obtain honour and money.'

Earlier that year, after a spell in Paris, Moscheles had gone to live in London, which became his base for continental concert tours. In 1846 he joined his ex-pupil Mendelssohn at the Leipzig Conservatory, where he spent the rest of his life. As he grew older, he found full Romanticism difficult to follow and never really got to grips with Chopin or Liszt. Franzi, whose concert repertoire at this time consisted of the work of Hummel, Moscheles himself and his own improvisations, played for him, and the older man was impressed enough to write him a warm letter of recommendation. It was only later that both their styles drew far enough apart for the mature Franz Liszt to write that 'as he grew older he became too old-womanish and set in his ways'. Moscheles died in Leipzig in 1870.

Munich's premier concert venue, the National Theatre, had burnt to the ground in January of that year, five years after its completion. It had been situated on the east side of the Maximilian-Joseph Platz, at right angles to the royal Residenz on the north. It was a severe blow to the Court, and the King was inconsolable, wringing his hands and moaning 'My beautiful theatre.' Nestled in the corner between the two edifices was the Hof Theatre. This small venue, with its exquisite Baroque interior and ornate exterior, crowned with statues, known also as the Cuvilliés Theatre after its designer, was affected by the heat and smoke. It was due for renovation anyway, and by March the ceiling had been replaced, the boxes repainted and the gold ornamentation renewed. It was then designated the chief venue for concerts while the National Theatre was being rebuilt. On 10 October Moscheles gave his concert, delayed to attract beer festival tourists, at the sparkling new theatre, and the stage was clear for Franzi to follow suit. Under the circumstances the smaller venue was a good thing, for Franzi's audience on Friday 17 October was not great, and the larger venue would have seemed awesomely empty. He was an unknown following on the heels of the renowned Moscheles. However, the King came over from next door to attend, accompanied by his daughters.

Advance notice of the concert by eleven-year-old Franz Liszl [sic] appeared in the *Münchner Politische Zeitung* on 16 October. The programme described the concert-giver as Franz Liszt, a Hungarian boy, the son of an Esterházy official, and a pupil of the renowned Carl Czerny, on his way to Paris and London. The public were also invited to supply a theme for improvisation. The concert began with Franzi's rendition of Hummel's B minor Concerto, which was followed by a selection of highly topical drinking songs arranged for a male-voice quartet. The first half ended with Weber's Clarinet Concertino, played by Herr Schulein. The second half opened with Franzi playing Czerny's Tragic Introduction and Variations in E flat for piano and orchestra. This was followed by Miss Pesl with an aria from Rossini's *Italian Girl in Algiers*, and Franzi concluded with an improvisation on the theme of the Fantasia for violin by Royal Concert Master and later musical director to the royal court of Württemberg, Wilhelm Bernhard Molique, which Franzi heard the composer playing at Moscheles's concert. He finished with a free rendition of 'God Save the King', which may or may not have been directed at the personage in the royal box. The noise of the applause belied the size of the audience. *Flora* reviewed the concert on 19 October: 'On Friday 17 the young boy Liszt gave a concert. This boy, with the claim in years to childhood, is a musical phenomenon, who arouses great astonishment and wonder and, we might well say, leaves every other clavier player behind him. Agility, skill, taste and confidence are evident in his playing, which was heard with the greatest applause.'

A second concert was scheduled for Friday 24 October and was a sell-out, and Adam had to close the box office when all the seats had gone: 'The gathering', recorded *Flora*, 'was so numerous that many people could not find a place.' Again the King was there. Franzi opened with Hummel's A minor Piano Concerto; Franz Xaver Lochle then sang an aria from *Carassa*, and Herr Stahl finished the first half with a performance of his own Variations for violin. For the second-half opener, Franzi chose Moscheles's Variations in G, after which Miss Schechner sang an aria from *Rassolini*. Franzi closed with an improvised free Fantasia.

'Both the Hummel Concertos [*sic*],' reported *Flora* on 31 October,

> the Czerny Variations and those of Moscheles, appeared to us as though it was his own spirit coming out, with a depth of emotion which always came at the right moment in his performance; the mastery alone in overcoming all difficulties would certainly put him in the first rank of today's living clavier players. Above all, he surpassed himself in his free fantasy, and this was truly the highest point of all. It testified to his inherent genius, was proof of his knowledge of harmony and justified great hopes for the future.

Adam wrote to Czerny that the Munich Court orchestra, conducted by Spagnoletti, was excellent, an opinion echoed by *Flora*. This was hardly surprising as the director was Peter von Winter. He went on to say that Franzi's Hummel was done matchlessly, adding, perhaps with a dash of *schadenfreude*, that 'Moscheles has outlived his renown in Munich, and people do not speak of him with due respect. I thought he played his concerto [in E major] unsurpassably, but his improvisation – if it could be called that – was empty. What lost him respect more than anything else was that he charged double prices.' Moscheles's hopes of exploiting the beer festival had not been entirely successful, and his concert was not a sell-out, although *Flora* added that 'the unusually high prices did not frighten away our culture-loving public'.

Franzi was a hit with everyone. People crowded round him to ask whether Herr Czerny had any more like him. The King, according to Adam 'this kindliest of kings', bestowed two audiences on Franzi. 'So you, young fellow,' beamed his Majesty, 'had the courage to appear after Moscheles?' Whereupon he gave Franzi a kiss.

Franzi also found friends in two Hungarian brothers, Karl and Anton Ebner, aged eleven and twelve respectively – both violinists at the Royal Court of Prussia. They arranged for Franzi to take part in a concert they were planning, scheduled for Monday 27 October. 'In response to a pressing request from the directors of the Theatre Royal,' wrote Adam to Czerny, 'I allowed Franzi to appear a third time . . . he had to repeat, by public demand, your Variations in E flat with orchestra.' Apart from Czerny's Variations, Franzi's contribution was a duet with Karl Ebner, Variations for violin and piano – a joint item that the two boys had prepared. Franzi brought the concert to an end with a solo free Fantasia.

Also on the programme was 21-year-old Catherine Sigl-Vespermann, von Winter's star pupil and protégée and, according to Holmes, 'one of those lavish productions of nature, a real singer'. She sang an aria from *Pucitta*. 'Mademoiselle Vesperman', continued Holmes, 'fell sacrifice in her twenty-first year [she was twenty-six] to the blunders of an ignorant physician, who negligently allowed a simple disorder to become a malignant one.' She died, in her prime, in 1828.

Franzi received no reward for taking part in the Ebners' concert, having done so purely out of support for his fellow Hungarians; he and Karl became very close friends. The King commented on his kindness towards them, and Adam wrote that 'we earned immortal glory for ourselves in return'.

Franzi also earned a sharp rebuke from *Flora* in its issue of 30 October: 'Modesty and good manners are virtues which are especially fitting for boys. The public consequently found it not fitting that the young Liszt, on his entrances and exits, nodded to the numerous gathering in a lackadaisical and offhand manner. This could have had unpleasant consequences from a less tolerant public.' The conductor, Spagnoletti, also aware of this deficiency, afterwards took Franzi aside and taught him how to bow properly.

Czerny was heartened by the popularity of his Variations. Not so Salieri in Vienna, who had nothing to be heartened about. The rumours of his having poisoned Mozart accelerated his decline, and by that October he was a broken man. He was dragged to the General Hospital, struggling and protesting vehemently at the expense.

The day after the Ebners' concert, Tuesday 28 October, the Liszts left Munich with fond memories of three very successful concerts in a lively and friendly city and a kiss from 'the kindliest of kings'. That same evening they arrived in Augsburg, the birthplace of Mozart's forefathers.

While still in Munich Adam had been arranging the next stage of Franzi's concert tour. On 28 October *Flora* reported that 'he will continue his journey to Paris without stopping, but if connoisseurs and the inhabitants of Augsburg request to hear him, then arrangements will be made to stop there one day and give a concert'. The connoisseurs and inhabitants of Augsburg did request it, and the one-day projected stop-over turned out to be a week. On 30 October Franzi gave the first of two performances at Augsburg's National Theatre and included the Ebner brothers. The programme is not known, apart from an improvisation on a theme which had been written out for him on a piece of paper. A second concert took place at the Harmonie on 1 November. 'Today,' wrote Adam to Czerny the following day, 'Zisy [the latest of Franzi's nicknames] will play for free at a concert for the poor, and tomorrow we leave for Stuttgart.'

The *Schwabische Chronik* of 5 November mentioned the 30 October concert.

Local music lovers had a great treat: a concert given by Franz Liszt, a young Hungarian. . . . This boy possesses in the highest degree, facility, expression, precision, execution, etc. etc.: in fact all the qualities that reveal a distinguished pianist. To this may be added the profound knowledge of counterpoint and fugue passages which he disclosed when performing a free fantasia. . . . All this justifies the affirmation that this boy already equals the first pianists in Europe, perhaps already surpasses many of them.

Also a review of Franzi's first Munich concert appeared in the *Augsburger Allgemeine Zeitung*:

A new Mozart has appeared unto us, Munich announces to the musical world. Young Liszt played Hummel's Concerto in B minor with a facility and purity, with a precision and power, with such deep and true feeling, that even the boldest imagination would not dare to expect anything similar at so tender an age. We have heard Hummel and Moscheles, and do not hesitate to affirm that this child's execution is in no way inferior to theirs. But what carried admiration to the highest point was an improvisation on given themes. . . . It is not to be wondered at that the numerous and delighted audience could set no bounds to their applause.

On 9 November *Flora* noted that 'the young clavier player has been heard with the greatest applause. Afterwards he greeted the assembly very decently and respectfully.' Spagnoletti's pep talk had borne fruit. On 12 November *Flora* included the Ebners in its review: 'Little Liszt gave two public concerts and produced in both such style on his instrument that excited the greatest wonder. The two young Ebners were no less interesting to hear, as such skilful development on these difficult instruments at such a tender age is remarkable and rare.'

Adam found Augsburg expensive; food, carriage costs and, particularly, wine dented the family budget; but at the end of the day he recorded a net profit of 921 florins. The time had come to look ahead, and he began making arrangements for the next port of call, Stuttgart. He then heard of Salieri's ignominious removal to the General Hospital, and the news upset him considerably. 'God grant that it is not true, what I have heard about Salieri,' he wrote to Czerny, 'and although I do not want to be kept in the dark, I ask you not to let me know until we get to Paris.'

On 9 November the Liszts set off, now warmly clad, westwards along what is today Route 10. The road went through Günzburg and crossed a young, barely navigable Danube into Ulm and the Kingdom of Württemberg. After Ulm the scenery changed as the coach passed among the bleak fields and vineyards along the hilly landscape, crossed the River Neckar and into Stuttgart, the capital and seat of the Court of King Wilhelm I.

Like Bavaria, Württemberg became a kingdom in 1806, and former Elector Friedrich II became king. The state had a tradition of military posturing going back to Duke Karl Eugen, who founded a military academy, the Karlsschule, at the Castle at Ludwigsburg, just to the north of Stuttgart.

During the Napoleonic wars Friedrich II defied popular opinion, fought against France and suffered defeat and devastation on a massive scale. After a deal involving reallocation of territory, he went over to Napoleon's side and joined the Confederation of the Rhine. But the military ethos remained, which King Wilhelm used as a symbol. 'Soldiers seemed to be more numerous than the inhabitants,' wrote Vincent Novello, 'I have an invincible repugnance to these outward signs of the power of the privileged few.' Württemberg was a poor but very picturesque kingdom, dominated by the forest-clad Swabian highlands, through which the River Neckar meandered to join the Rhine at Mannheim. A third of the kingdom was covered in forest full of wildlife, and hunting was a favourite pastime for the privileged. Where Munich was a beer-drinking region, Württemberg was noted for its wine. The vineyards on the slopes astride the River Neckar were renowned throughout Germany for the production of a white wine, which, according to Holmes, had 'a strong resemblance in colour, smell, and taste, to the gargle which physicians prescribe for a sore throat'. The following day, 10 November, Franzi gave a concert at the Royal Court Theatre and another on 18 November. There are no further details about them. Winter was taking hold of Europe when the Liszts continued on their journey. The next stop was Strasbourg, in France. The post road went by way of Karlsruhe, in the Grand Duchy of Baden, along what is today Route 10. The road skirted to the north of the mountains of the Schwarzwald, or Black Forest, which, although one of Germany's most picturesque regions, was unsuitable for coaches. At Karlsruhe travellers to France changed coaches for the three-hour drive south, parallel to the Rhine, to the frontier crossing point at Rastatt. Vincent Novello jotted down some notes: 'Apathy and indifference of the people at the Bureau of Diligence. Frenchman nearly lost his portmanteau in consequence of their being too indolent to look for it, although it was in the carriage all the time.' On 25 November the Liszts' coach reached the bridge over the Rhine at Rastatt and continued down the west bank and through the 'Porte Dauphine' into Strasbourg.

Passport formalities at Strasbourg were awkward and verged on corruption. The Novellos, also on their way to Paris, had to surrender theirs to be sent on to the capital, and temporary passports were issued, at a cost of two francs, to tide them over until Paris. 'This appeared to be an excuse', wrote Vincent Novello, 'to extract money from travellers and is a piece of paltry meanness totally unworthy of any government pretending to be conducted upon liberal practices. It is a contemptible and mean imposition.'

The Liszts experienced a completely different welcome to Strasbourg when they booked in at the Hôtel de l'Esprit at 6 quai St Thomas. Discovering the name, Sieur List, on the list of new arrivals, the Prefect demanded immediate action at the Town Hall, to ascertain whether this was Professor List, a dangerous criminal sought by the Police. Inquiries resulted in the written reply that 'the traveller, whose name resembles that of the infamous Professor Frédéric List (liberal economist) of Stuttgart, is Adam Liszt, travelling with his wife and son, eleven-year-old François Liszt, a musical artist said to possess a talent as rare as it is precocious'.

For the past nine years France had been getting back to a semblance of normality after twenty-five years of revolution and war. The Bourbon Monarchy had been restored in 1814, with the coronation of Louis-Stanislas-Xavier, the Comte de Provence and younger brother of the executed Louis XVI – with a slight hiccup following Napoleon's escape from Elba and his final adventure on the field of Waterloo. The new King assumed the title of Louis XVIII (ten-year-old Louis XVII died in captivity in 1795) and reigned over a country that had heaved itself into the new century. Apart from a period in which a 'White Terror' wrought revenge on prominent revolutionaries, the Napoleonic infrastructure – a great improvement on the pre-revolutionary scenario – remained largely intact. France had become an ideological melting-pot where religion, monarchy and liberalism strove to find the right level for a functioning nineteenth-century state.

Both the Liszts and the Novellos found in Strasbourg a beautiful, historic city situated at the point where France and Germany meet, physically and culturally. The Rhine traditionally represents the western reaches of Germany, with its many mythological connotations from the Rhinegold, through the Lorelei legend to the fantasies of the Brothers Grimm. The Liszts experienced a change of culture as radical as that between ethnic Germans and Magyars. There was much to see in the city centre, built on an island in a complex of waterways and canals, including the River Ill, a tributary of the Rhine. The Novellos attended Vespers at the Cathedral. 'The Cathedral at Strasbourg', wrote Mary Novello, 'pleases me much more than any other I have seen. It is in fine preservation, even the ornamental part, and if the other tower were complete would be perfect. The interior is very grand and many fine stained windows.' 'No last voluntary on organ,' wrote her husband, 'which I was less sorry for, as I was sure the performer would only have spoilt any movement of the dignified class which he might have attempted.' The organ was built by Gottfried Silbermann, who was in the van of pianoforte development in Germany.

Another visitor to Strasbourg at this time was the future – as from October 1825 – King Ludwig I of Bavaria. Born in Strasbourg, he was now on a nostalgic visit to his native city. In the marshy, Rhine-side terrain just to the north of the city stood the Château de Pourtalès, the residence of city councillor Paul-Athanase Renouard de Bussière and his wife Frédérique. She ran a lively salon which caused Stendhal to describe her as the 'Mme de Récamier of Strasbourg'. She organized a grand reception in the Prince's honour at the Château, at which, through the Liszts' connections with the Bavarian royal family, Franzi was asked to perform. He wanted to play Moscheles's Rondo brillant for piano duet, 'The Charms of Paris', which was dedicated to the Prince – but who to play it with? Madame de Bussière suggested her twelve-year-old nephew, Ferdinand de Turckheim, who was an excellent musician. So a carriage was sent to the Pension Redslob, where the boy was doing his studies, to fetch him. The two boys played with true empathy and delighted everyone with their brilliant display. They were consequently plied with cakes and sweets.

Ferdinand, later Baron de Turckheim, recalled this event on the occasion of his 100th birthday in 1911, embellishing his story with a Chopin Ballade. The Château de Pourtalès is still there, in the northern suburb of La Robertsau.

On Friday 5 December Franzi gave his first concert at the Salle de l'Esprit, situated in the Hôtel. This was the venue of the Société des Amateurs, which was run by two local musicians and teachers, the French horn player and composer Antoine-Aloise Laucher and the clarinettist Ernest Betz 'for the sole purpose of stimulating enthusiasm in their pupils and to accustom them to orchestral playing'. The programme is not known.

The next day the *Affiches de Strasbourg* gave notice of Franzi's second concert:

> THÉÂTRE DE STRASBOURG. Today, Saturday 6 December, M. Liszt, aged eleven, pianist, will have the honour to give a concert in which he will be heard for the last time. The enthusiasm which this young virtuoso has aroused has made it necessary to arrange this concert ... so that the inhabitants of this town might have the chance to hear this phenomenon.

The programme began with *La Jeunesse de Henri V*, Alexandre Duval's comedy in three acts. Franzi opened his set with Hummel's Piano Concerto in B minor and Moscheles's *Grand Variations on Alexander's March*, with orchestra, to follow. He concluded with an improvised Grand Fantasia.

A review of his performances appeared the following year in the *Allgemeine Musikalische Zeitung*:

> On 3 December [*sic*] in the Salle de l'Esprit, and on the 6 at the Théâtre, we were amazed by eleven-year-old Liszt, who, with his skilful and expressive piano playing evinced great applause, especially with his free Fantasia. Among other items he played the Piano Concerto in B minor by Hummel, and in addition the Alexander March Variations by Moscheles with amazing facility and feeling. He set out from here to Paris with his father.

The Liszts stayed in Strasbourg for about a week, and after the second concert they set off on the final stage of their journey to Paris. The diligence passed through Nancy and Châlons-sur-Marne and took four days. The final stretch into Paris hugged the banks of the River Marne, crossing over to the south side at Épernay. The Liszts arrived in Paris on 11 December and booked in at the Hôtel d'Angleterre in rue du Mail, today No. 10. Their apartment, overlooking the street, consisted of two rooms on the ground floor and a pair of adjoining drawing rooms upstairs. The rent was 120 francs per month; not cheap, but, Adam reflected with satisfaction, they could afford it. The Liszts settled in, happy and relieved to have completed their 1,250-kilometre journey from Vienna.

Paris had all the appearance of a thriving, modern city, thanks to Napoleon, who had great tracts redeveloped. Largely gone were the narrow slums where misery and resentment once festered and germinated into the storming of the Bastille and its consequences. Rue du Mail was a fashionable street, close to the centre. Opposite the hotel was the Maison Erard, the showroom, workshop and recital salon of the Erard family, perhaps the most forward-looking piano manufacturers in Europe at the time.

The Erard brothers, Jean-Baptiste and Sébastien, were born in 1745 and 1752 respectively in Strasbourg, of German origin. In 1768 Sébastien went to Paris where he worked in harpsichord manufacture. He found a patron in the Duchesse de Villeroi, who provided him with a workshop, where, in 1777, he built his first piano. By this time Jean-Baptiste was also in Paris, and in 1785 the brothers teamed up, established their own piano factory, and were granted a patent by Louis XVI. The following year, keen to expand, Sébastien went on a fact-finding trip to London; when he returned he built a piano for Queen Marie-Antoinette, who was taught by Gluck as a child. By the time the French Revolution took place Sébastien had paid a second visit to London, and the firm had moved to 37 rue du Mail, where the brothers made over 400 pianos a year.

In 1792 Sébastien emigrated to London, where he established a showroom at 18 Great Marlborough Street, leaving Jean-Baptiste in charge of the Paris branch. In 1794 Sébastien obtained the patent for the newly developed escapement mechanism, and in Paris the same year Pierre was born to Jean-Baptiste and his wife. As the century turned, Erard pianos were firmly established as among the best; their customers included Haydn, Beethoven and leading Paris musician Ferdinando Paër. Sébastien returned to Paris, and the brothers bought up Nos 17 and 39 rue du Mail, and the London branch was overseen by Pierre. The technical qualities of Erard pianos came to a head in 1822, with the patenting of the double escapement mechanism, one of the most important developments in pianoforte manufacture, which allowed notes to be repeated at great speed.

Late on 11 December 1823, Sébastien, his two sisters, Barbe and Elyse, and Pierre, who was in Paris at the time, received a visit from the family of Adam Liszt, who had just arrived from Vienna at the Hôtel d'Angleterre opposite. Adam had immediately exploited the coincidence and went over with Anna and Franzi to introduce themselves. The five-storey palatial building was a stack of annexes, apartments and turrets placed one on top of the other at various angles and built around an arched courtyard, giving an air of well-maintained but eccentric architectural anarchy. Within there was every sign of a successful business, and the Salle Erard was an opulent recital room with rows of chandeliers. The Erards received the Liszts cordially and showed their range of instruments, which included harps, a popular alternative to pianos at the time. Franzi was excited and overwhelmed by such a treasure trove and needed no encouragement to try out the pianos. Pierre Erard was amazed by Franzi's prowess, and the scene was set for the type of partnership between manufacturer and artist on which the technicalities of virtuoso Romanticism were built.

Adam explained that they had spent two and a half months earning their way to Paris from Vienna, giving concerts, and now he intended to enrol Franzi at the Conservatoire and to visit London. Erard approved the idea and offered to accompany them to the Conservatoire the next day and introduce them to the Director. The following morning Adam gathered up his letters of introduction from Prince Metternich, Salieri, Moscheles and banker's wife Mme Eskeles-Fliers and set off with Franzi to the Conservatoire to see Director Cherubini.

Luigi Cherubini was born in Florence in 1760, the son of a musician. Although no prodigy, he had a love of his native Italian opera and a singular understanding of counterpoint. Having established a start as an opera composer by the time he was twenty, he chose to seek his fortune abroad, and travelled extensively between Italy, Paris, Vienna and London, before finally settling in Paris in 1788. The following year the Revolution interrupted his composing, as there was little call for operas at that particular time. When the Terror of the early 1790s gripped France, the only musical work he could find was as triangle player in a band. When the situation had subsided, and the new regime set about restoring a semblance of order in France, Cherubini continued composing operas and church music and enjoyed considerable success. He was much admired by musicians as well as the public, including Haydn and Beethoven, who held him in the highest esteem. As an expert in counterpoint and theory, he involved himself in transforming the Garde Nationale Music School, in rue du Faubourg Poissonnière, into the Conservatoire de Musique – a task that through hard work he eventually made his own. In 1805, during a trip to Vienna, he visited Eisenstadt, where he met Adam Liszt.

He met Napoleon before the latter became First Consul, and the two struck up a relationship which ended in mutual dislike. Both men shared the same box one night, when a Cherubini opera was being given. 'My dear Cherubini,' said Napoleon, 'you are certainly an excellent musician, but really your music is so noisy and complicated that I can make nothing of it.' 'My dear general,' replied Cherubini, 'you are certainly an excellent soldier, but you will excuse me if I don't find it necessary to adapt my works to your comprehension.' After Napoleon's exile in 1814, Cherubini pointedly recognized the restoration of the French monarchy by writing a Coronation Mass for King Louis XVIII.

In 1822 he achieved his ambition and became director of the Paris Conservatoire, which he ran with a mixture of musical enlightenment and petty tyranny. His regulations managed to irritate academics and students alike. Some, like the 20-year-old Hector Berlioz, who had been using the Conservatoire library that year prior to enrolling, had little respect for him, a feeling that was mutual. 'He looked as if he had eaten some mustard,' Berlioz wrote in his *Memoirs*, commenting on his somewhat grim disposition. This brilliant young student from near Grenoble, in the Savoy Alps, was proving to be a wild genius who lived in a musical and spiritual fantasy world of his own, in which theories of harmony and counterpoint were but one part. Cherubini, although born in the Classical era, had enough understanding of the new trends to see the way music was going, but, like Salieri and Czerny, he advocated care and restraint; for Berlioz unleashed, he reserved a stark pomposity and grim manner that were totally absent from the methods of Czerny and Salieri.

Berlioz recorded some anecdotes in his *Memoirs*, which might
have served as advance warning to Franzi. Having on one occasion entered by the 'wrong' door, the unrepentant Berlioz was
chased all over the library by an enraged Cherubini, knocking over
tables and chairs. 'One does not go out of the Conservatoire',
admonished Cherubini on another occasion, 'as if it were a stable.'
'Why not,' replied Berlioz under his breath, 'if we are treated like
horses?' 'I have seen something of egoism in high places,' he also
wrote, 'and how the young are cold-shouldered from fear of competition.'

The generation gap may have caused resentment among some
extreme progressives, but for all that the Paris Conservatoire was
now reputedly Europe's finest music school. Competition was fierce,
notably in the climate of the new Romanticism, and hopeful young
pianists like Franzi arrived by the coach-load from the far corners
of the continent to seek enlightenment, fame and fortune in the
French capital. Cherubini and his committee feared that the Paris
Conservatoire would be swamped with foreign pianists, and they
decided that, as from the end of that year, admission to the piano
course would be restricted exclusively to French students. With
only two weeks to go before the regulation was due to come into
effect, Adam and Franzi, accompanied by Sébastien Erard, first
called on the Minister of Education, M. Lauriston, and then on
Director Cherubini.

Nervously, Adam and Franzi entered the portals of the
Conservatoire and made their way to Cherubini's office. Vincent
Novello jotted down that Cherubini had 'a fine head with long
hair and long, grave and intelligent face, but careworn as if he
were not happy'. He received the newcomers stiffly but politely.
Adam submitted the letters of introduction and recalled their meeting
at Eisenstadt eighteen years previously. The Director regretted that
he did not remember the occasion. He skim-read the letters, without even raising his eyebrow at the signatures: Prince Clemens
Metternich, Ignaz Moscheles, Antonio Salieri. He then declined
to take Franzi on the grounds that the new regulation disqualified
all foreigners automatically from enrolling on the pianoforte course,
in view of the vast numbers applying from all over Europe. After
a stunned silence Adam begged Cherubini to at least listen to the
boy, but the Director was deaf to all entreaties and pronounced
the interview terminated.

'Regulations,' he said.

FIVE

Ferdinando Paër's Paris
1823–24

F ERDINANDO PAËR was born in Parma in 1771. A pianist, cellist and composer, notably of operas, he had his first success there with his *Orfeo ed Euridice*. Several operas later he was appointed maestro di cappella in Rome before moving to Venice. In 1797 he went to Vienna and took the post of director of the Kärntnertor Theatre. In 1801 he became Kapellmeister in Dresden, where in 1806 he caught the ear of the victorious Napoleon, who offered him a future in music in Paris. Paër accepted and was soon appointed director of the Opéra Comique. In 1812 he took over the Théâtre Italien from Gaspare Spontini. In 1822 he had a major hit with his *Le Maître de Chapelle*, which represented the apex of his musical career. He was still basking in the glowing aftermath of this production when, towards the end of the following year, a M. Adam Liszt came to see him with his son, armed with a letter of introduction from Prince Clemens Metternich:

My dear Paër,
This letter will be brought to you by the father of a young pianist who is worthy of your attention. Normally I do not care for early genius, however, I make an exception with young List [*sic*]. He will surely astonish you as he has astonished me. You would do me a great kindness if you can help him to give a concert. The father needs assistance so that his son may continue with his training, and I recommend him to you as I have no effectual interest in his regard. Adieu, my dear Paër, I have not seen you for a long time, but my feelings for you remain the same. Metternich.

Paër listened to Franzi, and was as astonished as Metternich wrote he would be. He took Franzi under his wing and soon after began to give him lessons. He could not replace the technical workouts of Czerny, nor the lessons in counterpoint of Salieri, but he was enough of an all-rounder to teach Franzi the four things he knew well: French, commercial pianism, counterpoint and the art of Opera. He listened appraisingly to Franzi's playing, and promised to look into the possibilities of a concert at his Théâtre Italien, pointing out that, although he was musical director there, bookings all had to go through official channels.

Sébastien Erard had one of his new seven-octave, export-special square pianos moved across the road for Franzi's use. Franzi was now set to continue with his studies and practice, which had been to an extent suspended while on tour. This he did with great vigour, for he had become obsessed with his technique and sometimes worked ten hours a day at the keyboard. The word spread quickly round Paris, and within four days of the Liszts' arrival the first bookings started to come in for Franzi to play at soirées.

Since the Restoration salons were a growing trend in France, providing a forum for artists, including musicians, writers and painters. Among the new patrons that year was eighteen-year-old Marie de Flavigny. She was a striking-looking girl, tall, slender, with fair curls framing a perfectly oval face. She had come out that year, having just completed her education at the Convent of the Sacre Coeur. Writing in her *Souvenirs* decades later, she described the musician's role at the salon scene of the time:

> Composers and singers still had their place apart; in spite of the eagerness to have them, they appeared in the salons only on the footing of inferiors. If someone wanted to give a fine concert he went to Rossini, who, for a recognized fee . . . undertook to arrange the programme and see to the carrying out of it. . . . Generally he added an instrumental virtuoso – Herz or Moscheles, Lafont or Bériot, Nadermann (the leading Paris harpist), Tulou (the King's first flute), or the wonder of the musical world, the little Liszt.

All the artists arrived at the side door at the specified hour, and were ushered to their place beside the piano. They were always kept apart from the guests, sometimes even roped off. After their performance they all left together, having been complimented by the master of the house and a few genuine music lovers. Franzi found this segregation distasteful, as did Beethoven before him. He did not yet have the nerve to answer back to a Prince, as did Beethoven according to legend, that 'there are princes and there will be thousands of princes more, but there is only one Beethoven'. The latter was known for his cantankerous attitude, whereas Franzi was renowned for his generous spirit and kind personality, but their attitudes to privilege and aristocracy were the same. The usual fee for a complete 'package' of the kind supplied by Rossini was 1,500 francs. By the middle of March 1824 Adam further recorded that Franzi had made thirty-eight appearances. For each of his performances he received between 100 and 150 francs. This brought in between 4,500 and 5,000 francs in their first three months in Paris, an average gross income of 1,600 francs per month. The total outlay at the Hôtel d'Angleterre, including rent, heating, meals and service, came to just over 600 francs per month. Adam could theoretically bank a net profit of 3,000 francs over this period from the soirées alone.

Franzi's repertoire consisted largely of Czerny's compositions and his own improvisations, nearly always on themes from operas. Both proved enormously popular. The journal *L'Étoile* ran a piece on Franzi in its issue of 22 December:

> Paris possesses at this moment a real phenomenon in an eleven-year-old Hungarian named Leist [*sic*]. This child already displays pianistic talents of the first order; but his playing is distinguished not only for the rapidity of his fingers, which is what is admired in a number of performers; with perfect lightness and firmness he unites an expression lacking in other artists, even those of high reputation. That, however, is what is least astonishing in the talents of this extraordinary child. He composes in the style of the greatest masters; and on themes given to him he improvises with a facility made all the more marvellous in that his power and grace of his ideas never fail him. Since Mozart, who astonished several European courts at the age of eight, the world of music has certainly witnessed nothing so surprising as young Leist.

L'Étoile added, optimistically, that he was already fluent – and stylish – in French. Franzi, who had never managed his native Hungarian, had actually made a good start on the language that was to become his first as an adult.

The French Royal Family had two branches, the House of Bourbon and the House of Orléans. King Louis XVIII, younger brother of the executed Louis XVI, was of the former line. The head of the latter line was his cousin Louis-Philippe, the Duc d'Orléans, a cultured socialite whose salon at the Palais Royal attracted the cream of Parisian society and featured the capital's finest artists. Among them was Franzi, who performed in front of an admiring aristocratic gathering on New Year's Eve. So successful was his performance that, before the winter was out, he was recalled twice more to the Palais Royal. On one occasion, the Duc asked Franzi if there was anything that he would like as a reward. Franzi looked about the room, and his eye fell on a marionette belonging to the little Prince de Joinville. He made his choice. The Duc took the marionette and gave it to Franzi, who placed it on the piano and announced to a delighted audience that he was going to give it a piano lesson. Having thus charmed Parisian aristocracy, and presumably upset the little Prince de Joinville, it became customary for the aristocracy to bring baskets of toys to his performances, to the bemused chagrin of his mother, who did not know where to put them all.

Among regular visitors to the Palais Royal was Caroline, the Duchesse de Berry. She was born in 1798, the eldest daughter of King Francis I of Naples. She married King Louis XVIII's nephew, Charles, the Duc de Berry, the heir to the French throne: the King had no children of his own. On 13 February 1820, a radical saddler, Louis Louvel, pounced upon the Duc and the Duchesse de Berry outside the Opéra as they were getting into their carriage after a performance. The Duc was stabbed and mortally wounded, leaving a frantic, frightened 22-year-old widow bespattered with his blood and pregnant with his child. Seven months later, Henri, the Duc de Bordeaux and Comte de Chambord, was born, a new heir to the throne of France. 'On one occasion,' wrote Adam to Czerny on 17 March, '[Franzi] played at Madame la Duchesse de Berry's, where the entire royal family was present, and he improvised four times on themes given to him.'

The Palais Royal was built by Richelieu in 1632, and in 1780 it passed into the hands of the Orléans dynasty. It was taken over by 'the people' after the Revolution but handed back to the house of Orléans at the Restoration. The official residence of the royal family was the Palais des Tuileries, beside the Louvre. The Duchesse de Berry and the little Duc de Bordeaux had apartments there. Franzi was taken to see these apartments and was shown the three-year-old heir to the throne and his toys. 'An angel of a prince,' wrote Adam. The Palais des Tuileries was destroyed in 1871 and was not rebuilt.

On 15 January M. Chapellon, a composer and member of the

Société Académique des Enfants d'Apollon, invited Adam and Franzi to a society chamber concert given by the Conservatoire's cello professor Charles Nicolas Baudiot, the oboe professor Gustave Vogt and the pianist M. Woest. After the performance Franzi could not resist going to the piano and attending to a theme from the Trio he had just heard in his own inimitable manner. Improvising on another musician's performance can have unfortunate consequences; it had been a trick of Mozart's, who often enraged lesser composers by subjecting their prize compositions to his instant 'improvements'. It was not the case on this occasion. 'Every transfixed listener thought himself transported by a dream into a place inhabited by the god of harmony,' read the Société's minutes. 'The clamour did not stop until Liszt said that he wanted to rest.' Franzi was then spontaneously and unanimously elected as a member. To commemorate the event the Société commissioned a lithograph by François Villain, after Xavier Leprince, of Franzi seated at an Erard square piano. The original lithograph is now at the Bibliothèque Nationale in Paris.

Mme Cresp-Bereytter, herself a singer, ran a salon at 16 rue Louis-le-Grand, at which it was becoming not unusual for artists and guests to mingle on equal footing. On 17 January she invited Franzi to join violinist M. Philippe and singers M. Larochelle and Mme Casimir in a musical soirée.

On 8 February Franzi gave a concert at the Salle Erard, where Adam netted 'a clear 2,000 francs' after Franzi played a solo version of Hummel's B minor Concerto on Erard's brand-new seven-octave model.

Ten days later he was due to perform again at Mme Cresp-Bereytter's, but at the last minute he became ill and could not attend. The assembled gathering were sorely disappointed, although they got their chance on 21 February when Franzi, having recovered, delighted the gathering with his improvisations.

That was not the only occasion that Franzi was forced to decline a booking. 'To give my boy some rest,' wrote Adam to Czerny, mindful of Franzi's still frail health, 'and so that his studies may not be neglected, I have had to turn down several invitations.'

Bureaucracy has always been the French way of doing things, before, during and after the Revolution, as Adam discovered when trying to organize Franzi's first formal concert. The venue was the Salle Louvois, in the Théâtre Italien, Paër's workplace as musical director and the capital's leading concert hall. The Théâtre Italien,

known familiarly as 'Les Bouffons', was situated in the Boulevard
des Italiens. Hiring had to be done through the correct channels,
which meant obtaining formal permission from the Minister of
State, Lauriston, and applying to the violinist and opera director
François-Antoine Habeneck for approval, in case of any clashes
of interest. Franzi's growing reputation, and connections with the
royal family, were the best guarantee of all. The only competition
at this time was a small contingent of child piano prodigies. They
included the fifteen-year-old Bavarian-born Anne de Belleville,
who had been a pupil of Czerny just before the Liszts' arrival in
Vienna and who went on to become a pianist of renown, and ten-
year-old George Aspull, who returned to his native England after
his Paris tour.

The hall was made available, free of charge – on condition that
Franzi also performed at the Concert Spirituel. This annual institution marked the start of public concerts in 1725, initially to pro-
vide public music during Lent, when opera performances were
suspended. At the time concerts were all but banned on the grounds
that they constituted competition for the Opéra, which was a state-
protected monopoly, but as the rules became relaxed with time
they became a traditional springtime event, with a religious bias.
They were initially held in the Salle de Cent Suisse, adjacent to
the Louvre, which was destroyed in 1871 and not rebuilt, but at
this time their venue was at the Académie Royale de Musique, on
the corner of rue Grange-Batelière and the Boulevard des Italiens,
which was also the Opera House. Of the waiving of the hire fee,
Adam acknowledged that 'this was a special favour which we owe
solely to the high protection of the Duchesse de Berry and the
royal minister Lauriston'.

Adam hired the services of the Théâtre Italien's resident orchestra, which he wrote was 'the best in Europe and France'. On
1 March the journal *Le Corsair* advertised the event in eulogistic
terms. The day of the concert, 7 March, was a Sunday. The Salle
Louvois was small, but the audience was Franzi's most eminent
so far and consisted of the cream of Paris aristocracy and academia,
and all the boxes were reserved a week in advance. Whereas
Viennese and German audiences were largely dilettante, in spite
of the presence of important personages, those of Paris were far
more sophisticated and knowledgeable. Adam commented on the
Parisian arts scene: 'This one example will suffice to show you
how superior the French are to others in generosity and in regard

to the arts. . . . He who has talent must come to Paris, for artistic understanding is here the norm; here the artist is esteemed, honoured and rewarded.' Franzi certainly enjoyed esteem, honour and reward on 7 March. The programme consisted of a concert, followed in the second half by an opera performance.

The concert opened with a Haydn symphony, after which Franzi played to an appreciative audience Hummel's B minor Concerto on Erard's latest model, which had been specially installed, and Czerny's Variations for piano and orchestra. Their incredulity spread to the orchestra, who, apparently entranced, failed to come in at the end of a bravura solo passage. This unprofessional lapse was forgiven by the good-natured and understanding audience, who clapped and laughed it off. To conclude, after a mood-setting introduction – a device that he had adapted from both Czerny and the recitative that often preceded an aria – Franzi led into an improvisation on 'Non più andrai' from Mozart's *The Marriage of Figaro*. At the end Adam wrote that 'my boy received an ovation impossible to describe'. The orchestra joined in the applause, with the string players beating their instruments with the back of their bows. Between Franzi's items, Laure Cinti and M. Pellegrini performed Italian arias. The second half consisted of a performance of Act 3 of Rossini's *Romeo e Giullietta*.

Alphonse Martainville's review of the concert appeared in the 9 March issue of *Le Drapeau Blanc*:

> I cannot help it: since yesterday I am a believer in metempsychosis. I am convinced that the soul and spirit of Mozart have passed into the body of young Liszt. . . . This child is beyond compare; he is the first pianist in Europe, Moscheles himself would not feel offended by this affirmation. . . . Mozart, in taking the name of Liszt, has lost nothing of that interesting countenance which always increases the interest a child inspires in us by his precocious talent. The features of our little prodigy express spirit and cheerfulness. He comes before his audience with exceeding gracefulness, and the pleasure, the admiration, which he awakens in his hearers as soon as his fingers glide along the keys he seems to find extremely amusing and diverting. . . . He scarcely looked at the music. . . . His eyes wandered continually round the hall, and he greeted the persons he recognized in the boxes with friendly smiles and nods.

On the final improvisation, Martainville writes that 'if, as I have said, Liszt, by a happy transmigration, is only a continuation of Mozart, it is he himself who provided the text'.

The event was a financial triumph for Adam. After an initial outlay of 343 francs, the cost of orchestra, lighting, posters and tickets, he showed a clear profit of 4,711 francs. He was now in a position to transfer 6,000 florins for banking and investment in Vienna and Eisenstadt.

Franzi appeared again at the Théâtre Italien on 26 and 28 March, supplying improvisations as intermezzi between theatrical productions.

Adam, riding high on a crest of euphoria at his son's spectacular success, wrote two long letters. The first, dated 17 March, was to Czerny, in which he proudly described Franzi's successes – and his earnings – to date. 'In society my boy plays your things most of all,' he wrote, 'and they are heard with great pleasure.' He added that many people were keen to make the acquaintance of this composer and Franzi's teacher. 'Won't he be coming to Paris, they ask?' Adam implored Czerny to visit Paris, pointing out how much more the French value a true artist than do the Viennese.

His second letter, dated 20 March, was to his friend at Eisenstadt, Ludwig Hofer. 'If you have a chance to speak to my father,' he wrote, 'please tell him that I shall shortly be sending a sum of money to Vienna and will arrange its transfer. Tell him he can be pleased with his grandson.' Since 1819 Georg List was in Pottendorf, first working in a clothing factory, and in 1821 he was back with the Esterházys as organist and choirmaster in the village church. The following year Prince Nicolaus gave him a piano. Franzi had now added his erratic grandfather to his list of dependants.

A journal, *La Pandore*, pointedly commented on this fact: 'The parents of young Liszt are poor, and he supports them by the product of his talents.' This enraged Adam, who promptly wrote an open letter to *La Pandore* explaining precisely his position and standing with regard to the House of Esterházy and that the family were in Paris with Prince Nicolaus's approval. 'At the same time,' concluded the letter, 'I have not neglected to take advantage of the eagerness testified by the Parisians to hear his performance, in order to indemnify myself for the expenses necessarily attendant upon a long journey, and the removal of my whole family.' Adam's letter started a wave of speculation on the nature of parental exploitation of young talent, which the Liszts could well have done without.

Adam was further brought down to earth by Czerny's reply of 3 April:

To my little friend and pupil Zisy I will say, he should meanwhile study hard with redoubled effort, so that through exag-
gerated praise (which is as much a danger as approbation) he
must not go astray; he should consider that though he can in-
spire instant enthusiasm with his youthful vitality and astound-
ing improvisations, yet the perfectly and consistently accomplished
execution of the classical repertoire will lead to a more lasting
glory of which the world will never be satiated, and he should
cultivate his talent for composition as much as possible, and
not neglect to use the metronome in his practice, and finally,
not to forget that, the higher one stands in public opinion the
harder and more necessary it is to stay there.

Franzi took serious note of Czerny's advice, and used it as his
personal guiding star for the rest of his life. 'When you have attained
the heights of virtuosity and intellectual possibilities, you have not
finished your work,' Franz Liszt told Carl Heymann in 1869. 'For
to remain at this dizzy altitude of artistic possibility, you have to
continue your daily slavery, otherwise your highly trained muscles
and nerves and brain will relax to a more normal tension.'

On 12 April Franzi fulfilled his promise to perform at the Concert Spirituel at the Académie Royale. The programme opened
with a Haydn symphony, followed by an Italian aria by Paër, sung
by leading bass at the Opéra, Nicolas Levasseur. This was followed by Rodolphe Kreutzer's Symphonie Concertante for two
violins, in which the soloists were Auguste-Joseph Tolbècque and
M. Belon. Laure Cinti sang an Italian air, which was followed by
a piano concerto – probably one of Hummel's – played by Franzi.
A 'Benedictus' of Beethoven closed the first half. The second half
began with Méhul's Overture to *Timoléon,* followed by a duet from
Rossini's *Armide,* sung by Cinti and a Théâtre Italien tenor who
was also singing professor at the Conservatoire, Giulio Bordogni.
Franzi then gave an improvisation on the song, 'Il pleut, bergère',
and the concert concluded in solemn style with extracts from
Mozart's Requiem. The orchestra and chorus were conducted
by Habeneck.

Life was good for the Liszts. Adam's taste for wine was considerably enhanced by French offerings, and he spoke of 'the noble
grape of Alsace and Champagne that one drinks gladly'. Anna
basked in her son's reflected glory, and Franzi himself enjoyed the
pampering, the etchings, the presents and the praise, learning to
balance the arts of pianism and showmanship with taste. He possessed

enormous reserves of the ingredients for both. His ten hours a day at the keyboard paid high dividends in his technical skills, and his modest and simple charms seduced everyone who saw and heard him. He was a singularly handsome boy, whose disarming smile of delight when applauded showed surprise, where it might have shown arrogance in a lesser personality. Of his germinating power over women there was no doubt; the doting Duchesse de Berry was his latest victim. This power still appealed to the maternal instinct, but at twelve years of age the transition to sexual attraction was only a matter of a few short years away. There was a 'star quality' about Franzi with which he held any audience, enthralled, in the palm of his hand, yet he had the natural, innocent modesty to be as yet unaware of the power of his spell. Czerny was well aware of these qualities and knew that the brilliant and beautiful child would one day become an adult professional composer and performer of the best of the Classical repertoire; and the foundations for this were not to be ignored.

The Liszts were visited by the 66-year-old Viennese founder of the science of phrenology, Franz Joseph Gall; it was his discipline that gave rise to the ghoulish custom of stealing skulls of eminent people for study and culminated in the gruesome activities of Messrs Burke and Hare at the medical school at Edinburgh University in 1826. Gall, who had lived in Paris since 1805, merely wished to take a plaster cast of Franzi's head – working on his theory that talent and brain functions could be inferred from the shape of the skull.

Winter thawed into spring, and Franzi continued composing. A Waltz in A (S 208a) is believed to have dated from this time. He wrote an *Allegro di Bravura* (S 151), a *Rondo di Bravura* (S 152) and two sets of Variations. The first set were on a theme from *La Donna del Lago* by Rossini (S 149), and the second, Eight Variations in A flat (S 148), were dedicated to Sébastien Erard. The last of these variations features semiquavers repeated at speed – in acknowledgement of the Erard double escapement action. The first theme of the Allegro, one motif from the Rondo, and the theme from the Erard Variations were included in the early 'Third Concerto', which ended up in bits scattered throughout Europe. The style, though immature and awkward, points to Czerny and Hummel. Also dating from this time was an *Impromptu brillant* on themes of Rossini – *La Donna del Lago* and *Armida* – and Spontini – *Olympie* and *Fernand Cortez* (S 150); it opens, innovatively, with an original scene-setting introduction, a device that Franzi used in his improvisations, suggesting recitative leading into an aria. A *Rondo and Fantasia* is now lost.

He also wrote songs – now lost – for use in the salons, but it is not known who wrote the words. His interest in vocal music was largely the result of his studies with Paër, whose overriding passion for opera rubbed off on Franzi. Opera was the bread-and-butter form of entertainment for Parisians, who enjoyed going to the latest offerings by Rossini, Spontini, Paër and Gluck. Only modern opera was fashionable; Mozart, for instance, was heard only in piano arrangements.

Franzi had attended many operas and enjoyed reading the scores at home, particularly those of Gluck. He selected arias and choruses as themes for his workouts as well as improvisations for his audiences. Like all Parisians, he loved opera as a matter of course and even considered writing one of his own. To Paër's delight and approbation the initial idea turned to determination, and Paër arranged for two aspiring dramatists, Messrs Théaulon and de Rancé, to adapt a tale by Jean-Pierre Claire de Florian as a libretto. During the spring, sitting at the piano with the libretto in front of him, Franzi played and sang various tunes that suggested themselves by the words, and *Don Sanche* germinated.

On 27 May Franzi attended a concert at his 'club', the Société Académique des Enfants d'Apollon, given by Antonin Reicha. Born in Prague in 1770, Reicha was a youthful friend of Beethoven; they were both the same age. He became a flautist, prolific composer and author of a treatise on composition. He spent most of his life in Paris, where he was professor of composition at the Conservatoire. He was one of the torchbearers of the Romantic movement and shared with Franzi an interest in folk music. Adam approached him about teaching composition to Franzi. Reicha agreed, and, at that stage, only tentative plans were made for formal tuition. Reicha died in Paris in 1836.

While Franzi scoured the keyboard for ideas for his opera, Adam was planning the next stage of his son's concert tour: over the next two years they would take in Holland, Switzerland and Germany, before returning home to Vienna in 1826: but, first, England, specifically Pierre Erard's London.

SIX

Erard's London

1824–25

K ING GEORGE IV had been on the British throne for only
four years, although he had been acting Regent since 1811,
when his father, George III, was declared insane and unfit to reign.
The Regency was an era of elegant and stylish dissipation, in which
fine architecture flourished alongside abysmal poverty. Napoleon's
adventures did not encroach on British soil, and British heroes
played significant parts in his downfall. Unlike mainland Europe,
Britain was not laid waste by twenty years of war, and the population could afford to be blasé. In 1820 George III died, and his
son, then fifty-eight, finally acceded to the throne. His Coronation
in London the following year was a splendid affair; the age of the
dandy had produced a fashion for stylish and often outrageous
clothes, but on that occasion every sartorial effect was completely
upstaged by the Austro-Hungarian ambassador, Prince Paul Anton
Esterházy. His dress, cut in the dashing Hungarian style, was
covered in diamonds: its cost could only be speculated on. The
35-year-old son of Prince Nicolaus II was a profligate spender
who was ultimately responsible for the collapse of the Esterházy
fortunes.

The Paris–London run was one of the great European round
trips, and was *de rigueur* for everyone of note. Philipp von Neumann,
Prince Paul Anton Esterházy's chargé d'affaires, took over seven
hours to reach Calais from Paris in the winter of 1822. The post
road passed through Rouen and Boulogne. At Calais he stayed at
the Hôtel Bourbon, where he waited three days for the weather to
clear. When at last he embarked on the steamer, the crossing took
nine hours. 'I don't remember ever having to have suffered more. . . .

I slept at Dover.' The road to London, which passed through Canterbury, was excellent.

Anna did not accompany her husband, son and Pierre Erard to London. She had befriended Barbe and Elyse Erard and was quite content to stay at rue du Mail, where she could cross the road at any time for a gossip over a cup of coffee or a glass of wine. As the all-male trio were travelling at the very beginning of May, they would not have endured the winter tribulations suffered by von Neumann and arrived at the Erards' establishment at 18 Great Marlborough Street, where they stayed, in the prime of a London spring. Erard's was just off Regent Street, the elegant, curved thoroughfare designed and built by the architect John Nash and completed only five years previously. With them came a new, seven-octave Paris-made square piano for Franzi's use. As the London representative of the family, Pierre was on home ground, and was able to show Adam and Franzi around 'his' city, and introduce them to the music scene. He had also done some advance publicity and displayed a picture of Franzi in the window of his shop.

Adam's initial foray into the soirée scene proved negative; they were late, the season was under way, and most bookings had been made. Undeterred, Adam solicited the artists on the off-chance, but, with the exception of Ferdinand Ries, he got nowhere. Perhaps it was not surprising, as they were all competing with one another. Concerts were thick on the ground, and Clementi, Cramer and Kalkbrenner had their own venues to worry about. 'Yet, as you know,' wrote Adam to Czerny, 'good material does not remain suppressed for long,' and Franzi's first performance – apart from some late-booked soirées – was at the invitation of the Royal Society of Musicians, a philanthropic organization which arranged musical events of note. The event was a dinner held by the Society at the New Argyll Rooms. This venue, one of London's leading halls where concerts, balls and dinners were held, was rebuilt on the site of the old hall and incorporated by Nash into his Regent Street development on the corner of Little Argyll Street. It was the official venue of the Philharmonic Society, founded in 1812 by a group of eminent British and immigrant London musicians and trendsetters of the London scene: the Cramer brothers, violinist Franz and pianist Johann Baptist, founder of a piano manufacturing concern; Muzio Clementi, whose Third Symphony contained a fantasia on 'God Save the King', in tribute to his adopted country; opera conductor and composer of, among other things, 'Home Sweet Home', Henry Rowley Bishop; conductor, organist, music professor and choirmaster Sir George Smart; Thomas Attwood, organist and pupil of Mozart; and musicologist, traveller, diarist and leading member of the publishing dynasty, Vincent Novello.

Franzi had a letter of introduction to Vincent Novello, who welcomed the Liszts warmly at the Novello home at 66 Great Queen Street, where they became frequent visitors to compare views on music and the post roads of Europe. It was there that Franzi added the joys of mint sauce to his gourmandise, which he took not only with lamb but also with fish and pudding.

The date of the Society's dinner was 5 June. Franzi improvised on his imported Erard for twenty minutes. The *Morning Post* of 7 June was literally lost for words: 'To do justice to the performance of Master Liszt is totally out of our power; his execution, taste, expression, genius and wonderful extempory playing defy any written description. He must be heard to be duly appreciated.' The *Quarterly Musical Magazine and Review* was more analytical:

> There were the marks of acquirement vast at any age, but prodigious at his, and of talent that requires only the assistance of a larger share of acquired knowledge. His genius brightens his face, and particularly when any thought first rises to his mind. There was an eminent proof of this previous to the commencement of a fugue with his left hand, which he worked with much skill. He feels every note he touches.

Franzi's first public concert was also at the New Argyll Rooms on 21 June. Adam was taking a chance, as the renowned soprano, Giuditta Pasta, was giving a concert of her own at the theatre on the same evening. He recorded the outlay: the hall cost thirty guineas, the London Philharmonic Orchestra, led by Nicholas Mori and conducted by Sir George Smart, charged thirty-five guineas. Advertising placards and printing of tickets were singularly expensive, at twenty-six guineas and nine and a half guineas respectively. Tickets to the concert cost half a guinea each.

It was a very full concert, with the orchestra backing a number of mostly Italian singers, french horn player Giovanni Puzzi and harpist Théodore Labarre, foster-brother of the future Napoleon III and second-prize winner of the Prix de Rome in 1823. The opening item of the first half, or 'Act', was a Grand Symphony by Haydn – it was not specified which one. Franzi's two items in the first half were interspersed with arias and Puzzi's horn Fantasia. He played a Hummel piano concerto and a new item in his repertoire, the Variations for mandolin and piano of Joseph Mayseder, in which the mandolin was played by Signor Vimercati, a virtuoso on an instrument which was enjoying great popularity at the time: both Hummel and Beethoven had written for it. The first 'Act' finished with a recitative and aria by Handel, 'Deeper and deeper' and 'Waft here, Angels', sung by the Englishman John Braham.

The second half opened with Weber's Overture to *Der Freischütz*. This was followed by various arias and a harp Fantasia from Labarre, and Franzi was joined in Czerny's Variations by the orchestra. Franzi also gave the première of a new set of Variations by Winkhler – one of the fifty composers who had written a Diabelli variation. At the end Sir George Smart invited the audience to submit a theme for Franzi to improvise on. A female voice suggested 'Zitti, Zitti', from Rossini's *The Barber of Seville*. 'The little fellow,' wrote the *Morning Post* two days later,

> though not very well acquainted with the air, sat down and roved about the instrument, occasionally touching a few bars of the melody, then taking it as a subject for a transient fugue, but the best part of this performance was that wherein he introduced the air with the right hand, while the left swept the keys chromatically; then he crossed over his right hand, played the subject with the left, while the right hand descended by semitones to the bottom of the instrument.

The correspondent found it needless to add that his efforts were crowned with the most brilliant success.

In the audience, Adam noted with satisfaction, since he had invited them, were Clementi, Cramer, Ries and Kalkbrenner. Also present were two protégés and champions in London of Beethoven: the pianist and former pupil of John Field, Charles Neate, and Cipriani Potter, who led the applause for Franzi. Cipriani 'Little Chip' Potter, pianist and composer, was one of the guiding lights of the London music scene, with an ear to what was happening on the continent. He was born in London in 1792. He went to Vienna, where he became an admirer and friend of Beethoven. Appointed principal of the Royal Academy of Music in 1832, a post he held till 1859, he also championed the piano works of Liszt and Chopin. In later life he was admired by Wagner. He died in 1871, leaving some chamber works and nine symphonies, which have enjoyed a limited revival after a century of oblivion. During the Liszts' stay in London, 'Chip' Potter often helped out with Adam's soirée arrangements for Franzi, including one at the house of a Mr Tunno, of 18 Bentinck Street, at the end of May. The concert netted a clear profit of £90 – approximately 720 florins by Adam's calculations. In addition, soirées, which paid from five guineas for an ordinary evening's playing to twenty pounds at the French Embassy, had brought in £172 – 'roughly 1,376 florins'. Adam tried for another public concert, but the season was so full that it was impossible to find a venue, 'because', wrote Adam, 'there were already too many others'.

John Braham had performed at Franzi's concert, and a week later, on 29 June, Franzi returned the compliment and played as a favour at 'Mr Braham's Night' at the Theatre Royal in Drury Lane. John Braham – born Abraham in 1774 – was one of London's longest-standing and most enduring tenors, having started his career as a boy soprano. He was a mainstay of English vocal music – notably Handel – in a climate where Rossini and Italian opera reigned supreme. The event was a full programme of music and theatre which included an opera, *Devil's Bridge*, in which Braham sang the leading role, and a farce, *What Next?* The evening finished with a collection of essentially British items in which Welsh composer, singer and conductor John Parry on the flageolet, and various singers – including Braham singing 'Scots wha ha'e wi' Wallace bled' – were accompanied by Mr Horn on the piano, and 'For this night only, the incomparable MASTER LISZT has in the most flattering manner consented to display his inimitable powers on the New Grand Piano Forte invented by Sébastien Erard.' A few days later Franzi received a very warm and congratulatory letter of thanks from Braham.

The Drury Lane Theatre, as the Theatre Royal is familiarly known today, is London's oldest theatre. It was originally founded as part of the royal household of King Charles II in 1662. It was destroyed and rebuilt several times and its present form dates from 1812, although improvements, such as gas lighting five years later, have been made since. The twin staircases are today named the King's side and the Prince's side, commemorating the occasion when King George III slapped the Prince Regent across the face there in a fit of anger. The theatre is today renowned primarily for the production of musicals.

Franzi had heard a great deal of opera in London; Braham,

Pasta and Angelica Catalani were some of the great stars of opera in London during that summer. The atmosphere was right for Franzi to immerse himself further into his opera. He was enjoying writing for orchestra as well as for voice. He had further taken to reading scores at the piano, a skill originally learned from Salieri, notably of Gluck operas, vast chunks of which he memorized. *Don Sanche* was making good progress.

Shortly afterwards Adam began negotiating with the violinist Andrew Ward of Manchester for Franzi to play at two concerts in England's greatest northern city. On 22 July the dates and terms were agreed by letter: the concerts were to take place at Manchester's Theatre Royal on 2 and 4 August, the fee would be £100 for the two performances – a fee few top performers would even contemplate charging – plus board and lodging for himself and Franzi for the duration. Adam himself would pay the travelling expenses.

On 15 July the Austrian ambassador Prince Paul Anton Esterházy arrived in London from Paris, just before the end of the London season. The King left town for Windsor and the rest of society left for their out-of-town estates. Adam wrote that 'we are looking forward to being back in Paris. . . . For the moment there is nothing to be done in London because everyone is in the country.' He was only waiting for the Manchester concerts, when a late invitation came from the King requesting Franzi to play at a small soirée at Windsor on 29 July. The invitation was at the behest of Prince Esterházy, who had gone to Windsor and saw an opportunity to hear for the first time the legendary son of his father's employee from Raiding. The King was taken by the idea, and Adam and Franzi were presented at the enormous, walled castle that was the King's 'summer palace' on the River Thames.

Franzi was the only musician booked. He had barely started the Introduction to Czerny's Variations in E flat, when the King muttered that he had never heard anything like it in all his life. Franzi continued to enthral the gathering for over two hours, at the end of which time the King suggested the Minuet from Mozart's *Don Giovanni* as a theme for improvisation. 'This is quite unlike anything I have ever heard,' the King kept repeating in English, French and German – for the benefit of his guests. 'This boy surpasses Moscheles, Cramer, Kalkbrenner and all the other great players, not only in the actual playing, but in the wealth and development of his ideas too.' Adam reflected that this was praise indeed from a monarch who, although a dissipated sybarite, knew what he was talking about in matters of music. 'In His Majesty', wrote Adam, 'we have found the greatest, kindest and most humane monarch and true connoisseur of music.' 'I was very young at the time,' Franz Liszt told Rev. H. R. Haweis decades later, 'but I remember the King very well – a fine, pompous-looking gentleman.' On 31 July the *Windsor Express* reported the event:

> On Thursday evening the famous young pianist Liszt was presented to the King by Prince Esterházy. In the course of the evening he played various pieces of music by Handel and Mozart on the piano, with great skill, to the applause of his Majesty and the company. The Variations of Czerny were generally applauded. Very great applause greeted the Minuet from Don Juan which King George IV gave as a theme to the pianist, and on which he improvised.

The Liszts stayed overnight in Windsor and took the opportunity to do some sightseeing. 'A trip on the Thames surpasses everything,' wrote Adam. 'One can see from it what an abundance of water England possesses. Whether one sees a village, or a small or large town, everywhere there is wealth, cleanliness and order. Whoever has not seen England has not seen the world's greatest treasure. The people are most agreeable, and the countryside is a real paradise.'

By the weekend Adam and Franzi had returned to the capital – probably by boat, a normal mode of travel between London and Windsor, Adam with a draft for fifty pounds in his pocket.

The next stop was Manchester. The Erard was freighted off and arrived there on the morning of Sunday 30 July, 'as I [Adam] shall be glad for my son to play upon that instrument', and was taken to the Theatre Royal. That same afternoon Adam and Franzi climbed aboard the elegant 'Telegraph' parked in the courtyard of the White Horse in Fetter Lane, off Fleet Street. At three o'clock the coach set off northwards on its twenty-four-hour run to Manchester. The post route passed through Northampton, Leicester, Derby, Leek – the Liszts would have caught tantalizing glimpses of the Peaks to their right – Macclesfield, before pulling up at one of Manchester's two main post stages, the Mosely Arms or the Star Inn. They were met by Andrew Ward, who verified Franzi's programme, assured Adam that the Erard had arrived safely and took them to his home, where they stayed.

The two concerts turned out to be something of a prodigy gala, and Franzi found himself on both occasions competing with a girl harpist who was 'not yet four'. The INFANT LYRA and MASTER LISZT were the two featured stars with only their names on the playbills in capital letters. Both concerts also included orchestral items from a 'very full band' and glees and songs by a variety of artists.

For the first concert Franzi selected one of Hummel's piano concertos and Moscheles's *Fall of Paris*, both with orchestra, and for the second he opted for the Czerny Variations and an improvisation on a written theme submitted by the audience. *Cowdroy's Manchester Gazette* of 7 August reported that 'the performances of Master Liszt on the pianoforte were really astonishing; and though only 13 years of age, the brilliancy of his execution we have never heard equalled by professors of the oldest standing and highest reputation'. The Infant Lyra merited a longer write-up, as the correspondent described in some detail how the little girl went through some cute theatricals before exhibiting 'a proficiency which, in one who has not been in existence more than the time that might be required to learn, was surprising. The simple airs were given not merely with accuracy, but with feelings.' As one might expect, some of her efforts at the more physically demanding chords fell short of the mark and 'afforded some amusement', but the correspondent admitted that the easier parts were played elegantly, 'and the soft notes fell with a liquid sweetness from her tiny fingers'. Despite having given a typical, brilliant performance, Franzi found the Infant Lyra an impossibly cute act to follow, and he found himself, for a change, thoroughly upstaged.

After the second concert Adam, with £100 in his pocket, took Franzi back to London. The Erard was despatched back to Paris and the trunks were packed for the return. They said goodbyes to Pierre Erard, and to the many people who had supported Franzi during their stay, and promised to return the following year. A week after their return from Manchester Adam and Franzi caught the coach for Dover. As Adam watched the lush countryside of Kent – the Garden of England – go by, he reflected on the past three months. Franzi had learned to speak English and had undoubtedly conquered the nation with his talent and charm. Adam would have liked more concerts, but London was full to bursting with pianists even though he assured Czerny that 'piano-playing here is still almost in its infancy'. He added that 'the nation, especially the women, are extremely fond of music, and in every home instruments and pieces of music can be found to excess'. He was not over-impressed with English musicians, and found them to be envious and jealous.

Franzi had come up against competition from children of his own age, not only from the Infant Lyra but also, in London, from the eleven-year-old Manchester-born pianist and Rossini favourite George Aspull. Adam had read about his Paris tour earlier that year; now he had given two concerts in London during the season. Adam and Franzi had been to his second concert, and George had also called on them. The two boys amused themselves at the piano cross-fertilizing some variations together. Adam found George a nice, well-behaved but shy boy and concluded that 'in his playing I found nothing of what I had read about. . . . The lad has much talent but is not having the right teaching, and if he continues with it he will achieve nothing outstanding.' George Aspull did achieve outstanding fame but died of tuberculosis in 1832, aged nineteen.

The Channel was rough. Franzi, having learned the meaning of seasickness the hard way, was very glad when the steamer finally moored off Calais on 12 August.

In the middle of August Adam and Franzi returned to the Hôtel d'Angleterre, to the devastating news that while they were in England *Don Sanche* had been rejected by the committee for the sanctioning of operas. 'What,' laughed the chairman, Cherubini, mirthlessly, when aspiring writers Théaulon and de Rancé announced who would be writing the music to their libretto, 'do you think that writing an opera is as simple as playing a piece on the piano? Permission refused.' Paër's intercession on Franzi's behalf was useless. Cherubini ensured that his clique on the committee agreed with his decision. Franzi was inconsolable. He had completed the Overture and most of the main arias, and it only remained for him to score it for orchestra – for which he would have to enlist Paër's help – write the recitatives and mould the work into a flowing whole. Now, it seemed, it was all for nothing.

When he read Adam's news, Czerny had words to say about how it was in the world of opera:

> You must surely know how the success of such a work depends on so many circumstances of chance. A poor subject, a miserable singer, lack of show and display (to say nothing of cabals) often cause excellent operas to fail through just one small de-

tail. So I beg you, rehearse every single piece beforehand in front of a small, select circle, with a quartet accompanying the piano, pay attention to the result and do not ignore the suggestions of friendly critics.

Adam had learned a great deal about how things were done in Paris, how to pull the right strings, and how to play people off against each other in a cut-throat atmosphere of factionalism, petty jealousies and generation wars. Swallowing his anger with Cherubini, he bided his time, and waited for the right opportunity. 'I remained indifferent, playing the philosopher,' he wrote.

The opportunity soon arose, and he arranged for Franzi to play some excerpts before the Director of the Royal Opera and Minister for Arts, Viscount Sosthène de la Rochefoucauld. He was France's greatest landowner and was responsible for lengthening the skirts of ballet dancers and introducing the fig-leaf to the sculptures at the Louvre in the name of decency. Adam was not bothered with the fact that de la Rochefoucauld knew absolutely nothing about opera: he once asked Cherubini whether he had ever considered writing one, which caused a perpetual feud between the two men. 'I achieved my goal,' continued Adam triumphantly, 'and for the moment we are pleased because we have the assurance of his high protection.' This protection, dubious but official, later included permission for Franzi to go in and out of the Académie Royale de Musique – the Opéra – to listen to rehearsals and attend concerts, free of charge, to enhance his knowledge of music, as suggested by Paër.

With *Don Sanche*'s prospects revived, Franzi continued his taxing regime of composition and practice, interspersed with some preliminary rehearsals and try-outs of completed sections. His passion for studying and playing Gluck operas from the score was enhanced by their performances, which he attended. On the piano front he was also augmenting his repertoire with the sonatas of Beethoven, Jan Ladislav Dussek and – interestingly – Daniel Steibelt. Born in Berlin in 1765, Steibelt was the devastatingly good-looking pianist, composer, showman, deserter from the Prussian army and all-round crook who died that year in St Petersburg aged fifty-eight, a fugitive from the laws of several European states. He left a legacy of operas, chamber music, eight piano concertos and some 400 piano sonatas, many replete with often cheap special effects – his tremolando chords are heard on honky-tonk pianos to this day. Some of his virtuoso tricks found their way into Franzi's methodology, as became evident with his developing technical showmanship.

Czerny added to this fresh material by sending him a parcel containing a thick wad of manuscripts and publications: three *Allegri di Bravura*. 'They are brilliant and very difficult,' explained Czerny, ever the teacher who would not let his star pupil go, 'but Franzi will find it a bagatelle to play them in a correct tempo and with his special clearness and lightness of touch. I recommend that he pays strict attention to the pedal of No. 3 and to play all of them with much show (Do not forget the metronome).' Also in the parcel were the published Diabelli Variations, 'wherein Putzi's figures most creditably'; his Grand Concert Variations for piano and orchestra on Haydn's 'Gotte erhalte Franz der Kaiser' – from his 'Emperor' String Quartet in C, Op. 76 No. 3, and later the Austrian and German national anthems, 'that Zisy (after some practice) will perhaps play. I have tried to incorporate as counterpoint Ries's [Variations on Arne's] Rule Britannia on the noble theme.' Finally, the parcel contained a Piano Sonata 'that I believe is one of my best works.... At the moment I am working on a concerto.' Czerny had an ulterior motive in sending this package. Haslingers were not willing to publish his works in Vienna on the grounds of their not being commercial, and he thought that with Franzi giving them an airing in public they might have more luck in Paris. Adam hawked them around successfully and was able to send Czerny a draft for 213 florins, reiterating his invitation to come and stay with them in Paris, where he would be sure of the recognition he deserved. Czerny ruefully replied that as his ageing parents were unwell, he could not leave them at this time.

The King was also unwell. His health deteriorated and on 16 September he died. Paris ground to a halt and all public performances were put on hold as a period of mourning ensued. The funeral took place on 25 October at the Church of St Denis, at which Cherubini's Requiem in C was sung. Louis' debonair but reactionary younger brother acceded to the throne as Charles X.

Rehearsals of *Don Sanche* continued that autumn. They were effectively workshops round the piano with singers and added instruments, attended by friends and friendly critics, as Czerny had suggested. The catchy – if derivative – march that is *Don Sanche*'s opening arias, 'Aimer, aimer, voilà toute ma gloire', and is heard again as an orchestral March later, caught everyone's attention, and soon it found its way into the repertoires of various regimental bands in Paris: there were several garrisons in the north of the city. Its fame spread to Vienna, where Czerny read about it and promptly tried to get hold of the music. He was quite confident that the opera would sell in both Paris and Vienna.

By the beginning of November the Liszts had moved to an apartment in the Hôtel Strasbourg at 22 rue Neuve, near the church of St Eustache. This road no longer exists. By 15 December Paris had returned to normal, and Adam thought it was time Franzi gave another concert. He wrote to de la Rochefoucauld requesting the Salle Louvois under the same terms as before – offering in addition to play at the Concert Spirituel at the Tuileries at Easter. This offer was refused.

Franzi's first public concert of 1825 was at the Académie Royale on 25 January. A number of eminent performers, including singers Pasta, Cinti, Adolphe Nourrit, Dabadie, and violinist Pierre Baillot, flautist Jean-Louis Tulou, trombonist Vaubaron and Franzi gave a charity performance in aid of victims of a fire. The concert was followed by the ballet from Rossini's *La Cenerentola*.

Adam reapplied for a concert at the Salle Louvois and this time secured a booking for 13 March. Franzi played a Hummel piano concerto and improvised. The concert opened with a symphony and closed with the third act of Rossini's *Otello*, with operatic arias sung by Cinti, Bordogni, Pellegrini and Zucchelli.

On 20 March Franzi took part in a vocal and instrumental soirée given by Mme Cresp-Bereytter at her salon. Among the other performers was the eminent violinist Charles Lafont, and the singers included the hostess herself, Zucchelli, Pellegrini, Cinti and Pasta – who was in London at the same time as Franzi and whose enormous range and dramatic style were renowned throughout Europe.

Felix Mendelssohn could not understand why. He admitted she had plenty of expression, verve, fire and a wealth of embellishments and looked good, but her voice was rough and unclear. The fifteen-year-old pianist and composer arrived in Paris on 22 March and commented on the French capital's musical scenario in his letters home with the blasé disdain of a clever teenager developing his critical faculties. He found the salons, at which he played, boring and frivolous. The ladies talked through the music, guests kept swapping seats and interspersing the performances with spontaneous cries of 'Charmant!' and 'Délicieux!' His audience 'quite liked' his own improvisations, which, he admitted, consisted of stringing a few pianistic tricks together without even having to think. He met Rossini – whom he referred to as 'Master Windbag' – at Comtesse de Rumford's.

Mendelssohn heard Franzi Liszt for the first time at the third Concert Spirituel at the Académie Royale on 1 April. The programme opened with a Beethoven symphony – probably No. 2 – being given by the combined orchestras of the Opéra and the Théâtre Italien, followed by the 'O Salutaris' of François-Joseph Gossec, sung by Nourrit, Prévost and Dabadie. Henri Brod's Trio followed, with the composer on oboe, M. Barizel on bassoon and Franzi at the piano, gaining experience in the chamber music that was his latest growing interest. Pasta then sang a Paër aria, and Lafont played his violin concerto. The first half finished with Mozart's 'Ave Verum'. The second half opened with an overture, and Tulou's air with variations for flute. A sung duet by Ricciardo followed, after which Franzi first improvised, then played his own Seven Variations on a theme of Rossini with the orchestra (S 149), which he had written the previous year. The concert ended with Haydn's chorus, 'Fuit Jesus'. The chorus and orchestra were conducted by Habeneck. Mendelssohn found the strings of the orchestra at the Théâtre Italien excellent, unlike the winds, especially the brass, who were mediocre at best. Despite Habeneck's efforts to hold back, the orchestra ran away with the Beethoven symphony at breakneck speed. On hearing Franzi play, Mendelssohn admitted that he played very well and had 'many fingers but few brains'; but added that his improvisations were 'absolutely wretched'.

He also reported the feud between Cherubini and de la Rochefoucauld. Cherubini had been baying for the Minister's immediate sacking since the time that he made an appointment to see him, and was kept waiting. When he finally entered, de la Rochefoucauld asked the apoplectic Cherubini who he was. Mendelssohn found Cherubini dried up and wizened, and peevish beyond measure and found that often it was difficult to get any reaction from him at all. His sarcasm towards the younger generation is on Mendelssohn's record: one young musician who played for him was asked whether he was a good painter – an earlier version of the modern advice wryly given to aspiring artists: 'Don't give up your day job.'

On 7 May Antonio Salieri died at the General Hospital in Vienna, a broken man. He was given a state funeral, and mourned by the whole Viennese musical establishment.

SEVEN

Don Sanche

1825

FRANZI PLAYED at two more soirées that spring, in which he joined several singers as well as the flautist Tulou, the oboist Henri Brod and the violinist and composer Charles-Auguste de Bériot, on 17 April at Erard's, and on 22 April in the Salle Cléry at 21 rue Cléry.

Also giving soirées at Erard's – four in all – was Hummel, who was one of a veritable contingent of pianists who had descended on Paris that spring. 'Those who attended his soirées,' wrote Adam, who had arranged for Franzi to turn his pages at one of them, 'found his improvising dry' – of course, as Franzi now always played without music. 'Hummel did not attend [Franzi's soirée],' gloated Adam, 'probably so as not to have to see for himself that someone else can have a larger audience than he.' Hummel's engagement book – and audiences – were sparser than he would have liked; he had priced himself too high for a performer approaching fifty competing with the new, gilded generation of young pianists of Paris.

There was fourteen-year-old Ludwig Schunke of Stuttgart, the son of Gottfried Schunke, principal horn at the court of Württemberg. He had been giving concerts in Vienna, where he had a crash course from Czerny. 'The papers made him out as a rival to Franzi,' Czerny wrote. 'His talent misses a little, but what discipline! He has greater ability in playing than in fantasias and composition.' Schunke, who was almost Franzi's double in appearance, mannerisms and style of playing, continued as a renowned pianist and later became Schumann's friend and co-editor of the *Neue Leipziger Zeitschrift für Musik* in 1834, the year he died of tuberculosis, aged twenty-four.

Another product of the Czerny stable now in Paris was sixteen-
year-old Anne de Belleville and, according to Adam, not doing
very well. 'She did very bad business like all the rest, as she deserved,' he wrote to her former teacher, perhaps tactlessly, but
with the relish of *schadenfreude*, 'smudges the piano rather than
plays it and seeks her bravura in nonsensical runs and leaps'.
Czerny replied that 'her talent does not make such a stir as it
should and could do', and asked Adam to reproach her for not
keeping in touch.

There was also Camille Moke, whose reputation as a brilliant
pianist was later matched by her beauty and the subsequent atten-
tions of – among others – Berlioz, Hiller and Franzi himself, whose
clandestine tryst, after her eventual marriage to the pianist and
piano manufacturer Camille (by coincidence) Pleyel, in Chopin's
apartment caused some considerable friction between the two
giants of pianism.

Apart from Hummel and the 'beautiful' teenagers, Moscheles,
Kalkbrenner and Johann Peter Pixis were in Paris as well. All,
young or established, were having a lean spring. Franzi concen-
trated on putting the finishing touches to *Don Sanche*. No date
had been fixed, but anyway the King's coronation got in the way.
On 24 April Adam wrote to de la Rochefoucauld thanking him
for giving permission for Franzi's opera to be performed, but asked
for a postponement, 'since the opera singers are engaged in rehearsals for the opera for the King's coronation'. *Don Sanche* was
put off until the autumn. King Charles X was crowned with all
due pomp and ceremony at Rheims Cathedral on 29 May.

Three days later Moscheles officially launched Sébastien Erard's
new double escapement model grand piano. Erard pianos were
going from strength to strength, and the new action was set to
revolutionize piano manufacture. 'The perfection of Erard pianos
has reached the point that it is a century ahead of its time, and
impossible to describe,' wrote Adam to Czerny. 'One has to see
and hear it for oneself and play it oneself too.' Franzi's seven-
octave square piano, hailed as a brilliant instrument, was about to
become obsolete. The complex double escapement action took three
years to perfect since it was first patented in 1822, and it was
now ready for manufacture and marketing. 'The quicker action of
the hammer seems to me so important that I prophesy a new era
in the manufacture of pianofortes,' wrote Moscheles. Franzi was
familiar with the double escapement action and had already

anticipated it in his 'Erard' Variations of the previous year. The strings of repeated semiquavers would have been effectively impossible to play on the older models.

As Moscheles was putting Erard's new invention through its paces, Adam and Franzi were in London once more, again staying with Pierre Erard, whose new brief was to market his uncle's invention. There was a sense of *déjà vu* about the Liszts' second visit to England, although initially many of London's leading families were in Rheims for the Coronation. During their stay Adam and Franzi went to St Paul's Cathedral, where they listened to a choir of between seven thousand and eight thousand children from the Charity Schools singing psalms and hymns. Mass hymn singing was very common at this time, and the occasion had a deeply spiritual effect on Franzi. Very few dates are on record, but some of Franzi's venues are known. He took part in a soirée at the Duke of Devonshire's residence overlooking Piccadilly and played again for King George IV at Windsor. As in the previous year, the King was amazed by Franzi's prowess and attended his concert – about which no details have survived – at the Theatre Royal at Drury Lane.

Franzi's star turn took place at Apsley House, the Duke of Wellington's residence – today the Wellington Museum at Hyde Park Corner. On this occasion a number of distinguished performers were present; the flautist Charles Nicholson, whom Adam compared to the Dutch virtuoso Philip Drouet, brought his own Fantasy with Variations to play; Giovanni Velluti, one of the last of the great operatic castrati, renowned for his luxuriant embellishments of the melody lines, had the piano tuned a semitone lower to suit his flagging voice; Cipriani Potter was there in his capacity as accompanist. Franzi's and Velluti's contributions went off smoothly, but Nicholson's Flute Fantasia ground to a halt after a few bars. 'Your flute is sharp,' complained Potter. 'Then you will have to transpose,' replied Nicholson, 'as I cannot lower my flute.' 'What?' cried Potter in alarm. 'The piece is in C. Do you expect me to transpose it to C sharp? I dare not try it.'

Adam took up the story. 'The gentlemen argued for a long time, in the end drawing everyone's attention to them, because the interval had already lasted too long – but the refrain was always – I dare not risk it.' Potter finally went up to Franzi, who was standing nearby. 'Can you transpose a little?' he asked. 'Yes, a little,' rejoined Franzi, casting his eye on the piano score. 'And I believe that to transpose this will be no great hazard.' 'Good,' sighed a relieved Potter, 'do try it, because I don't want to risk it in front of such a large audience.' Franzi obliged, and gave a flawless accompaniment to the première of Nicholson's Fantasia and Variations in C (and C sharp) for flute and piano before an astonished audience.

In the middle of June the Liszts were again in Manchester at the instigation of Andrew Ward. Once more his beloved Erard was waiting for Franzi on 16 June, when he took part in the first of two concerts at the Theatre Royal. This time there was no Infant Lyra to batter at his psyche, but Andrew Ward, ever the proponent of infant prodigality, had included his star violin pupil, nine-year-old Master Banks, in the programme. The concert opened with the Overture to Weber's *Der Freischütz*, played by a 'large band' conducted by Mr Cudmore; among various ensuing vocal items in the first part, Franzi played Czerny's Air and Grand Variations for piano and orchestra – possibly the new set that Franzi had received from his former teacher earlier that year – and Hummel's Piano Concerto in A minor. 'Master Liszt elicited the most rapturous applause,' reported *Cowdroy's Manchester Gazette*, 'indeed it appears to us to be scarcely possible for any human being to attain a greater mastery of the instrument than was shown by young Liszt upon this occasion. His slender fingers ran over the keys with astonishing ease, rapidity and precision, and produced turns of unequalled brilliancy.'

The second half introduced Mr Ward's star pupil. 'Master Banks,' continued the *Gazette*, 'was a pupil of Andrew Ward's and led the orchestra in the Overture to Rodolphe Kreutzer's *Lodoïska* – which evinced thunderous applause.' Franzi's second-half contribution was an improvisation, for which he was open to suggestions of a theme. 'A gentleman in one of the boxes', continued the *Gazette*, 'suggested the Scottish air "We're a'Noddin".' Franzi was not familiar with this song, so Andrew Ward quickly jotted the melody line down for him, whereupon 'the young Apollo commenced a most beautiful discourse from it on his instrument, running through all the intricacies and windings in the manner of the major and minor modes, and at intervals sliding into the simple text. This *chef d'oeuvre* of improvising drew down loud and long continued plaudits.'

The second concert was on 20 June, and marked Franzi's formal début as a composer, as principal violinist Mr Cudmore conducted the première of the Overture to *Don Sanche*. This was followed by Master Banks, conducting the orchestra from his position as first violin, in the Overture to Rossini's *Tancredi*. After some ballads, Franzi returned with the Air and Grand Variations by Henri Herz, followed by improvisations. The concert closed with a Grand Quintet by Ries, in which Franzi was joined by Messrs Cudmore, two Sudlows and Hill.

After Manchester Adam and Franzi, having stopped over at 18 Great Marlborough Street, headed for Dover. Once over the Channel, they travelled the short stretch of coast road from Calais to Boulogne, where they had arranged to spend a fortnight, possibly at the recommendation of their London friends Vincent and Mary Novello. On 2 June Adam had written, 'Sir [this may have been addressed to John Holt, proprietor of the Hibernian Hotel in Boulogne, at 36 rue Neuve-Chaussée, a favourite with British visitors, including the Novellos], We will finish our business in London on the 23rd, and reckon to be in Boulogne about the 25th, and stay for two weeks to take the waters. If possible, we should like to fulfil a proposal that you had the goodness to suggest to us, to give a concert there, for which we would be particularly grateful.'

Boulogne was sunny and very agreeable at that time of year. It had been a gruelling month in England, with a tight schedule, and Franzi and his father only wanted to unwind and, in Adam's words, to 'wash away our exertions'. They spent most of their time enjoying being with each other on the beach, talking, basking in the sunshine, bathing in the sea and going for long walks along the sand, collecting seashells, and watching the fishing boats go by from the casino on the waterfront, where all the fashionable tourists used to go. The casino had a piano in the salon, and 'we always entertained ourselves very well'. By popular request, they gave a soirée, which developed into a 'ball'. Everyone had a marvellous time, and the evening brought in enough money to pay their holiday expenses with 600 francs to spare.

Adam and Franzi arrived back in Paris in early July, refreshed. Waiting for them at the Hôtel Strasbourg was Anna, keen to hear news of Franzi's English exploits. They were hoping to relax, call on friends and generally take things easy, but on 22 July a letter, addressed to Monsieur Liszt, composer, from de la Rochefoucauld at the Ministry of Arts brought Adam and Franzi down to earth with a jolt. Franzi was required by the committee to bring his work to be inspected and heard by M. Louis Piccinni, chief chorusmaster at the Opéra, immediately. This put Adam and Franzi in a spot. The committee had already rejected *Don Sanche* and were now probably only paying lip service to de la Rochefoucauld. 'Nothing was copied out,' wrote Adam despairingly to Czerny, 'and not one singer had been prepared.' It began to look as though the 'Don' would be doomed after all, with all the odds stacked against him.

Adam asked for a two-week extension. This was refused, but the committee agreed to grant just a few days. Adam and Franzi galvanized themselves into action, wrote, copied, scored and rehearsed furiously at all hours over the next few days. Paër helped whenever he could with the scoring. Franzi managed to raise a 'draft' performance of the opera. Cherubini sat surrounded by his committee: Adrien Boieldieu, the opera composer whose *La Dame Blanche* became his most popular work; Charles Catel, a professor at the Conservatoire, a composer and accompanist at the Opéra; Jean Lesueur, self-taught composer of church music and operas, and professor of composition at the Conservatoire; Henri-Montan Berton, violinist, composer of opéras comique, and professor at the Conservatoire, who pronounced Berlioz's music unplayable. It was not an easy audition. To a man the committee were friends of Cherubini, and would not hesitate to agree with their chief on principle. They listened carefully as Franzi conducted his opera from the piano, always looking anxiously for reactions on the faces arrayed before him. When the opera was finished, Adam and Franzi were convinced that it would be rejected again, but their joy knew no bounds when *Don Sanche* was accepted with the greatest attestations of approval. Even the chastened Cherubini was enthusiastic. 'My dear friend,' wrote Adam to Czerny, 'now I regret that you are not a father; it would give me scope to say something about the happy feelings of parents, when all sorrows are forgotten. So the opera is accepted . . .' and early October was the suggested date for its performance.

This fitted in well with Adam's plans. 'In November we plan to go to the Netherlands, Berlin, Leipzig, and thence to Vienna,' he wrote to Czerny in August, adding that he hoped to be back by the following March. He also wrote to his father, who was still in Pottendorf, giving him an update on Franzi's successes, on life in Paris and on the projected tour and of their eventual arrival in Vienna once more. 'Franzi is almost as tall as I am,' he concluded.

It fitted in with Franzi's plans too. Free of the uncertainty, he went back to composing: 'His sole passion is to compose; it is this alone that gives him joy and delight,' continued Adam. His *Allegro di bravura* and the *Rondo di bravura* written the previous year, dedicated to Count Thadé d'Amadé, were published in Vienna by Diabelli. He also wrote two piano concertos: 'His concertos are too rigorous, and the difficulties for the player are immense,' wrote Adam. 'I always regarded Hummel's concertos as difficult, but they are very easy in comparison.' These two concertos are effectively lost, although one of them, the so-called 'Third Concerto', which contains the theme from the 'Erard' variations, has been painstakingly collated by Jay Rosenblatt into a playable study version. Having played chamber music, Franzi also tried his hand at composing it, and wrote a sonata for piano duet, a trio and a quintet which Adam informed Czerny 'should please you greatly'. As well as three piano sonatas, all these works are now lost.

That summer Franzi took time off from composing to play between items during two theatrical performances, both given in aid of victims of a fire disaster. The first, on 17 August, was at the Théâtre Madame, in the Palais Royal, where four plays were given, after which Franzi played Czerny's Introduction and Variations Brillantes with the orchestra. On 29 August *Le Rossignol*, an opera by Sébastien Lebrun, was given at the Académie Royale; Baillot, Tulou, Pasta and Franzi contributed to the music.

Rehearsals for *Don Sanche* had begun in earnest. Rodolphe Kreutzer was put in charge of the orchestra, and the eminent tenor Adolphe Nourrit took the title role. M. Prévost, and Mmes Grassari, Jaworek, Frémond and Sèvres of the Company took the supporting roles. The march from *Don Sanche* was still heard, serving as an unintentional 'trailer'. Its catchy, memorable tune held out the promise of more of the same. As always with opera, the cabals and factionalists came out of the woodwork, and the air of Paris was thick with comment. 'Curiosity is at fever pitch,' wrote Adam, 'and envy running at its highest.' Some accused Franzi of not doing his own orchestrations and suggested that either Paër or Kreutzer – or both – did them for him. Franzi never claimed that the orchestration was entirely his own work and recorded in later life that Paër – but not Kreutzer and Spontini – had helped him considerably with the scoring.

Gaspare Spontini had offered to help in any way he could. He was born near Ancona in 1774 and studied music in Naples, where his abilities as a composer of operas came to the fore. He went to Paris in search of fame and fortune, and in 1807 had a major success there with his *La Vestale*, which was highly praised by Napoleon. In 1811 he married Marie-Céleste Erard, Pierre's older sister. A few years later he became chief musical director in Berlin, where his fortunes wavered until he returned to his homeland. He died in Ancona in 1851. That autumn he was in Paris staying with his father-in-law's brother, Sébastien, at rue du Mail, and there were discussions about his doing an opera. Sébastien introduced him to the Liszts, and he and Adam became very friendly and dined out together regularly. Spontini heard Franzi play and was amazed by his improvisations, but his offer to involve himself in Franzi's opera came to nothing.

The idea of a thirteen-year-old writing an opera is essentially controversial but by no means impossible. A naturally musical child with no musical education is capable of holding quite complex music in his mind's ear, and his greatest problem lies in transferring the sounds in his head into sounds in real life. A teacher with a good ear and a mastery of musical syntax, harmony and counterpoint should be able to help bring this about with the minimum creative input of his own and ensure as far as possible that the work is his pupil's and not his own. There is no doubt that Franzi needed help with arrangements and orchestration, and there is also no doubt that Paër, as a matter of principle, would have kept within the parameters of Franzi's intended creativity and would not 'improve' on the basic concept.

The libretto of *Don Sanche* was a clumsily adapted reworking of de Florian's fable by Théaulon and de Rancé. Nothing is known of the latter, but Emmanuel Guillaume Théaulon de Lambert, who was born in 1787, worked in administration under Napoleon's minister, Cambacères. In his spare time, he put his name to over 250 plays and libretti, all of which are now lost, with the exception of *Don Sanche*. Théaulon died in 1841.

The story was designed to appeal to Franzi's sense of fairy tale. Don Sanche, a courtly Spanish knight, is in love with Princess Elzire, sung by Mme Grassari. But the Princess, her sights set on being one day Queen of Navarre, is betrothed to the Prince of Navarre, for whose castle her cortège is bound. Don Sanche arrives at the Castle of Love – the Château d'Amour of the subtitle – the residence of the magician Alidor, sung by M. Prévost, and asks to be admitted. Alidor's page, sung by Mlle Jaworek, refuses on the grounds that only those truly in love, and loved in return, may enter. Don Sanche, thinking that he is not loved because his beloved was on her way to marry another, contemplates suicide.

Alidor brings his magical powers to bear, and conjures up a storm. This causes Elzire's cortège to seek shelter at Alidor's castle. She is also refused admission on the same grounds – that she is not really in love with the Prince of Navarre. Don Sanche and Elzire meet outside the castle. Don Sanche declares his love, unsuccessfully, until he is challenged by Romualde, who threatens to take Elzire away. A duel ensues and Don Sanche is badly wounded. Elzire takes pity on him, and her pity turns to love. She rejects the prospects of being Queen of Navarre and declares her true love. Don Sanche is miraculously cured and together they enter the Castle of Love to the revelation that Romualde was really Alidor in disguise. The opera ends with a chorus of rejoicing.

On 17 October, five days before his fourteenth birthday, Franz Liszt's one-act opera, *Don Sanche, ou le Château d'Amour*, had its première at the Académie Royale. The opera was followed by a performance of *La Dansomanie*, a ballet-pantomine by M. Gardel, with music by Étienne Méhul. At the end of the performance Nourrit carried Franzi onto the stage – somewhat to Franzi's chagrin – and Kreutzer kissed him.

Reactions to the opera were mixed. No one disputed that it was a remarkable achievement for a thirteen-year-old, while at the same time pointing out that opera had to be essentially the product of finished rather than developing musicianship: 'Young Liszt is truly an extraordinary child,' reported the *Gazette de France*, 'yet he is still only a child, and so one cannot demand from him proof of an adult and formed talent without being unfair.' Franzi was up against Cherubini, Spontini, Boieldieu, Paër, Rossini and Gluck on their own ground. In the world of opera, comparison was essentially unqualified. As composer of an art form as multi-layered as opera, Franzi was just not in their league. One of his weaknesses was in his portrayal of adult emotions – sorrow, jealousy, hatred, melancholy and tales of woe – emotions that he could not yet understand at an adult level, which is what an allegorical tale of love required. The *Gazette* continued that *Don Sanche* 'contains many sections that our best-loved composers would not dismiss . . . above all, the Overture, the first chorus, the harmonically interesting Romance "C'est ici le château d'amour", and the aria "Repose en paix au milieu de l'orage", which appeared for us to be of a fine and sensitive character'.

The *Journal de Débats* pulled no punches: 'Young Liszt's composition is praiseworthy, but its promise has not fulfilled expectations . . . the whole work is cold, its inspiration curiously forced and unsatisfactorily written, though interspersed with some nice motifs.' *Le Constitutionnel* suggested that *Don Sanche* should have been in the first instance performed at a college, the Conservatoire, or among friends in a society among connoisseurs and critics. The journal singled out some arias and extracts as very agreeable.

Don Sanche ran for four nights, 18, 19, 21 (the eve of Franzi's birthday) and 26 October. Adam took a grand total of 170 francs and admitted that concerts brought in more. Théaulon and de Rancé partly blamed themselves – as did many critics – for the eventual demise of *Don Sanche* from the music scene. 'Young Liszt silenced our vanity as authors,' they said. No more has been heard of them since. The libretto and score of *Don Sanche* lay dormant – even believed to have perished in the fire which destroyed the Académie Royale in 1873 – until the discovery at the Opéra library of two beautifully bound volumes of the complete 1825 performance, in 1903. The first performance in modern times was in London in 1977.

Adam now considered the projected tour of the Netherlands, Berlin, Leipzig and Vienna. Anna, who had thoroughly enjoyed Paris and made many friends there, decided to forgo the rigours of touring and go straight back to Austria. She intended to go first to Graz to spend some time with her sister, Franzi's beloved Aunt Therese, before going to Vienna to prepare for Adam and Franzi's arrival. As soon as *Don Sanche* had finished, she said goodbye to her husband and son and to her many friends and left Paris.

At the end of November Adam took Franzi to Rouen. This bustling city, an important inland port astride the River Seine, was a thriving commercial centre. The Paris–Calais post road had been diverted to pass through it, so it offered added facilities to travellers, notably the English. Artists and virtuoso performers – such as Paganini and Chopin – made a point of playing there. The city often featured child prodigies; the previous year ten-year-old pianist Delphine Schauroth captivated the city. The Liszts put up at the Hôtel d'Europe, and Adam inserted an advertisement in the 28 November edition of the *Journal de Rouen*: 'It is announced that young Liszt, the celebrated pianist about whom all the Paris newspapers have expressed the most brilliant eulogies, has just arrived in Rouen, where he proposes to give a concert.'

The city's most prestigious venue, the Salle Saint-Ouen at the historic Town Hall, with seating for up to 500, became unexpectedly unavailable, so they had to settle for the beautiful, but much smaller, Gothic-Renaissance room at the Hôtel de Bourgtheroulde, at 5 Place de la Pucelle. The concert took place on 3 December. Franzi's programme included improvisations on themes from Weber's *Der Freischütz*. The following day the *Journal de Rouen* reported that the size of the venue was a double disadvantage:

> it prejudiced the interests of this astonishing pianist . . . and it deprived many people of the pleasure of enjoying his admirable talent. . . . One cannot think of anything more abundant, more rich in harmony and more graceful all at once, than the piece in which the artist, as he played, varied and combined, through all the keys, the two delightful motifs of the chorus and the waltz from Robin des bois [*Der Freischütz*].

While in Rouen the Liszts visited M. and Mme Eders, to whom Franzi wrote several years later, recalling his visit, expressing his special gratitude, apologizing for being 'that naughty little Liszt, who often made you furious' and offering to supply any music that M. Eders might require.

The Town Hall building, adjacent to the massive Gothic church of St Ouen, is unchanged to this day, and the Salle Saint-Ouen is the Salle de Mariages on the first floor. The Hôtel de Bourgtheroulde was damaged by a bomb in 1944 and was rebuilt five years later. The historic façade and the courtyard were repaired, but the main hall is now a modern bank.

Back in Paris, Adam's plans for a circuitous return to Vienna were scrapped in favour of a tour of southern France to promote Erard's new double escapement action piano.

EIGHT

A Tour de France
1826

THE GRAND Théâtre in Bordeaux was completed in 1780. It is today, as it was in January 1826, an imposing, four-square building with a grand Corinthian colonnade and a cupola, dominating the Place de la Comédie. Almost the whole building was given over to the unusually big auditorium to accommodate a very large audience. It was in this enormous venue that Franzi gave his first three concerts in the city. The Liszts put up at the Hôtel d'Angleterre.

L'Indicateur gave notice of the vocal and instrumental concert to be held at the Grand Théâtre on 5 January, at which 'the young Liszt will be heard on the pianoforte'. The concert – or rather, an evening of music and stage entertainment – opened with *Valérie*, a drama in three acts, followed by *Almaviva et Rosine*, a ballet in three acts. The evening finished with Franzi's performance of a Moscheles piano concerto and Czerny's Variations. Between his items, Mme Mercier, wife of the violinist-conductor of the Théâtre Orchestra and mainstay of the Bordeaux opera, sang an air from *Concert à la Cour*.

Present at this concert was the violinist and composer Pierre Rode. Franzi was familiar with his music; Léon de Saint-Lubin played his Variations in E at Franzi's first Vienna concert. Now Franzi became acquainted with the man as well as with his music. Rode was born in Bordeaux in 1774. He studied violin with Viotti and later enjoyed Napoleon's patronage. After extensive travels as a concert performer – Beethoven wrote his Violin Sonata in G Op. 96 for him – he returned to Bordeaux and retired from performing because of paralysis, which ultimately claimed his life in

1830. His legacy included a number of violin concertos, a set of twenty-four *Caprices*, one in each key, some string quartets and, most famously, the Variations in G, whose Air Franzi henceforth used as a springboard for his own variations. Rode had now taken under his wing a young violinist named Jupin, who was critically acclaimed as 'worthy of taking his honourable place among the most brilliant violinists'. Jupin attended Franzi's concert with Rode. On 7 January *Le Mémorial Bordelais* began a review of the concert with a short commentary on the nature of prodigies. 'Young Liszt is one of a very small number of these children blessed by Nature,' it continued; 'he pleases from the first instance. . . . I speak of those who applauded at his very first appearance . . . and the thousand bravos during all the pauses in his brilliant execution were not those of habit but of a universal enthusiasm. It would be difficult to give an idea of the extreme facility of this young virtuoso. His instrument seemed to be a part of himself, so natural, easy and rapid was his rapport with it.' The review continued that this was particularly evident in 'the Variations of Crauchy [*sic* – Czerny], fantasies full of grace and lightness, elements in which he can express everything he wants to, how he wants to. In more vigorous mode, he has not yet the verve which comes with age . . . but his execution of Moscheles's concerto with orchestra was such as to satisfy the most critical demands.'

L'Indicateur described how young Liszt, 'of scarcely fourteen springtimes', was heard by a numerous audience. 'This is a child who runs with great strides towards the reputation of a celebrated artist; he draws everything possible from the piano; he obtains from it the most noble and vigorous sounds; there is about him nothing mechanical; the fire in his looks, his attitude, his poses, everything goes to prove that his soul rests largely in the movement of his fingers, through which he displays a velocity which stuns, dazzles and provokes outbursts of applause.' The review mentioned Franzi's authorship of *Don Sanche*, saying that it was not a masterpiece, but what would one expect from one so young?

On 9 January Franzi gave his second performance at the Grand Théâtre, this time sandwiched between a comedy, *La Gageure Imprévue*, and the home-spun *La Fille Mal Gardée* in its original version. This anonymous compilation ballet first appeared in Bordeaux in 1789 and has gone through a number of metamorphoses since then, notably those of Paris chorus-master Ferdinand Hérold in 1828 and John Lanchbery in 1959. The music programme was interspersed with an aria by Cimarosa sung by Mme Mercier and the Horn Concerto of M. Clapisson, principal horn of the Théâtre Orchestra. Franzi's own programme, as recorded by *L'Indicateur* of 11 January, is ambiguous. The review noted that the Théâtre was not as full as before, and rued the loss to music lovers who did not attend.

It is impossible to hear anything more graceful than the concerto [*sic*] of Czerny, and the new variations which were given a new charm from the brilliant execution of this famous child. He has again surpassed himself in his improvisation on twin themes suggested by the audience, 'La Tirolienne' and the chorus from *Der Freischütz*. With what art each motif appeared alternately, over a fracas of percussive effects, a fireball of notes imitating storm and tempest, followed by the sweetest, smoothest and most melodious tones imaginable. The entire electrified audience paid, with its prolongued applause, a just tribute of its amazement and admiration.

Franzi's third appearance at the Grand Théâtre was on 12 January, slotted between the comedy *La Brouette du Vinaigrier* and the ballet *L'Amour et la Folie.*

On the corner of Alées de Tourny and rue Jean-Jacques Bel stands the building – today a commercial establishment – which was the former Hôtel de l'Académie Française. In 1826 it housed Le Museum – in which there was a small concert hall; it was here that, on 23 January, Franzi took part in a chamber concert. *L'Indicateur* of 26 January stated that it was a simple, small-scale affair, 'with no symphonies concertantes, often discordant ones at that'. It began with a piano trio by Mayseder in which M. Mercier, the conductor of the Théâtre Orchestra, played violin, M. Rouhier the cello and Franzi the piano. 'These three names united say more than anything I could add,' continued *L'Indicateur*. Two unnamed girls sang duos from *La Gazza Ladra* and *Pucita*, and Franzi concluded the evening with Czerny's Variations on a theme of Rode and his own improvisations on 'Au Clair de la Lune'.

The following evening, 24 January, young Jupin gave a concert at the Grand Théâtre. 'This young pupil of Baillot', commented *L'Indicateur*, 'will follow in his master's footsteps, as no difficulty stops him . . . Jupin of the violin will become the Jupiter of the violin.' Jupin played a Viotti concerto and some fantasies by Weber. The concert was badly timed. Jupin was certainly an exceptional violinist; however, there was not room in Bordeaux for two prodigies simultaneously, and Jupin came off second best. The *Revue Historique de Bordeaux* of 1917 recorded that Jupin 'suffered the disadvantage of playing in our city the day after a concert given by fourteen-year-old Liszt'.

The Société Philomatique de Bordeaux, the city's most prestigious arts society, met at the Waux-Hall. This complex of ballroom, concert hall, covered walkways and 'jardin anglais', built in 1770 on the model of the Vauxhall Gardens in London and demolished in 1851, stood at today's 26, 28 and 30 Cours de l'Intendance, at its western corner with rue Vital-Carles. Its entrance was situated beside rue de la Vieille Tour. At seven o'clock on the evening of 25 January, the Société, also known as the Société Musicale des Amis des Arts, held a public session and concert at the Waux-Hall. *L'Indicateur* described it as a splendid occasion, with music lovers, artists and ladies dressed in elegant splendour 'all bestowing the most flattering homage to the supernatural and precocious talent of the celebrated child'. Both Franzi and Jupin were honoured, although it was undoubtedly Franzi's night. The concert began with M. Mercier conducting the orchestra in a symphony by Haydn. This was followed by a Romance by Romagnesi, sung by M. Gromel, and an Air by Béniowski given by Mlle Legendre. The highlight was Franzi's renderings of Ries's Second Piano Concerto, the Czerny Variations and some improvisations to finish. M. Leupold, the president, then rose to his feet and addressed Franzi.

Sir, I present to you, in the name of the Société Philomatique, the medal awarded to you at its last general meeting. It was its wish that this solemn expression of its esteem for a talent which, at such a young age, you have brought to such a high level, should be offered to you in the very place of your triumph, to the noise of that unanimous applause which the pleasure of listening to you has spontaneously caused to burst forth from every part of this hall. Under the spell of brilliant inspiration and the enchanting effects of an art which appears to have been revealed to you, as you do not appear to have had the time to learn it, this assembly joins us to offer the most flattering homage, this *élan* of enthusiasm and universal acclaim. Judging others by my own feelings, I have no hesitation in saying that it is the entire assembly that places, through my hands, this crown upon your head. The Société Philomatique will be pleased to remember that it was the first to offer you one of the numerous laurels which await you in the brilliant career which you have been called to pursue.

The *Mémorial Bordelais* of 27 January reported that the presentation of the gold medal and the palm crown contributed to give the evening an air of solemnity hitherto unparalleled in Bordeaux. The session then continued with its literary deliberations. *L'Indicateur* of 26 January summed up Franzi's art in eulogistic terms.

Whether Liszt improvises or plays written music, his age disappears; he is no longer a child but a mature composer – perfection itself; not only does he enter the thoughts of the composer, he penetrates them deeply, and even unravels hidden beauties in the music before him; his own inspirations, alas but fleeting, are themselves masterpieces of grace and harmony; the music copyist, willing and quick enough to gather them onto paper would find not one dissonance in following the imagination and thoughts in the lyrical momentum. His is a prodigious fecundity, a miraculous digital dexterity which holds his audience in ecstasy.

The same issue also judged that Franzi's grand piano, the invention of the Erards, deserved special mention.

This instrument, infinitely more sonorous than any other, and whose mechanical combinations I could not begin to describe, combines all the advantages of pianos with and without escapement; touch tells in all the positions, and it is not necessary to let the note return to its normal position to obtain further notes. This facility, this promptness, are invaluable to the perfection of the trill and of an infinite number of passages requiring a delicate and light execution. This invention is as important to the piano as the double escapement movement is for the harp; it is a problem which M. Sébastien Erard has now resolved, and all pianists will appreciate its consequences and advantages.

Adam and Franzi then left Bordeaux for Toulouse, where they arrived at the end of January, and booked in at the Hôtel d'Europe, where Liszt also stayed in 1844. The building is still standing, in what was Place Angoulême in 1826, Place Lafayette in 1844 and is today 6 Place Wilson. Nothing is known about Franzi's stay in Toulouse in 1826. They stayed for about three weeks, after which they left for Montpellier and Nîmes.

Nîmes is famous for its Roman ruins, notably the 'Arènes', or amphitheatre, and the 'Maison Carrée', or Square House, a single-roomed cube with a colonnaded portico. Directly opposite the Maison Carrée stood the Théâtre, built in 1798, and it was there that

Franzi gave the second of his two concerts in Nîmes on 16 March. The first one took place the previous evening in one of the rooms at the Mairie, the town hall a short walk away, situated among narrow streets. 'It has been recognized', wrote the *Journal du Gard* of 18 March,

> that a remarkable talent can only be formed after long study. That of this virtuoso has reversed all calculations of reason in this regard. Like Mozart, on whom nature has bestowed such a superior genius, young Liszt stretches beyond the limits that which one might impose on one so young, and it is difficult to predict where such a rare talent might stop. We would only say of Liszt that nature seems to have done everything for him and that she had engraved in advance on his spirit lessons far exceeding those he might have received from the greatest masters. Whatever lofty ideas the journals of the capital may have conveyed about our new Orpheus, the Nîmes public would never have truly appreciated this marvellous talent, if it had not been for the witness of its senses. Those of our citizens who have had the rare pleasure of hearing him truly regret that he will not accord us another soirée to satisfy the wishes of the music lovers of our town.

During his stay in Nîmes, Franzi met Jean Vignaud. This self-taught artist was born at Beaucaire in 1775, and, after a short spell as teacher of drawing at the École Centrale de Nîmes, he went to Paris in 1795. He made a living with his sketches and paintings, which he exhibited in the Salons. He also worked in the studios of David. He returned to Nîmes in 1820, where he was appointed professor at the new school of design, specially created to serve the burgeoning textile industry, based on the twilled cotton fabric, 'serge de Nîmes' – today better known as denim. Vignaud took time off to paint a portrait of Franzi and died in Nîmes that same year.

The Mairie building, now the Hôtel de Ville, dates from 1700 and is still there, although the interior has been completely altered. The Théâtre burned down in 1952, and in its place, overlooking the Maison Carrée, stands the modernistic Carré d'Art Museum, Library and town archive. The painting of Franzi, long considered lost, is in the possession of the Musée du Vieux Nîmes.

Adam and Franzi arrived in Marseilles almost immediately after the two Nîmes concerts. The Mediterranean spring had arrived, and they stayed until the end of April. It was a very agreeable stay: the weather was pleasant, and Franzi gave six concerts altogether together, with which he conquered France's historic port city. There was much to see: sites with Napoleonic connections, fine buildings, the port and the Mediterranean Sea. Joseph Lecourt was a lawyer and music lover resident in the city. He had read all about fourteen-year-old Franz Liszt, and, ever distrustful and preju- diced against performers with big reputations, attended a soirée at which Franzi played, to see and hear for himself. In the small salon, cluttered with furniture, Franzi sat at the piano and played a polonaise by Czerny. Then, when he requested a theme for improvisation, Lecourt suggested the Andante from Beethoven's Seventh Symphony. Franzi used to play this in his younger days, but now declined to do so. He decided instead on variations on Rode's Air in G – the theme from his most well-known composi- tion, the Variations in G; one of Franzi's favourite devices was to do his own versions of published variations, including those of Czerny. Lecourt was not impressed, and later cornered him, and asked him why he had rejected the Beethoven. Franzi sat again at the piano, played the air in question, and said, 'How can one play something like this in front of donkeys?' After further persuasion, Franzi did promise to play the Beethoven Andante at his forth- coming concert.

This took place on 6 April. To Lecourt's chagrin, Franzi again eschewed the Beethoven and elected to 'improvise on some very indifferent tunes'. After the concert he confronted Franzi with his disappointment. Franzi admitted that he was afraid to tackle Beethoven, whom he held in supreme reverence. Lecourt was undeterred. 'One has to force the hands of some people,' he wrote to Mme Jenny Montgolfier in Lyon, 'but by warming their heads.' He warmed Franzi's by arranging for the orchestra to play the Beethoven Andante at the second concert, which took place on 11 April. The ruse worked. 'The child was overwhelmed,' continued Lecourt, 'his chest heaved, his eyes shone with admiration, and he ran to the piano and paid Beethoven a homage truly worthy of him.'

Whatever mixed impressions Franzi made on Joseph Lecourt, his improvisations evinced a eulogistic report in the *Journal de la Méditerranée* of 15 April:

> All the panegyrics in the world would not suffice to give a notion of his splendid talent; to analyse it one would have to define perfection. . . . The moment preceding his improvisation offered one of the most interesting spectacles imaginable. Music

lovers of all kinds, professors growing white with age and talent, were grouped about him, awaiting impatiently the moment when they could give free vent to their enthusiasm. . . . Surrounded by these most distinguished connoisseurs, Liszt began to improvise on some quite ordinary theme. It was then, when he was entirely given up to his imagination, that the obstacles and difficulties wholly disappeared, to make way for the sublime inspirations of his genius; at one moment could be heard the noise of the storm, above which a graceful melody arose; at another, exquisitely tasteful and skilful modulations in the harmony; and sometimes several themes, despite each being in a different time and of a contrasting character, were made to come together as one, as well as a crowd of innovations of which no idea can be formed except by those who have heard and enjoyed them.

The report throws some light on the nature of improvisation as seen in the context of the day. Playing tunes in different ways was not a new idea; the Variations principle, as perfected by Mozart half a century previously, was well established. Even lesser composers who composed by the book could come up with a standard set of variations using a standard set of formulae, which were taught in all the music schools. The advent and development of pianos brought about a new generation of performer, to whom the instrument was an extension of his personality. With a technique honed to perfection, he could use the piano in the same way as an orator uses his power of speech and create a continuous mesmerizing flow which could change direction, key, mood or speed at whim. A theme was not necessary. The article's mention of 'the moment preceding his improvisation' may well have referred to Franzi trying to think of a starting point, which could be anything from a single note to a phrase or a flourish. In any case, a key needed to be established. A familiar theme provided a useful starting point in the concert hall, as it delighted an audience to hear what an artist could do with it.

Among the first of the great improvisers were Mozart and Beethoven, followed by the early Romantics, specifically Hummel. By the time the next generation of high Romanticism had arrived, with Liszt and Chopin in the van, improvisation was a highly developed skill. Franzi did not just play a theme in different ways, he created an instant musical tone-poem, technically brilliant and exploratory, moody and directed at the audience, in which the theme figured enough to be a pliable yet recognizable backbone,

sometimes – tantalizingly – barely so. Franzi's early studies of Bach's
fugues played a part, specifically where the fugue subjects dis-
solve into episodes, only to emerge again at intervals, in any one
of the voices. Likewise, Franzi's themes took off at creative tan-
gents, only to re-emerge in a different mode, key, time signature
or voice. Franzi had further mastered contrapuntal improvisation,
and his fugal treatment of themes is on record. He took this skill
even further. Inspired by Czerny's technique of weaving different
themes together – as in the Variations where he superimposed
'Rule Britannia' onto Haydn's 'Gotte erhalte Franz der Kaiser' –
Franzi experimented with mixing themes together and playing them
off against each other, as he did with 'La Tirolienne' and the chorus from *Der Freischütz* in Bordeaux.

There was so much more to improvisation than what it sounded
like. With this natural skill perfected – it cannot be taught – an
artist could 'talk' to his audience, tease it, delight it and take it
through a whole gamut of emotions. Franzi explained to Lecourt
that he could play any music as well as anyone – except Beethoven.
Improvisation always has an undercurrent of parody and has been
used extensively as such by Mozart in disdainful mode. Franzi held
Beethoven in such awe that he almost felt it impertinent to tamper
with his music in any way. He aimed to honour rather than dep-
recate his subjects, and with Beethoven he was afraid of failing.

He had learned that through his skill he could hold a large number
of people in his thrall, an awesome power, yet at fourteen he was
only just beginning to realize it fully. Lecourt wrote that 'his very
faults please me, because they are inseparable from his youth'.
This innocence, combined with his generous nature, his technical
skill, his good looks, and the fact that he was the first of his kind,
were at the core of his genius at this time. All of this, combined,
turned a brilliant musician into a performer with that indefinable
factor of modern performance – star quality. Franzi was one of
the first 'superstars', but even these ultimate performers are subject to mood and inspiration, and the presence of an audience
does not necessarily activate the muses. Many indifferent fantasias
have been played at concerts redolent with atmosphere, and many
brilliant comets of creativity have come and gone for ever in the
privacy of a practice room. The soirée at which Lecourt first heard
Franzi must have been a dull affair, if Franzi declined to play
Beethoven 'in front of donkeys' and went on to play some 'mediocre variations'.

Since the decline of Romanticism, improvisation – and playing by ear – have been neglected by the musical establishment, possibly because of their lack of an essential discipline and a rule book, and their connotation with jazz and popular music, in which the skill is central.

Back in Paris, in the absence of Franzi Liszt, the prodigy juggernaut had unleashed its latest star. Charles Valentin Morhange was a thirteen-year-old Parisian Jew and a pupil of Joseph Zimmermann, professor of piano at the Conservatoire. The Morhange family shed its Jewish surname and changed it to Alkan, Charles's father's first name. 'Young Alkan' made his début at the showrooms of piano manufacturer Pape in rue des Bons Enfants with an Air and Variations of his own composition. The concert, which was blessed with a 100-franc subsidy from de la Rochefoucauld, took place on 2 April and launched Alkan onto the Parisian soirée scene.

In Marseilles Franzi's reputation had spread and there were loud calls for another concert. Marseilles wanted to hear some of this *Don Sanche* that had been recently given in Paris, so a third concert was arranged. A number of local singers came forward to learn some of the arias, and the orchestra were given the parts. The concert, or rather a performance of highlights from *Don Sanche,* took place on 19 April, starting with the Overture. Franzi also played Moscheles's Grand Variations and Hummel's Piano Concerto in A minor.

Franzi now spent two hours a day in practice, an hour in reading and the rest of the time in composition, and his most significant compositions to date appeared – a set of twelve Études. These were written purely for his own work-outs and were never intended for concert performance. Each one featured a particular technical skill, and, although they were not difficult compared to some of his later works, they served their purpose. Their inspiration lay firstly in Czerny's exercises; Franzi, obsessed with honing his technique to perfection, found Czerny's work-outs musically uninteresting. Yet he understood the value of a structured system of practice and wrote his own aesthetically more satisfying ones. His second inspiration lay in Bach; each of the twelve Études had the feel and continuity of a Bach prelude. In later years he rearranged them – twice – into the technically very demanding *Transcendental Studies.*

Franzi was very proud of the new Études and needed no en-

couragement to play them. One of their great admirers was the
hunchbacked Mme Lydia Garella, a local pianist. The two of them
got together to play duets – an added bonus to the joys of making
music being that she plied him with sweets. Franzi returned the
compliment by dedicating his Études to her. They were published
that year in Marseilles by Boisselot, and later in Paris by Dufont
et Dubois, as 'Études en douze exercises', Op. 1. The chaotic
Liszt numbering also marked them as Op. 6, but they are now
catalogued as S 136.

Franzi gave three more concerts in Marseilles, on 21, 23 and
26 April.

In May the Liszts were in Lyon, where they stayed for a month.
Franzi's reputation had preceded him, partly through the Marseillais
press reports and partly through the agency of Mme Jenny
Montgolfier, the recipient of Lecourt's detailed account of his Franzi
Liszt experience. On 23 May Franzi gave the first of his three
concerts at the Salle de Bourse in the Palais Saint-Pierre, and there
was much clamour for tickets – at three francs each. Franzi shared
the bill with violinist Baumann and the singer Mlle Folleville. In
attendance was the orchestra of the Grand Théâtre. Franzi's programme included music from *Don Sanche*, a Rondo by Mocker,
some Variations (probably Czerny's and Moscheles's), and some
compositions of his own – doubtless the Études. The concert concluded, as usual, with improvisations. Three days later the *Journal
du Commerce* reported that Franzi 'created an impression difficult
to describe', and the *Indépendant* wrote that 'he had excited a universal
enthusiasm'. Franzi's two other concerts, also at the Salle de Bourse,
took place on 31 May and 13 June.

The Palais Saint-Pierre is today the Musée des Beaux Arts, and
the intimate, arched Salle de Bourse, with its exquisite frescoes,
sculptures and bas-reliefs, is unchanged from the seventeenth century,
when it was the refectory of the Sisters of St Peter. Francisco de
Zurbarán's dramatic painting of St Francis was there on view at
the time of Franzi's visit, as it is today. He would certainly have
seen and been affected by this representation of his favourite saint.

On 5 June, while Franzi was in Lyon, Carl Maria von Weber,
composer of *Der Freischütz*, died in London of tuberculosis, aged
thirty-nine.

NINE

Crisis

1826–27

B Y THE middle of summer Adam and Franzi were back in Paris, after a very successful six months, in which Adam, apart from supervising his son's triumphs, was also able to indulge his taste for the wines of Bordeaux, Languedoc, Provence, the Rhône and Burgundy at source; and in which Erard's double escapement piano enjoyed the best possible exposure.

Franzi returned to some bread-and-butter soirées around the salons of Paris but no further concerts. By his fifteenth birthday in October he had become disillusioned with his audiences and had developed a hearty disdain for the wealthy, upper-class patrons – 'donkeys' he called them. The Comte de Montbel was present at a soirée given at his house by M. de Castelbajac and recorded his displeasure at what happened. Franzi gave his usual brilliant performance, which included variations on themes suggested by the ladies. Also present were two politicians, who persisted in talking throughout his performance. When reproached, one of them claimed to be totally disinterested in child prodigies, whereupon they continued their discussion on customs and excise in loud voices. Franzi had not yet gained the confidence that he summoned when, in a similar incident in later life, he stopped playing and informed Tsar Nicholas I of Russia that he would continue when His Majesty had finished saying what he had to say.

Harriet, the Countess Gower, later the Duchess of Sutherland, was an ardent music lover and patron of the London music scene. She was in Paris in November, and heard 'an extraordinary boy by the name of Lizt [*sic*] playing ... with the greatest execution and expression' at a soirée given for a group of ladies by Countess

Thérèse Apponyi, the wife of the Austrian Ambassador, Count
Antal Apponyi. Countess Gower recorded that they whispered and
yawned throughout.

This attitude was getting Franzi down and led to depression.
He was now a fully fledged teenager, with a teenager's growing
insight into the way things are. He began to acquire value judge-
ments of his own, which were different to his father's. Whether or
not Adam grovelled to the aristocracy for the calculated reasons
of getting what he wanted for Franzi, or whether forelock-touch-
ing 'to his betters' was ingrained in him, is not clear; his 'respect-
ful' letters to the hierarchies of Eisenstadt, Vienna and Paris suggest
the latter. Franzi decided in his mid-teens that he would never
pander to what the Romantic movement referred to as 'insensitive
bourgeoisie'. He also began to ponder on the nature of Art, and
the artist's place in the world, and he did not like his findings. He
was filled with repugnance for the way musicians were segregated
– even roped off – at soirées. Franzi applauded the action taken
by Queen Victoria's favourite singer, Luigi Lablache, at a soirée
in London, which brought the emancipation of the artist a step
closer. 'Lablache,' Franz Liszt told Haweis years later, 'entering
the music salon at a certain great house, observed the usual rope
laid down in front of him when he came on to sing in a duet. He
quietly stooped down and tossed it aside. It was never replaced,
and the offensive practice dropped out of London society from
that day.'

Franzi developed the teenager's *angst* and self-consciousness and
felt himself humiliated. As a prodigious talent, he might objec-
tively have considered himself a superior human being, endowed
with a singular gift from God with which to enchant Mankind,
and yet there were those aristocrats whose code forebade ever
thanking a servant – and that included hired piano players. The
later, more mature Liszt was able to consider and set down his
feelings at this time: 'I succumbed to a feeling of disgust for art,
which I found to be degraded to being a more or less profitable
trade, a mere amusement for the well-bred; and I would sooner
have been anything in the world than a musician in the pay of the
aristocracy, patronized and remunerated by them like a juggler, or
like Mumito the performing dog.'

Towards the end of 1826 Franzi started the long-awaited lessons
with Antonin Reicha, professor of composition at the Conservatoire.
The lessons were largely on counterpoint and took the discipline

to its ultimate frontiers. Another young hopeful who came under
Reicha's tutelage that year was Hector Berlioz, who enrolled as a
full-time student in August – despite his confrontations with Director Cherubini in the Conservatoire library.

In December Adam and Franzi again arranged the carriage of
the new Erard and left for a tour of Switzerland. The English
journalist Henry Reeve recalled his journey in 1820: 'We drove
from Paris to Geneva in a berline with three horses, same all the
way. . . . We were nine days on the road, sleeping at Fontainebleau,
Sens, Auxerre, Joigny, Dijon.'

Franzi's first stop was at Dijon, where he gave a chamber concert, with four other musicians. This took place on 18 December
at the Hôtel de Ville, situated in the complex of the Palace of the
Dukes of Burgundy. The opening item was Ries's Piano Quintet;
the *Journal de Dijon* of 20 December 1826 wrote, 'from the lively
and forceful manner in which the young pianist attacked the theme
of the allegro, one could immediately discern a knowledgeable
interpretation that was animated and vigorous. The predominant
qualities of M. Liszt are in truth his vigour and energy, which he
contrasted, where necessary, with the most pleasing lightness. He
united these qualities admirably in the Variations which followed.'
After these – no further details are given – came the Piano Trio
by Mayseder, in which Franzi 'has shown that his style extended
to every expression, and embraced every effect. But it was the
improvisations that were most eagerly awaited.' Franzi ended his
concert by superimposing a theme from *La Dame Blanche* onto
the waltz from *Der Freischütz*, in which the qualities of his Erard
came to the fore.

The gift of improvisation is here surely enchanced by the nature of the instrument. But in all good improvisations the discerning listener seeks to find argument, design, pleasing
modulations, movement without chaos and variety without confusion. The artist began with a theme from *La Dame Blanche*,
as had been suggested to him. A timely transition led to the
horn call of the hunter, and the theme from *Freischütz* appeared
beneath his fingers. Then all the fugal counterpoint and verve
of Weiber's [*sic*] music flooded forth. . . . He paraphrased his
subject with an ever growing warmth and flow until the moment
when he climaxed his theme with a graceful decrescendo freefall . . .
as if into sounds heard from afar. M. Liszt has shown, in this
improvised scene, the mind of a harmonist and the soul of a composer.

From Dijon Adam and Franzi continued, as did Henry Reeve, who wrote 'through . . . Poligny, &c. How well I remember these sleeping places, and the French country inns; and Antoine the driver, who was a fierce Bonapartist, and rather won my mother's heart; and the first view of the lake of Geneva from the Jura . . .' The details of the tour are sparse, save that it included Geneva, Lausanne and Lucerne and probably Bern and Basle.

During 1827 Zimmermann was arranging soirées all over Paris for his star pupil, Charles Alkan, whose reputation for technical brilliance was now spreading. One such soirée was at the home of Princess de la Moscova; also present at this soirée was Franzi. Charles gave a typically virtuoso performance, which, by the tremendous applause, established him as the undoubted star of the glittering soirée. Later in the evening Franzi played his piece in a display of virtuosity that Charles had not believed possible. He descended into a mood of sheer despondency as he realized that he was only second best. That night Charles cried himself to sleep. It was the first encounter of the great pianistic élite: Liszt, Chopin, Alkan, Hiller, Kalkbrenner and Herz, who would dominate Paris in the 1830s and set the standards of pianism for the remainder of the century.

On 26 March, Beethoven, Franzi's supreme hero, died in Vienna of liver and kidney failure, aggravated by alcohol misuse. Ten days later, on 5 April, Adam and Franzi set off for their third trip to London and arrived at their lodgings in Frith Street, Soho, on 8 April. Franzi's first performance took place at the New Argyll Rooms on 21 May. The concert was the seventh organized that season by the Philharmonic Society, whose members, notably 'Chip' Potter, were still smarting from the death of Beethoven. The previous year, having heard of the Master's plight and poverty, the Society had sent him a financial donation to ease his stress. Beethoven, in gratitude, began work on his Tenth Symphony, which was to be his 'London' Symphony. He died leaving only sketches, which lay in obscurity until their discovery and realization in a performing version of one movement by Dr Barry Cooper. It was given its première, aptly, at the Royal Philharmonic Society's concert at the Royal Festival Hall in London on 18 October 1988, by the Royal Liverpool Philharmonic Orchestra, conducted by Walter Weller.

The London Philharmonic Society's Orchestra accompanying Franzi's performance of Hummel's B minor Concerto was conducted by Henry Bishop. Moscheles was there and commented that he performed 'with rare skill, but restlessly'.

On 25 May Franzi played Hummel's A minor Piano Concerto at a concert given by former child prodigy violinist Nicolas Mori, the leader of the London Philharmonic Orchestra. Present at the rehearsal for this concert was the composer of Franzi's early pianistic workouts under Czerny – old Muzio Clementi, one of the co-founders of the Philharmonic Society, now seventy-five. 'The venerable appearance and benevolent expression of the bald-headed veteran, and the deference shown to him by all in that select assembly, attracted my attention, alert with boyish enthusiasm. . . . Keenly did I watch the aged Clementi's face, with intense interest, and his brilliant dark eyes glistening, he followed the marvellous performance.' Thus wrote the London representative of the prodigy juggernaut, the brilliant thirteen-year-old London-born Jewish pianist, Charles Kensington Salaman, about Franzi's playing at the rehearsal. 'His playing of Hummel's Concerto created a profound sensation, and my enthusiastic admiration made me eager to know this wonderful young pianist, my senior by a couple of years.'

A few days later Charles and his father went to Erard's to buy tickets for Franzi's next concert at the New Argyll Rooms on 9 June. They cost half a guinea each. They then called on the Liszts. Charles congratulated Franzi on his Hummel, and very soon the two boys were talking music, and Mr Salaman invited Adam and Franzi to dinner. Charles later recalled Franzi's exclamation of pleasure when one of his favourite dishes was served. 'Oh, gooseberry pie!' The evening was spent with Charles and Franzi at the piano, playing duets and exchanging virtuosities. Franzi played Charles his recently published Études. Charles was most impressed, so Franzi presented him with a volume, adding an instant rewrite of No. 6 in G minor.

Charles Salaman spent the rest of his life in London, where he pursued a career as a pianist, conductor and highly respected teacher. Unlike his Parisian contemporary and namesake, Charles Alkan, he maintained his faith in high profile and was a pillar of London Jewish society until his death in 1901. The manuscript of Franzi's rewritten Étude eventually found its way to the Royal College of Music, where it was discovered by Busoni in London in 1908. It is now known as the Scherzo in G minor (S 153).

The concert on 9 June at the Argyll Rooms was a long and varied one in two parts. The London Philharmonic Orchestra was there, led by Nicolas Mori, and conducted by Gottfried Schunke, who was on tour from the court of Württemberg at the time. A number of artists were featured, including some faces familiar from Franzi's previous visits. The spectacular opener was an arrangement for four pianos by Moscheles of the Overture to Cherubini's *Les Deux Journées*, in which Franzi joined Mr Beale, Mr Martin and Mr Wigley. This was followed by an aria from Mr Begrez and Beethoven's Harp Fantasie on Irish airs played by Théodore Labarre, which was followed by a Rossini duet from Miss Grant and Signor Torri.

Then came the first highlight, Franzi's Piano Concerto in A minor, which he played with the London Philharmonic Orchestra. Moscheles was in the audience and wrote that the concerto contained 'chaotic beauties; as to his playing, it surpasses in power and mastery of difficulties everything I have ever heard'. This concerto was one of two that Franzi had written the previous year. It is now lost, although it is possible that a rewrite in later years resulted in the now familiar mini-concerto, the *Malédiction* for piano and strings; it may also have been the legendary 'Third Concerto', which has been 'reassembled' by Jay Rosenblatt into a study version, using parts that were scattered throughout Europe.

The Concerto was followed by a song from Miss Stephens, a French horn solo from Schunke, an aria by Miss Betts and a duet, 'Amor, possente nome', by Miss Fanny Ayton and Mr Begrez, both by Rossini, and a Fantasy Duo for violin and piano by Mori on Rossini's *Semiramide*, a collaborative composition by Mori and Franzi, whose manuscript is now lost. Next came a scene from an opera by Nicola Zingarelli, sung by John Braham, to whose benefit concert Franzi contributed three years previously. Franzi closed the first half with an 'Extemporised Fantasy'.

The second half opened with the Quartet for voice, harp, piano and violin by Mayseder, performed respectively by Miss Stephens, Labarre, Franzi and Mori. Miss Ayton then sang Rossini's 'Una voce poco fa', Mr Huerta played his composition on guitar, Braham and Miss Stephens sang a duet, and Miss Love sang 'Had I a Heart'.

There followed a collaboration between Franzi and another boy, the flautist Master Minasi, in a duo Fantasia inspired by the example of Moscheles, 'The Fall of Paris: a Military Air with Variations'. This manuscript is also missing. Miss Grant then sang Crivelli's 'The Nightingale', and the concert finished with Franzi, in English mode, playing his own *Variations brillantes on 'Rule Britannia'*, with the orchestra.

Master Minasi was probably related to portrait painter James Anthony Minasi, of Italian origin, who was born in London in 1776. Franzi visited him at his home at 13 Praed Street, Paddington, where he drew his portrait. James Minasi died in London in 1865. Catholics in a staunchly Protestant land, Adam and Franzi sought out the company of people of similar convictions, notably the musical and Catholic Novellos, whom they often visited at their house at 66 Great Queen Street. Vincent Novello was born in London in 1781, the son of an Italian immigrant. He devoted his life to the pursuit of musicology and founded the music publishing house of that name. He was also one of the founders of the London Philharmonic Society, played the organ and composed church music. With his wife Mary and their seven children, the Novellos were among the most gregarious, generous and open-minded Catholic families on the London music scene. Their eldest, Alfred, was a year younger than Franzi. He grew up to be a fine singer and inherited the family publishing house, which thrives to this day. The youngest was nine-year-old Clara, who at the age of three sang Rossini's aria from Tancredi, 'Di tanti palpiti', after hearing it on a barrel organ. She grew up to be one of the mid-nineteenth century's most celebrated sopranos. In 1829 Vincent and Mary travelled to Salzburg to talk to Mozart's widow, Constanze von Nissen, and his sister Nannerl. They recorded the account of their journey and interviews in their diaries, which were discovered and published, aptly by Novello, in 1955, as *A Mozart Pilgrimage: Being the Travel Diaries of Vincent and Mary Novello in the Year 1829*.

By 1 July, Adam and Franzi had returned to Paris. Franzi's depression became worse. His disillusionment with the artist's life, fanned by his experiences in the salons of Paris, merged with his religious convictions, all of which led to a spiritual crisis. He asked the question which is the standard philosophical cliché lying like a trip-wire at the threshold of adulthood: 'What is it all about?' He was experiencing feelings of *déjà vu* at every turn: spring in London, summer in Paris, the Hummel concertos, the Czerny variations, the London Philharmonic scenario, the Paris soirées, the newspaper reports, the female adulation. At fifteen he was still sexually immature and unaware of the longer-term implications of his effect on women. Added to this teenage *angst* was the constant travelling, performing and practising which took a toll on his health. His concerts were taxing in the extreme; few modern concert pianists would give two concerto works as well as a solo item the length of an improvisation at one concert, as did Franzi in his early teens.

Franzi, physically and mentally exhaused, was close to a breakdown. He and his father found themselves with time on their hands in which to think and ask where to go next. He again felt the call of the priesthood, which came and went like a tide from a very early age. 'During the many years of my youth,' wrote Franz Liszt in later years to his mother,

> I dreamed myself incessantly into the world of saints. Nothing seemed to me so self-evident as heaven, nothing so true and so rich in blessedness as the goodness and compassion of God.... Nothing and nobody have ever been able to shake my faith in immortality and eternal salvation, a faith that I had won by my prayers in the churches at Raiding and Frauendorf, the Mariahilf church in Vienna, Notre-Dame de Lorette and St Vincent de Paul in Paris.

He found himself pulled in different directions by his art, his faith and his slowly awakening sexual awareness. Fortunately his father was there for him. Both were deeply religious people who found solace – as well as torment – in their faith. Adam advised strongly against the priesthood, reminding Franzi that his calling, his real vocation, lay in music; and that the path of the artist does not lead away from religion, but can be a path to both. 'Love God, be upright and good so that you will reach ever higher in your art. You belong to art, not the church.' Whether this was a wise and loving father guiding his son, or a middle-aged man looking for security in his declining years, is not clear. Perhaps he perceived that Franzi would never reconcile celibate priesthood with the sexual awareness to which he would one day – soon – awake.

Franzi was guided by his father, and his vocation to Holy Orders receded. But he spent many hours praying obsessively and examining his conscience. His reading consisted largely of religious books, especially the lives of the Saints. He was deeply affected by the writings of St Paul, St Augustine, St Teresa of Avila and, above all, *The Imitation of Christ* by Thomas à Kempis, a heavy theological work which effectively became his handbook on living. He tried to live by its very severe precepts, which advocate a dark

Raiding, Hungary, Liszt's birthplace

Adam Liszt, Franz's father. Gouache by unknown artist, 1819. National Museum of Budapest

Franz Liszt in Vienna, aged twelve.
Portrait by Baron Ferdinand
von Lutgendorf, c. 1823.
Liszt Museum, Budapest

Franz Liszt in Paris,
aged thirteen. Drawing
by A.X. Leprince,
1824. Bibliothèque
Nationale, Paris

Franz Liszt in Paris, aged thirteen. Lithograph by C. Motte, 1825. Liszt Museum, Budapest

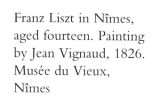

Franz Liszt in Nîmes, aged fourteen. Painting by Jean Vignaud, 1826. Musée du Vieux, Nîmes

Franz Liszt in London, aged sixteen. Drawing by James Anthony Minasi, 1827. Royal College of Music, London

Franz Liszt in Paris, aged twenty-one. Drawing by Achille Deveria, 1832. Bibliothèque Nationale, Paris

LISZT.

humility verging on nihilism. 'Love to be unknown,' Franzi read, 'and accounted as nought.' A strange piece of advice to be embraced by a consummate showman and superstar. It was almost as if Franzi, racked with guilt over his talent, was seeking oblivion in spiritual suicide.

The Novellos went regularly for their summer holidays to Boulogne, where they stayed with the Bonnefoys, a French family who ran a private school much patronized by English pupils wishing to learn French, including Alfred and later Clara. It may well have been the Novellos who had recommended Boulogne to the Liszts two years previously and who may have done so again. In the middle of August Adam and Franzi, feeling a need to relax and unwind, left the stifling heat of Paris for the sea air of Boulogne.

In Boulogne Adam and Frenzi put up at the Hibernian Hotel at No. 36 rue Neuve-Chaussée, an inn run by an Englishman by the name of John Holt. Adam retired immediately, as he had not been entirely well since his return from London. On arrival in Boulogne his condition suddenly deteriorated, his temperature rose and he became delirious. The local doctor was called and diagnosed typhoid fever. Adam was under no illusions; he knew that typhoid fever was a killer. In his lucid moments he talked to Franzi, and told him to write to his mother, who was still expecting them back in Vienna. This Franzi did.

Boulogne, 24 August 1827

Best of women, Mother,

At the very moment I write to you, I am anxious about my father's health. When we arrived here he was already feeling unwell, but it has got worse, and today the doctor told me that it may be dangerous. Father begs you not to lose courage. He feels very ill, and that is why he wants me to tell you in this letter that you may perhaps have to come to France. He thinks we can wait for a few days still, and he said to me: 'You can write to her later on, once we know something definite.'

He was very pleased to receive your letter. I thank you for your loving remembrance of me, and I will write to you again for sure in three or four days.

Farewell, we embrace you many times.

In haste,

F. Liszt

Anna immediately set off for Paris. As Adam grew weaker, he looked at Franzi and marvelled at his talent, his spirituality and his good looks and caught a glimpse of a possible future for such a boy. He feverishly mumbled to Franzi that his life would be dominated and troubled by women. It was merely the observation of the proud father of a good-looking, charismatic son, but it turned out to be prophetic.

Adam Liszt died at 8.30 on the morning of 28 August. The town hall was notified, and at ten o'clock the Deputy Mayor, Alexandre Lorgnier, issued the death certificate, which was witnessed by the town clerk Sylvain Bilot and landlord John Holt. The following day Fr Paque officiated at the hastily arranged funeral service at the church of St Nicolas after which his body was buried at the Cimetière de l'Est. *The Franc Parleur* reported the event in its issue of 3 September: 'The father of young Litz [*sic*], the celebrated pianist, died in Boulogne on Tuesday last, after several days of illness.'

Franzi was in a daze. Since his mother had left Paris, his father was all he had. Count Thadé d'Amadé, who only learned the tragic news the following spring, wrote a belated letter of condolence to Franzi:

> You have lost your first support, your best friend, he who concerned himself with your interests from your birth, and who loved you with the tenderest affection, long before you were in a condition to appreciate and deserve his love. Up to now, your life has been sweet. All you needed to do was to obey, and you could rest blindly on the care of your father. Now you have a more difficult task to fulfil. You have to acquire friends and become the support of your mother. You must thank heaven that it has saved for you the woman who, like your deceased father, will always be disposed to cherish and love you.

In later life Franz Liszt wrote to his mother:

> My father . . . hesitated not for a moment, nor did he yield to all the rational arguments of rational people. He had to sacrifice his secure position, give up comfortable habits, leave his own country, ask his wife to share a doubtful future, meet the costs of our modest standard of living by giving Latin, geography, history and music lessons; he had, in a word, to quit the service of Prince Esterházy, leave Raiding and settle in Vienna, so that I could take lessons from our good, excellent Czerny and thereafter face the risk of a very problematic career. And all this with savings of no more than a few hundred francs. Certainly, dearest mother, you are entirely right when you say that no one

father in a thousand would have been capable of such devotion, or of such persistence in that kind of intuitive stubbornness possessed only by persons of exceptional character.

Franzi knew what he had to do and set about assuming his responsibilities as the family breadwinner and supporting his mother. It was no easy task, for although he was only two months off his sixteenth birthday, he was still innocent and immature, having been sheltered all his life from the true ways of the world. He sought strength in prayer and from the belief that his father's soul was in heaven. He put on a brave face and took his first steps as a responsible adult, the first being to pay the expenses: three weeks in the hotel, nursing, doctor's fees, the grave, coffin, burial fees and prayers for the dead. The Rev. Haweis recorded the results of his conversations with the older Franz Liszt. 'Rousing himself from the bodily prostration and torpor of grief into which he had been thrown by the death of his father,' he wrote in *My Musical Life* published in 1896, 'Franz, with admirable energy and that high sense of honour which has always distinguished him, began to set his house in order. He called in all his debts, sold his magnificent grand Erard and left Boulogne for Paris with a heavy heart and a light pocket but not owing a sou.'

TEN
Caroline
1827–29

B ACK IN Paris, Franzi rationalized all his affairs, realized the
family savings from his concerts and soirées and wound up
the rue du Mail apartment. He found cheap, temporary lodgings
at 38 rue Coquenard, in the Poissonnière district in the northern
suburbs, in the heart of musical Paris: the Conservatoire, the Opéra
and the 'Bouffons' were all just a short stroll away. At one end of
the road there was a garrison, and just round the corner, in rue
du Faubourg Montmartre, was the church of Notre Dame de Lorette,
which Franzi adopted as one of his favourite places of worship;
the original church was rebuilt, and the present building was consecrated on 15 December 1836. His street was, approximately,
where the rue Lamartine is now.

His mother arrived soon afterwards, and they moved to a larger
apartment on the fourth floor at 7 bis rue Montholon, which was
virtually a continuation of rue Coquenard. Anna had prepared for
the triumphant return of her husband and her brilliant son, only
to find her plans dashed so tragically. The apartment was not
large, and there was no longer a piano – the Erard had gone towards paying off immediate debts. With his mother's help and
support, Franzi pulled himself together enough to start making a
living teaching music. In a short while the crisis had passed, money
began to come in, the investments in Vienna remained untouched,
and Franzi was soon able to buy another piano.

Franzi found he was good at his new job. That his grandfather
and father were teachers counted for nothing; he far exceeded
their capacities and soon gained a reputation as an enlightened
and brilliant teacher. By his sixteenth birthday in October, Franzi had

as many pupils as he could cope with. He went to their houses, and often returned to rue Montholon late at night, exhausted, and left untouched the supper that his mother had prepared before retiring. In order not to disturb her, he would sometimes sleep on the stairs.

He found a job at 43 rue de Clichy, teaching music at Madame Alix's Academy for Young Ladies – most of whom were doubtless delighted to be taught by a good-looking and talented boy of their own age. Among Franzi's private pupils were some English girls, for whom a spell in Paris was part of the finishing process: the daughters of the British Ambassador, Lord Granville, and Catherine Glynne, who later became Mrs W. E. Gladstone. Among his French pupils were the Comtesse Montesquieu, Herminie, the sister of seventeen-year-old Alfred de Musset (who had started to establish himself as a brilliant poet in the Romantic mould), and fifteen-year-old Caroline, the pretty daughter of Minister of Commerce the Comte Pierre de Saint-Cricq.

Franzi's workaholism was due partly to a need to achieve that which had to be achieved, to learn that which had to be learned before it was too late and partly as an opiate for his *angst* about his art and his place in the world. He kept a diary that year, in which he wrote quotations from his spiritual readings. Among them were such precepts as La Bruyère's '. . . those who use time badly are the first to complain of its brevity; those who use it well have time to spare', and, from Bouhours, '. . . at the hour of our death, what would we wish to have done? Let us do now what we would like to have done then. There is no time to lose; any moment may be our last.' Taken in conjunction with the harsh precepts of Thomas à Kempis, such as '. . . why seek you rest, since it is for work that you were born?', Franzi had imposed on himself a regime of almost medieval self-mortification.

Free of his father's management, Franzi eschewed all public performances and was content to become a 'celebrity' teacher. He earned up to 20 francs an hour, which compared very well with 10 to 20 francs for a soirée and his total income of 170 francs for *Don Sanche*. The income was regular, and he was appreciated by both pupils and employers alike, even though some only hired him on a short-term basis just to be able to 'name-drop' their daughters' teacher. Working on a one-to-one basis on his own terms, Franzi was in control, which suited him while he took stock of himself.

He continued to seek solace in his faith, and his reading extended to the fashionable philosophy of Saint-Simonism, a post-Napoleonic philosophy of social and religious reform which appealed to his liberalism and spirituality. Just down the road from his apartment in rue Montholon was the original church of St Vincent de Paul, which was built in 1804. The foundation stone of the present church was laid on 23 August 1824, off the nearby Place Bossuet. At the time of Franzi's arrival in the area, only the foundations had been laid; the following year, a financial crisis put a stop to further construction, and the new church was not consecrated until 21 October 1844. The Place Bossuet has now been renamed Place Franz Liszt. Franzi visited the old church every day. The parish priest was Abbé Guillaume Cayla, although Franzi established a strong, spiritual rapport and a close friendship with Abbé Jean-Baptiste Bardin and was a frequent visitor to his house at 4 rue Montholon.

On the down side, Franzi took up smoking and drinking, vices that he pursued for the rest of his life. He had also lost interest in composing.

One of the most flamboyant figures on the Paris music scene was Vienna-born Henri Herz. Noted for his spectacular piano technique, good looks, eccentric dress sense and a total devotion to commercialism, he made a very good living playing what people wanted to hear and teaching, for which he charged exorbitant fees. On Christmas Day he arranged a full, orchestral concert at the Théâtre of HRH Madame and invited Franzi to take part. Franzi went against his inclinations and accepted. The programme included Weber's *Oberon* Overture, given in Paris for the first time, the Overture to Méhul's *Le Jeune Henri* and Herz's own Piano Concerto. Among other singers and instrumentalists were the violinist Lafont and the clarinettist M. Schott. The concert was brought to a close in spectacular style with the Grandes Variations Concertantes, an arrangement for two pianos eight hands by Henri Herz of a chorus from *Il Crociato in Egitto* of Meyerbeer, in which he was joined by his older brother Jacques and by Pixis and Franzi.

This concert nudged Franzi back onto the performing circuit, but only in a limited capacity as an extra pianist or accompanist. He was in action again on 27 January 1828, when the piano maker Jean Henri Pape gave a soirée at his showrooms in rue de Valois, beside the Palais Royal. The programme featured the flautist Aristide Farrenc, accompanied by his wife, Louise Farrenc, who was a former pupil of Moscheles and Hummel, teacher of piano at the

Conservatoire, prolific composer and early proponent of feminist achievement. Among the singers were Giulio Bordogni, Fortunata Marinoni and the celebrated mezzo-soprano, Maria Malibran. The programme included a Fantaisie for eol-harmonica – one of the experimental piano-harmonium hybrids beloved of inventors at the time – and two guitars, by M. Schulz, and played by himself and his two sons. Franzi's friend from Munich, the sixteen-year-old violinist Karl Ebner, on an extended visit to Paris from the Prussian Court, played a Polonaise by Mayseder, with Franzi at the piano. The concert concluded, again in spectacular fashion, with an arrangement, by Paër, of Mozart's *Magic Flute* Overture, for three pianos twelve hands, those of Franzi and Paër, Pixis, Rhein, Schulz and one of the Schunkes: there were two unrelated pianists named Schunke on the concert circuit, Charles and the ex-Czerny pupil Ludwig, who was on a concert tour in Paris with his father and younger brother at this time.

On 23 February the award-winning piano maker Johann Dietz gave a small-scale soirée at his showrooms in rue Neuve-Augustin, at which Mme Durand and M. dell'Oro sang, and guitarist Fernando Sor played two of his Fantaisies; Franzi and Ebner played a duo and an *Air Tyrolien* for violin and piano, and Franzi closed the programme with an improvisation.

On 29 March he accompanied the young violinist Camillo Sivori in his second and final Paris concert at the Salle Chantereine, in rue Chantereine – today rue des Victoires. The following day he was again at the Salons Pape where the horn player Gottfried Schunke was giving a concert with his two sons, pianist Ludwig and horn player Ernst. The opening item was Paër's twelve-hand piano arrangement of the Overture to Mozart's *The Magic Flute* again – this time played by Paër, Franzi, Wojciech Sowiński, George Osborne, M. Rhein and Ludwig Schunke.

With the coming of spring, Franzi's heart grew lighter. The cause of this was his piano pupil, Caroline de Saint-Cricq. A year younger than Franzi, she had poise, delicate features, dark eyes, black hair and a slim figure. 'Caroline', confided Liszt to Rev. Haweis, 'was lithe, slender, and of angelic beauty, and a complexion like a lily flushed with roses, impressionable to beauty, to the world, to religion, to God.' The piano lessons, on the de Saint-Cricqs' Erard, were a joy and lasted as long as they felt like continuing. Caroline's invalid and terminally ill mother, the Comtesse Jeanne-Clémence, chaperoned the lessons, but also took an active interest in them and joined in the music talk. She became very fond of Franzi, and he of her. While Franzi introduced Caroline to what was finest in the piano repertoire, she, in turn, introduced him to her favourite writings of Victor Hugo, Alphonse de Lamartine and Dante. The poetry of the latter two affected Franzi especially, and his preoccupation eventually gave rise to the symphonic poem after Lamartine, *Les Préludes*, and the 'Dante' Symphony and the Fantasia quasi Sonata, 'Après une lecture de Dante' from the *Deuxième Année de Pèlerinage*. It was soon obvious to the Comtesse that her pretty daughter and the handsome piano tutor were in love, a fact that filled her warm heart with pleasure. The love affair developed before the Comtesse's discreet eyes, which were often turned away to allow the youngsters to hold hands or steal a kiss. Franzi was invited in the evenings to the de Saint-Cricq house in extra-curricular circumstances. The Comte, always busy with his Ministry, did not take much notice and assumed that his wife had the 'meaningless little flirtation' under control.

It was an idyllic time for the young lovers during the Paris spring of 1828. There was so much to share; both loved music and literature, both were spiritual, both aspired to what was highest and best, and both were very much attracted to each other. Caroline had introduced Franzi to literature, and he became aware of enormous gaps in his general education and tried to remedy this defect by reading more widely and expanding his knowledge of the great French writers.

April was particularly busy for Franzi, as his concert appearances increased. He even composed two Hungarian Recruiting Dances, *Zum Andenken* (S 241), based on works by László Fáy and Johann Bihari. On 4 April, at the Académie Royale, he played the Rondo from Hummel's B minor Concerto at the second Concert Spirituel, at which Beethoven's oratorio *Jesus at the Mount of Olives* was the main item. On 7 April Franzi gave his own concert at the Salle Chantereine. He opened with Hummel's Grand Septet for piano, flute, oboe, horn, viola, cello and double bass and again accompanied Ebner in Mayseder's Polonaise, finishing the first half with an improvisation on three themes, from a Beethoven symphony, from *The Siege of Corinth* and from *La Muette de Portici* by Auber. The second half again featured the horns and piano of the Schunke family. Throughout the items were interspersed with airs from Mlle Rigal, M. Dommange, Margarethe Stockhausen and Auguste Panseron. The concert ended with another chance to hear Herz's Meyerbeer chorus, played by the Herzes, Franzi and Ludwig Schunke.

On 10 April Franzi and Ebner filled in the time between theatrical acts at the Théâtre of HRH Madame with Mayseder's Polonaise and Franzi's improvisation. On 12 April, Charles-Auguste de Bériot, first violinist at the Court of the Netherlands, composer and later husband of the singer Maria Malibran, gave a concert at the Salle Chantereine, at which Franzi accompanied the concertgiver in a performance of his Fantaisie on motifs from Rossini's *Moïse*. In the second half Franzi played Henri Herz's Grand Variations on motifs from Beethoven's *The Siege of Corinth*. The violin items were interspersed with arias. The following day Franzi took part in a charity vocal and instrumental soirée at the Salle Cléry, organized by the singer Mlle Amigo for the benefit of an 'unfortunate family'. Taking part were the guitarist Sor and the violinist M. Haumann. Franzi's contribution was an improvisation on themes from Rossini and Auber.

On 18 April Julia Robert gave a soirée at the Salle Chantereine, at which Franzi joined Charles Schunke in the latter's Duo for two pianos, on the march from Rossini's *Elizabeth*. Sor and Haumann also took part. On 20 April Charles Schunke arranged a concert at the Salons Pape. Franzi and Charles opened with another performance of Charles's Duo, and the concert ended with Henri Jerome Bertini's arrangement, for two pianos eight hands, of Beethoven's Seventh Symphony, in which the arranger was joined by Franzi, Charles Schunke and Sowiński. On 30 April the singer Mlle Rigal gave a largely vocal soirée at the Petite Salle at the Conservatoire, at which Franzi contributed an improvisation.

After this Franzi decided he had had enough performing, and gave up altogether to concentrate on his teaching and reading. The three-month spell did not tax him in the least. Instead of formal performances of the Czerny Variations and the Hummel, Moscheles and Ries Concertos, he had turned up at small venues to knock up some lightweight improvisations or to join with other pianists in multi-hand arrangements. Besides, it brought in that extra money which was always useful. In early May Count d'Amadé's letter of condolence on the death of his father arrived. Born in Pressburg in 1783, d'Amadé was known as the 'Musical Count' because of his ability to improvise; he was taught piano by Hummel. Franzi and Anna considered him the kindest and most supportive of the Pressburg Six, and his encouraging letter was eagerly read and his advice acted upon. Count d'Amadé died in 1845. Franzi and Caroline watched, hand in hand, as spring turned to summer. Everything seemed to be going well, money was not in short supply, and the strain of performing was lifted from Franzi's shoulders. Franzi bought two more pianos – one of them specially made and extremely unresponsive, designed to make practice as strenuous as possible. A dark cloud appeared in June, when Comtesse Jeanne-Clémence's health deteriorated, and she died on the last day of the month, aged fifty-eight. Before she died, she begged her husband to look kindly on their daughter's love for Franzi. 'If she loves him,' she said, 'let her be happy.'

But the Comte de Saint-Cricq had other plans. While permitting Franzi to continue calling on Caroline in the evenings, he had already arranged her marriage to his friend, the Comte Bertrand d'Artigaux, who had an estate at Pau, in the foothills of the Pyrenees. He then needed an excuse to dismiss Franzi. This came after Franzi overstayed one evening until midnight and had to summon a servant to let him out and lock up after him. The servant did so, but Franzi failed to tip him, so the next day the servant reported the matter. Franzi was duly summoned by the Comte, who thanked him politely for his music lessons, which he said were no longer necessary, as Caroline would be marrying, as befitted her status, the Comte d'Artigaux, and dismissed him peremptorily. Franzi left, shattered at the fact that marriage between him and Caroline would have been impossible anyway because of a difference of status. Before they parted, the young lovers pledged to think about each other every day thenceforth at the hour of the Angelus. Caroline was devastated, refused to countenance marriage to Bertrand d'Artigaux and became very ill. When she recovered she asked to enter a nunnery.

Franzi took the break-up very badly. 'Love, grief, religion, all struggling together for victory in that young and fervid spirit, at last seemed to fairly exhaust him,' wrote Rev. Haweis. 'His old haunts knew him not, his pupils were neglected, he saw no friends, shut himself up in his room; and at last would only see his mother at meals.'

Franzi lost all interest in life and suffered a nervous breakdown. For the rest of the summer and into the autumn he had stopped looking after himself, and often went all day without eating, numbing his senses and gnawing hunger with wine. Anna, obviously very concerned, was powerless to do anything for him; sometimes he would sit, motionless, at table and stare through his supper without touching it. He managed to keep going at Mme Alix's Academy, if only to bring in some money. Otherwise he devoted himself entirely to religious reading and daily visits to the little church of St Vincent de Paul, where he would spend his time confessing, praying and meditating. His feelings of lost love tormented him all the time. Since the death of his father, he had grown up very quickly, and his sexual awareness, dormant even a year ago, had turned into a raging turmoil of desire that he could not reconcile with his faith. He turned to the Abbé Bardin and asked for enlightenment about the sixth and ninth commandments and why it was that the expression of true love should be a mortal sin. What he learned filled him with trepidation and conjured up images of eternal damnation from Dante's *Inferno*.

He finally announced to his mother and to Abbé Bardin his intention of entering the Paris Seminary and of taking Holy Orders. Both Anna and the Abbé agreed to stop him from doing so, which they did after a great deal of persuasion.

The only friend he could face was Chrétien Urhan, a musical mystic who fasted every day till six in the evening and whose ideas on self-mortification were even more extreme than Franzi's. He was, with the permission of the Archbishop of Paris, first violinist at the Opéra, a job that he undertook without ever looking at the stage in case he was corrupted by what he saw. He also played the viola and was organist at the Church of St Vincent de Paul and played in many of the same concerts and soirées as did Franzi.

The strain told, and Franzi's health began to decline seriously. The cataleptic fits of his childhood recurred, during which he would lose consciousness for worrying periods of time. The climax came at the time of his seventeenth birthday, when he had a seizure that lasted two or three days. His metabolism virtually stopped, and premature rumours of his death leaked to the Paris press. Pictures of Franzi, inscribed with the legend 'Franz Liszt born Raiding 1811 died Paris 1828', were on sale in the streets. *Le Corsaire* actually announced his death and on 23 October printed his obituary.

Young Liszt has died in Paris. . . . With this extraordinary child one more name is added to the list of precocious children whose appearance on earth has been all too fleeting; they are like hothouse plants which bear some delicious fruit and then die from the expenditure of effort. . . . He is a child, people remarked at each of his successes, and envy was patent. But had he grown to manhood, had the divine spark which inspired him been allowed to develop, people would have looked at him with an eye more critical, would have denied his merits, and – who knows? – might perhaps have gone so far as to censure him.

It was a tactless piece of journalism, and not the kind of obituary Franzi would have cared for. Mme Alix read the piece with amazement and shock. She angrily contacted the press to assure them that her music teacher, if not actually well, was alive.

Franzi recovered from his seizure – and his obituary – but never got over the trauma of losing Caroline, and the question of social status gnawed at his psyche. It was precisely that kind of thinking that was beginning to cause rumblings of dissent and talk of revolution and social change in the cafés and the more liberal drawing-rooms of Paris. Franzi's status as jobbing piano player to the moneyed classes was rollercoasting to an end, even though he did not know it.

Caroline succumbed to the age-old traditions of her class and entered a loveless marriage with Bertrand d'Artigaux. She and Franzi never forgot one another, and Franzi stuck to his pledge to think of her at the hour of the Angelus every day. His first love lasted to the end of his days. During the French upheavals two years later, the Comte de Saint-Cricq incited his constituency to vote against government policy and was sacked from his post; this brought his political career to an end.

In November there arrived in Paris a young hopeful from the Russian city of Riga – today the capital of Latvia – the nineteen-year-old pianist Wilhelm von Lenz. 'It was a great time, and Paris was the centre of the world,' he wrote. 'There lived Rossini and Cherubini, also Auber, Halévy, Berlioz and the great violinist, Baillot; the poet Victor Hugo . . . and Lamartine.' With hope in his heart and a trunkful of music, notably of Weber, his intention was to take lessons with Kalkbrenner, whose Sonata for left hand he had prepared as his audition piece. But he was soon disappointed in the pianistic scene of Paris. 'What did the piano repertoire consist of?' he wrote. 'That smooth master-joiner, Hummel; the Herzes, Kalkbrenner and Moscheles; nothing for the piano that was plastic, dramatic or eloquent. Beethoven was not yet understood. . . . The five last sonatas . . . were regarded as the monstrous freaks of a German ideologue who knew nothing about writing for the piano . . . Mozart was too old-fashioned. In this realm of the mediocre dwelt Liszt.'

Von Lenz's first sighting of the name was on a handbill in the street advertising his forthcoming performance of Beethoven's Piano Concerto No. 5 in E flat. He immediately changed his mind, on the grounds that anyone who played a Beethoven concerto – a rare event in Paris at the time – had to be a better bet than Kalkbrenner. 'The Parisians,' continued von Lenz, 'a year after Beethoven's death, for the first time heard something of him.' At Schlesinger's music shop he was given Liszt's address – von Lenz recorded that they pronounced his name Litz.

'Liszt was at home,' wrote von Lenz. 'That was a great rarity, said his mother . . . her Franz was almost always in church, and no longer occupied himself with music at all. . . . In Liszt I found a thin, pale-looking young man, with infinitely attractive features. He was lounging . . . on a broad sofa, smoking a long, Turkish pipe.' Von Lenz noted three pianos, on which he offered to play Kalkbrenner's Sonata for left hand. 'That I will not hear,' scoffed Franzi. 'I don't know it and I don't wish to.' Von Lenz decided on Weber's *Invitation to the Dance*, which Franzi asked him to play on his special piano. Von Lenz tried but could hardly get any sound out of it, no matter how hard he played. 'I ordered it on purpose,' explained Franzi, 'so as to have played ten scales when I had only played one. It is an altogether impracticable piano. It was a sorry joke of mine.' Franzi motioned to his Erard: 'There, that is one of the finest instruments in Paris.'

Franzi, whose knowledge of Weber did not go beyond *Der Freischütz* and the *Momento Capriccioso*, which he played five years previously in Pesth, was overwhelmed by the piece. His enthusiasm caused him to join in, and together they began to discuss Weber's piano music in general. Von Lenz brought out the Sonata in A flat, after which there was no stopping the two of them.

> We thus brought two minds to the task. So great grew my teacher's restlessness during the first part of the opening allegro that before I had reached the end he shoved me aside with the words, Wait! What is that? I must try it for myself. . . . The first part he tried out again and again in the most different ways. At the passage in E flat at the end of the first movement, he said, It is marked legato, but perhaps it would be better to make it pianissimo

and staccato? It is also marked leggermente. He experimented in all possible ways. And in this manner was it given to me to observe how one genius looks at and turns to account another.

Von Lenz also learned of Franzi's compulsion to alter and add to other composers' works, a habit that riled Mendelssohn. Von Lenz never looked back, and it was as though Kalkbrenner had never existed. 'In the andante of the Sonata,' he wrote, 'I learned in the first four bars more from Liszt than in years from my former good teachers.'

Franzi's teaching methods were born of an unbounded enthusiasm which rubbed off on his students. The lessons were not so much teaching sessions as masterclasses, in which both participants were as equals in the creation of excellence. Interpretation was discussed and illustrated, and both parties would dissect and analyse the works together, phrase by phrase; and at the heart of it all lay the ecstasy of music. Franzi took von Lenz on purely because he had introduced him to the breathtaking new world of Weber's piano music. Von Lenz played a significant part in Franzi's mental recovery, and when Chrétien Urhan came with his violin one of their pleasures was to play Weber's *Invitation to the Dance* in an arrangement for violin and piano.

Paris had to wait a further year to hear Beethoven's E flat Concerto. Franzi's concert, a full-blooded affair with orchestra, singers and Karl Ebner, scheduled for Christmas Day 1828, was cancelled at the last minute. Franzi had gone down with measles and spent the turning of the year in bed.

He was now seventeen and beginning to take his place in the adult world. The transition had been quick, violent, and fraught with anxiety. His character changed, and in many respects he was considered a strange youth, even weird, although his basic good nature and charm always shone through his erratic behaviour. He understood the warning in his ill-placed obituary that the adult Franz Liszt would be differently judged from Franzi the beautiful child. Von Lenz to an extent pointed the way: the Paris piano scene had become philistine, with eight-hand arrangements and improvisations on given themes assuming the character of a circus.

But change was at hand. Almost fifteen years had passed since the Congress of Vienna had established peace in Europe, and a new generation was growing up that had not known war. But it was a reactionary peace, breeding a philosophical void in which art found certain constraints and thought was fettered. Many young minds were looking for new ideas and fresh philosophies to hook onto and free them from the constrictions of an increasingly reactionary Establishment. A new intellectualism was now sweeping Paris, and discontent was rife in all walks of life. There was a need for social and artistic reform: Franzi was not alone in feeling the injustice of his status. The writings of the Comte Claude Henri de Saint-Simon found eager readers in the young, who failed to relate to the reactionary social order headed by King Charles X. Saint-Simon devoted his life to revolution and social change, but it was only after his death, aged sixty-five, in 1825, that his philosophies began to take hold.

Saint-Simonism advanced ideas of social equality, the emancipation of women, the phasing out of hereditary rights and the creation of a classless society based on achievement rather than heredity. Saint-Simon advocated the humanization of established religion by divorcing it from government control and sought to elect scientists, industrialists and achievers in general as the leaders of the new society. Many came together to live in communes, including the one at Ménilmontant, on the western outskirts of Paris, the property of a leading member, Father Barthélemy-Prosper Enfantin, where they wore their distinctive uniform of bleu-barbon coat and red beret. They soon became a thorn in the side of the Establishment, who could not countenance their socialist philosophies. This early version of communist ideology, of Napoleonic principles reborn in another guise, appealed to Franzi, and he began to attend some of the meetings held by chief advocate Armand Bazard at the Saint-Simonist headquarters in rue Monsigny and to take note of what was said.

Franzi also began to socialize and meet people, a skill that he had never acquired from his father, and he was now learning quickly, through sheer necessity. He continued to read voraciously, in an attempt to catch up with his lost education, and an encyclopaedia was never far from his elbow. Caroline had introduced him to Lamartine and Hugo, and now he read everything there was to read by them and sought out similar writings. But reading was not enough. He needed to get out and meet these people, to converse, to air views and compare opinions – above all, to learn. His early excursions into society were marked by the awkwardness and inferiority complex of a young man lacking in self-confidence.

This lack was totally absent when Franzi sat at a piano, and after a gap of almost a year he made an appearance at the Salons Pape on 22 March 1829, in which he again played the twelve-hands three-pianos version of Mozart's Overture to *The Magic Flute*, this time with Paër, Pixis, Rhein, Plich – and Ferdinand Hiller. This brilliant virtuoso was two days younger than Franzi. He was born in Frankfurt-am-Main and studied with Hummel in Weimar. He arrived in Paris the previous year in search of fame and fortune. His talent, charm and intelligence shone through, and he soon became a popular mainstay of the Paris Romantic set. He counted among his friends Balzac and Hugo, the painter Delacroix, and all the musicians from old Cherubini to Berlioz. He and Franzi met and became close friends that year.

On 1 April Franzi accompanied the violinist Haumann in a Duo at a full benefit concert for young orphans at the Société de la Morale Chrétienne. He again played a Duo with Haumann, *L'Enfant du Régiment*, written by Herz and Lafont, at the Salons Dietz on 7 April. Later in the programme Franzi played some Variations on 'La Tirolienne' from *La Fiancée*, a new opera by Auber that had just been given its première in Paris. The theme inspired Franzi to compose again, and that year he wrote the *Grande Fantaisie sur la Tirolienne de l'opéra La Fiancée*, which he revised twice (S 385i/ii/iii). The concert ended with a curiosity: a concoction on themes from *The Barber of Seville* by a 'young amateur' on the polyplectron – a hybrid keyboard instrument of Dietz's invention. On 11 April Franzi contributed a solo item at a soirée given by Panseron at the Hôtel Fesch in rue Saint-Lazare, where Mlle Berlot held her Salon. On 11 June Franzi and Ebner provided some entr'actes at the Théâtre Italien, where the first two acts of Boieldieu's *La Dame Blanche* and a one-act comedy, *Die Wiener in Berlin*, were mounted. Franzi gave no more performances in 1829 until 15 December, at the Salons Dietz, when he accompanied Antonio James Oury, a London-born violinist who married the pianist Anne de Belleville in 1831 and later became professor at the Royal Academy of Music, London. They played a Duo for violin and piano, and Franzi concluded the programme with an improvisation.

That spring Franzi began to meet the fashionable Romantic set. He already knew Alfred de Musset, the 'infant prodigy of litera-ture', through his sister, whom he taught the piano. On 5 May he was invited to dine at Hugo's; Prosper Mérimée was there. Wher-ever he went, Franzi tried to soak up knowledge so that he could converse with these brilliant minds at their own level. He read encyclopaedias and dictionaries with the same enthusiasm as the works of Lamartine and Hugo. Always aware of an intellectual inadequacy, he asked the historian François Mignet to teach him everything there was to know about French literature. Mignet was heard to mutter, in reply, that 'there is a lot of confusion in that young man's head'.

ELEVEN

Adèle

1830–31

FRANÇOIS MIGNET was right. By his eighteenth birthday Franzi's mind was a seething hive of conflicting forces, and he hardly knew which way to turn. On the spiritual level he had to reconcile his need to expiate his sins in penance and self-mortification, with the encouragement of Chrétien Urhan, with his more worldly tastes for luxury and the finer things in life. He found himself balancing his love of God with his love for Caroline de Saint-Cricq – and his now fully awakened and undoubted appreciation of pretty girls. He had to choose between the priesthood and the expression of his art. Both Abbé Bardin and his mother reinforced his late father's view that Franzi's vocation was to serve God through the talent that God had given him – and, incidentally, to be a support for his mother. Yet his art was going nowhere. His brilliant pianism had as much value in society as that of a performing dog – his clever tricks with themes by Rossini and Auber and his exploits at the piano in multi-hand arrangements of Mozart and Meyerbeer scoring more points with the public than his concert performances of the Hummel, Ries and Moscheles piano concertos. He was forced to weigh his gift for showmanship with à Kempis's admonition to 'strive to be as nought'. His composing, generally erratic and lacking in method, had virtually ground to a standstill. Even then, apart from a *Petit Morceau* for violin and piano of 1829, now lost, and an Introduction and Variations on *The Siege of Corinth* in 1830, of which only the Introduction survives (S 421a), it had hitherto consisted largely of his interpretation of other people's works. His two almost exact contemporaries, Chopin and Mendelssohn, were already established composers.

The year 1830 began with an exceptionally sharp frost. On 22 January Franzi took part in a concert given by Pixis at the Salons Pape, in which the newcomer Ferdinand Hiller joined Franzi, Pixis and Paër in the latter's eight-hand arrangement of Beethoven's *Fidelio* Overture. Franzi also joined Pixis in the latter's Duo Concertante. On 2 February Franzi took part in a soirée at the Salle Petzold, in the Académie Royale de Musique, for the benefit of a 'Spanish family'. Among the artists was Camille Moke, the future Mme Pleyel, with whom Franzi later had an affair. On 28 April, at the Salle Chantereine, Henri Herz gave a concert, at which he and Franzi played Herz's Variations for piano duet, and the following day Charles Schunke gave a soirée at the Salle Erard, at which Paër's twelve-hand arrangement of Mozart's *Magic Flute* Overture was played by the arranger, Charles Schunke, Franzi, Hiller, Sowiński and M. Fessy.

Franzi's moods swung from depression to the occasional highs, as when von Lenz appeared and introduced him to Weber. The Paris artistic set witnessed all these moods and understood. *Angst* and depression were essential features of the Romantic movement and were expected, so the tortured young pianist was readily welcomed into their circles, where the true meaning of art and its future in the new world order as envisioned by Saint-Simon were often the basis of discussion. He played in no further concerts for two years, preferring to talk to his fellow artists, rather than play to them.

Thus Franzi assimilated himself into these circles. Already among his fellow pianists on the social circuit were the Herz brothers, who earned enough to lack the Romantic capacity to suffer, the newcomer Hiller, who soon took up with the brilliant and beautiful seventeen-year-old Camille Moke, Charles Schunke (Ludwig had left for Stuttgart, eventually to join Schumann in Leipzig), Alkan, Kalkbrenner, now in his forties, whom Franzi viewed with some suspicion, and von Lenz. Painters included Achille and Eugène Devéria, Eugène Delacroix and Ary Scheffer, whose later portrait of Franz Liszt today hangs in the Liszthaus Museum in Weimar.

The biggest contingent were the writers, who set the literary tone of the Romantic movement. Honoré de Balzac achieved success with his complete picture of modern civilization in his *La Comédie Humaine* and later dedicated his *La Duchesse de Langeais* to Liszt. Others included Charles-Augustin Sainte-Beuve, critic and contributor to *Le Globe*, the mouthpiece of the Saint-Simonists, and author of a collection of poems, *Les Consolations*, which later inspired Franz Liszt's set of piano pieces of the same name; artist-turned-writer Théophile Gautier; poet, historian and statesman Alphonse de Lamartine, whose *Les Préludes* later inspired Liszt's symphonic poem of the same name; Alexandre Dumas père, whose play *Henri III* at the Théâtre Français was a great success in 1829; the introverted poet Alfred de Vigny, who had a brief affair with a beautiful young Parisian socialite, Marie de Flavigny, before she married the much older Comte Charles d'Agoult in May 1827; the civil servant, cynic and writer Prosper Mérimée, whose masterpiece, *Colomba*, was still ten years away; Victor Hugo, whose *Hernani*, mounted in February 1830 at the Théâtre Français, was an instant success and whose *Mazeppa* inspired Liszt's later, similarly titled work; and the well-travelled former ambassador to Berlin and London and established writer, François-René de Chateaubriand, on whom his mother had 'inflicted life' one stormy night in St Malo in 1768, whose works were among Franzi's favourites and whose *René* had such a profound effect on him.

During the early part of 1830, the theories of Saint-Simonism dominated the heated political debates about society and the direction it was taking. The King made little secret of his vision of a France returned to a pre-Revolutionary state, with an absolute monarchy at the summit. His announcement that he would 'sooner hew wood' than accept a constitutional monarchy on the British model did not enhance his popularity. The intelligentsia, largely weaned on Napoleonic and Jacobin principles, saw this as a giant step backwards and refused to countenance such a move. Dissent had been steadily growing since 1824, when some provocative measures were taken; enormous compensation was awarded to émigrés who lost their properties in the upheavals, strict censorship was introduced, publishers were fined and there were attacks on university professors. Saint-Simonists were hounded mercilessly, their writings were censored, and some were imprisoned. In August 1829 the King appointed the ultra-royalist Prince Jules de Polignac first to be in charge of foreign affairs and three months later as President of the Council, which was generally interpreted as a step towards the overthrow of the Constitution.

The artistic set were divided: some, like Lamartine, were staunch royalists, while others, including Sainte-Beuve and Franzi himself, were against the ruling order. Things came to a head in the summer of 1830, when on 26 July the July Ordinances proclaimed the dissolution of the Chamber, the abolition of the freedom of the press and the modification of the electoral law, whereby the electorate was reduced to just 25,000 landowners. Reaction was immediate in the torrid heat of the city. All printers went on strike; journalists protested in the streets and were soon joined by armed bands, and barricades were set up all over Paris. These erupted into riots, and cries of 'Down with Polignac! Long live the Charter!' were heard everywhere, accompanied by sounds of gunfire.

Prince Paul Anton Esterházy's chargé d'affaires, Baron – he had just received the title on 27 July – Philipp von Neumann, was in London at the time but recorded the events in Paris, as they reached him, in his diary.

30 July: Received news from Paris that on the 27th there was a great massacre there; the royal guard stood firm but two of the line regiments went over to the popular party. 31 July: Heard of another massacre on the 28th, chiefly at the Hôtel de Ville, which was taken and retaken three times between the national guards, the students of the Polytechnic schools, the people, and the King's bodyguard, which last were obliged to yield and had to march out of Paris to St Cloud, where the King and his ministers are. Two regiments went over to the insurgents. . . . A committee was formed at the Hôtel de Ville composed of Général Gérard, the Marquis de Choiseul, Général Lafayette [the famous Lafayette of the Revolution], M. Odier and M. Casimir Périer [grandfather of the future President of that name]. The tricolour is floating from the Tuileries.

The twelve-year-old Clara Novello, daughter of Franzi's English friends Vincent and Mary, was at school in Paris at the time, staying with other girls at the staunchly royalist house of Madame Tardieu in rue Bayeux. She listened, terrified, to the ferocious sounds of battles in the street. Over the next three days everyone cowered in terror, expecting the house to be sacked by insurgents. When she saw three bloodied and half-naked men rush through the portals of the house she sat herself astride the second-floor window, half in and half out, ready to throw herself into the garden should these ruffians barge into the room with rape in mind. The door did open, but it was only her mother's friends come to tell her that she was safe and that it was all over. The bells of Notre-Dame proclaimed that the people had won.

In rue Montholon Franzi was beside himself with excitement. To his mother's amazement he rushed out to join a jostling crowd yelling for the downfall of the King. He jostled and yelled with them, before returning home to his worried mother. He sat down at the piano and poured out his feelings in heroic improvisation. Urhan arrived, full of concern for his young friend, but found him in excellent spirits at the piano. Gone was the apathetic despondency which had been Franzi's hallmark for over a year. 'It was the guns that cured him,' explained Anna; 27, 28 and 29 July came to be known as the 'Three Glorious Days'. The King was taken unawares, having underestimated the size and strength of the opposition. Von Neumann's diaries continue:

> 2 August: The news received from France today, 31 July, says that a provisional Committee has been established and that the Duke of Orléans has accepted the offer to be Lieutenant-General of the Kingdom which has been made to him, and has hoisted the tricolour. Nobody knows exactly where the King is. 3 August: The King is at Trianon with 4,000 of his guards, and there are about 7,000 of them between the bridges of Sèvres and Neuilly. The Dauphin [the Duc d'Angoulême – the King's eldest son, who had declined to be heir] is with him.... Calm was established on the 30th. General opinion is strongly in favour of the new order of things in France and against the recent acts of Charles X. 5/6 August: The King ... has now positively abdicated in favour of the Duke of Bordeaux and has gone to Cherbourg.

The little Duc de Bordeaux, whose nursery Franzi visited when he first arrived in Paris, was the son of the heir to the throne, the Duc de Berry, who was assassinated outside the Opéra, while the Duchesse was one of Franzi's most enthusiastic patrons. The offer was not acceptable to the insurrection. Von Neumann's diary continued: '9 August: Received the news that the crown has been offered to the Duke of Orléans and that he has accepted.'

Franzi recalled his soirées at the Palais Royal, where he had played to the very appreciative Duc, the head of the Orléans side of the Bourbon dynasty. Von Neumann recorded that everything in France tended towards republicanism and observed, prophetically, that 'a prince raised to the throne by the will of the people can be as easily overthrown when he no longer suits them. The Duke of Orléans has given a pension from his private purse to Rouget de l'Isle, the author of the Marseillaise, to the sound of which his father Égalité was led to the scaffold. If this is the price he has to pay for popular favour, this hymn may easily bring him to the same end.'

Charles X, deposed, left for exile in England, accompanied by the Duc and Duchesse d'Angoulême, the Duchesse de Berry and the ten-year-old Duc de Bordeaux – who later came to be referred to by the Royalists as 'Henry V'. King William IV, who had succeeded to the British throne just over a month previously on the death of his brother George IV, placed Lulworth Castle, in Dorset, at their disposal. In Paris the Duc d'Orléans was proclaimed Louis-Philippe, the 'citizen King of the French'. His populist attempts to 'relate' to his subjects by calling them 'brother' and 'comrade' were initially well received, as was his unpretentious habit of walking along the streets with his umbrella under his arm.

Anna's claim that the guns had cured Franzi was largely true. Franzi's euphoria at the downfall of a loathed social order bore some fruit, even if unripe. Riding high on the events of that summer, he had in mind a Revolutionary Symphony, to be dedicated to General Lafayette. He worked on his initial improvisation and began to craft it into a whole. But the months after the Revolution went by, and Franzi became disillusioned with the 'bourgeois king' as a fraud and a compromise. Appearances may have changed, but the same old establishment was running things at the top. He lost the inspiration for the symphony, which ground to a halt at a piano draft of the first movement, and some orchestral sketches; he then shelved it for nearly twenty years. It eventually materialized, transformed, as the *Héroïde Funèbre*, now counted among his Symphonic Poems. A sketchy version of the E flat Concerto and the *Malédiction* for piano and strings appeared; both were revised years later as finished products.

The year 1830 constituted a watershed in the story of Romanticism, as germinated in Paris. Until then it was a largely disparate movement, experimental, and pursued in the face of reaction, both artistic and political. Despite the unpopularity of this reaction, it still had some powerful champions. In Warsaw there was growing unrest as Poland's Russian overlords were planning to send Polish troops to restore Charles X and to suppress the rebellion in Belgium – which would have been anathema to the almost genetically anti-reactionary Polish nation. The December insurrection caused an exodus of Polish artists, among them Chopin – who was in Vienna at the time – and the poet Adam Mickiewicz. Both headed for Paris, as did German-Jewish poet and 'democratic' politician Heinrich Heine. It was the dawn of the heyday of Romanticism, when the salons of the Faubourgs St Germain and

St Honoré blossomed and the nature of art and society was re-evaluated. The boundaries between writers, painters and musicians became blurred, and Franzi was not alone in striving to be the 'total' artist, with an overall appreciation of other disciplines. His art crossed into painting and, especially, literature, and he often recommended reading lists to his pupils to enhance their understanding of the music, such as Hugo's *Jenny* as a supplement to playing Moscheles.

Franzi had found a new lease of life in the growing knowledge that he was not only a true Romantic, but was in the van of Romanticism's musical expression. Only one other musician in Paris had found the leading path to take the movement further, and that was Hector Berlioz. He had just been awarded the Prix de Rome which necessitated a two-year stint in the Italian capital – an inconvenient prospect for him at this time. The two giants of Romanticism met on 4 December 1830, when Franzi called on him at his house at 96 rue de Richelieu. Berlioz introduced Franzi to Goethe's *Faust*, a formative experience that eventually culminated in his 'Faust' Symphony. 'We felt an immediate affinity,' wrote Berlioz in his *Memoirs*, 'and from that moment our friendship has grown ever closer and stronger.'

The following day, at two o'clock, Berlioz gave a concert at the Conservatoire. It included his Cantata, *Sardanapalus*, which had earned him the prize, the Overture to *Les Francs Juges* and the first performance of the *Symphonie fantastique*. Franzi was there and, as Berlioz wrote to his father, 'dragged me off to have dinner at his house and overwhelmed me with the vigour of his enthusiasm'. The object of Franzi's excitement was the *Symphonie fantastique*, which, despite its length and format, pointed the way to Franzi's own format for programme music, the Symphonic Poem.

Their friendship was put on hold, as Berlioz left – screaming within – for Rome on 30 December, leaving behind a tangled web of romantic intrigue. He was in love with the English actress Harriet Smithson but had seduced Camille Moke away from Ferdinand Hiller and was now unwilling to leave her.

Franzi's love life was also in meteoric ascendant. Having discovered the joys of love he never looked back and included its extensive study as part of his 'total' life experience. Affairs came easily to him, and there was no shortage of beautiful women who were ready to give themselves to him on any basis from life to an hour. He possessed every quality that was attractive to women in

abundance; he was exceptionally good-looking, he had an irresist-
ible charm and a generosity of spirit which made everyone feel
that they were special, he was witty, and enormously talented.
How he reconciled his amorous activities with the precepts of the
sixth and ninth commandments, which had been so carefully explained to him by Abbé Bardin, remains one of the great contra-
dictions of the Liszt story, although there is no evidence that his
amorous activities actually culminated in sex.

There are mentions in letters of a Hortense and a Madame G
at this time, but it was with Adèle, the 34-year-old wife of the
elderly and disinterested Count Laprunarède, with whom he had
engaged in what he later called 'exercises in the lofty French style'
– a sideways comment on the prevalent French custom of clandestine extra-marital affairs. They met on the salon circuit, and in
the winter of 1830–31 Franzi was invited to stay at the Laprunarèdes'
castle at Marlioz, in the Savoy Alps, some twenty kilometres south-
west of Geneva. The stay was longer than anyone expected, as
they were snowed in. This was not a problem for Franzi and the
Laprunarèdes, as the castle had all the comforts needed for a pleasant
stay. 'They laughed, jested, read, made music,' wrote Liszt's friend
Lina Ramann much later, omitting details of any nocturnal activities which no doubt also took place, 'and only when the approaching
spring had kissed away the snow and ice from doors and paths
did the young artist journey back to Paris.'

After this episode Franzi kept in touch with Adèle, and eventually the affair became very messy and its consequences lasted for
many months; although only the most tantalizing hints can be
gleaned from a necessarily secretive history. In later life she became Comtesse de Fleury.

At some time that year, Franzi and his mother moved to 61 rue
de Provence.

In September 1831 Chopin arrived in Paris. He was in Vienna
at the start of the Warsaw Insurrection and was torn between
returning to Warsaw to be with his family and countrymen and
emigrating to the West as musical ambassador for Poland, as everyone advised him to do. When the Insurrection failed and was suppressed, Chopin took the advice and made for the mecca of Paris.
He found lodgings on the fifth floor of 27 Boulevard Poissonnière,
'a little room beautifully furnished with mahogany . . . from which
I can see from Montmartre to the Panthéon'.

Chopin found post-revolutionary Paris a city of extremes, where reaction and radical liberalism had found a *modus vivendi*, side by side.

> There is the utmost luxury, the utmost swinishness, the utmost virtue, the utmost ostentation; at every step advertisements of venereal disease; shouting, racket, bustle, and more mud than it is possible to imagine.... You can walk in the streets in winter, dressed in rags, and frequent tip-top society; one day you can eat the most hearty dinner for 32 sous in a restaurant with mirrors, gilding and gas lighting, and the next you can lunch where they will give you enough for a dicky-bird to eat and charge you three times more.

With Chopin's arrival in the French capital, the stage was set for the Parisian heyday of the great Romantic pianists, which was to last until the deposition of King Louis-Philippe and the coming of Revolution throughout Europe in 1848 – a year in which a new brutalism dispelled the magic of that particular era for ever.

By the middle of December Chopin had met Rossini, Cherubini and Paër, so he wrote of high hopes that 'with time, I may get on well'. He had also got to know the pianists: the Herzes ('just wind-bags who will never play any better'), Hiller ('an immensely talented fellow, full of poetry, fire and spirit'), Sowiński ('not fit to hold a candle to poor Aleks [probably Aleksander Rembieliński – the Warsaw pianist much admired by Chopin, who died young]'), and Franzi: 'they are all zero beside Kalkbrenner . . . the first pianist of Europe, one whose shoe-latchet I am not worthy to untie.'

Friedrich Kalkbrenner's tenure as Paris's top pianist was now in question. He was the most successful survivor of the great pre-Romantic quartet of himself, Field, Moscheles and Hummel. Field was a spent force, and the latter two, though still great, had passed their prime. Kalkbrenner lasted long enough to continue setting the tone of Paris pianism of the nineteenth century. This great showman had the dramatic foresight to be born in a stagecoach near Kassel, northern Germany, in 1785. He trained first in Paris in 1798, then in Vienna in 1800. He went to live in London, where he took further lessons from Clementi, and made a considerable name for himself as a brilliant pianist and a teacher. He was a social climber, who liked to refer to the rich and the titled by their Christian names. He heard Franzi for the first time in 1824 at the New Argyll Rooms; that same year he left for Paris, where he settled for good. His major composition, *Effusio musica*, is a virtuoso work full of extremely difficult passages, which he played faultlessly. Alhough this and his other output have faded into oblivion, of his pianistic ability there was no doubt. 'Polished as a billiard ball,' wrote Ernst Pauer, 'undisturbed, unexcited, he controlled his obedient fingers as a captain of a company of well-drilled soldiers.' To which Louis Moreau Gottschalk added that his style was tedious; Charles Hallé wrote that 'in Kalkbrenner's playing there reigns a clearness, a distinctness and a neatness that are astonishing'.

As a teacher he was very much in demand, and it was Chopin's initial intention to study with him. But his superior manner, an extension of his natural showmanship, made him disliked by many, notably in England, where social pretension was seen through and looked down on. Clara Schumann, who watched Kalkbrenner at a concert as he was listening to one of his works being played, wrote that 'he looks as though he were saying, Oh, God, I and all mankind must thank Thee that Thou hast created a mind like mine'. Franzi did not know Kalkbrenner's Sonata for left hand, neither did he wish to, when von Lenz offered to play it for him. He often accused him of plagiarism, and Mendelssohn, learning that Chopin was to take lessons from him, sneered that Chopin was far better than Kalkbrenner anyway.

Mendelssohn arrived in Paris in December 1831, having largely grown out of the blasé teenage attitude with which he graced his first visit to Paris in 1825. He stayed only until the following April. During those four months he met Franzi, about whom he had then written disparaging comments. He also met Chopin to talk to – they had stared at one another across the room at a scientific convention in Berlin in 1829, when both were too shy to approach one another. Along with Hiller the four youngsters struck up a hearty friendship.

One day, Mendelssohn and Franzi went to Erard's to look at pianos. Mendelssohn had with him the barely legible score of his Piano Concerto in G minor, which he placed in front of Franzi to look at. Franzi sight-read it to an amazed Mendelssohn. 'Though it was barely legible,' he said, 'he played it off at sight with the utmost perfection – absolutely marvellous. I was not surprised, for I had long known that Liszt played most new things best the first time, because then they gave him enough to do. The second time he always had to add something, if the piece were sufficiently to interest him.'

In 1869 Franz Liszt recalled the occasion to one Anton Strelezki:

You know that Mendelssohn, who was the most jealous musician that ever lived, always had a dislike for me, and on one occasion, at a soirée, he drew a picture of me on a blackboard, playing his G minor Concerto with five hammers, in lieu of fingers, on each hand. The truth of the matter is that I once played his Concerto in G minor from the manuscript, and as I found several of the passages rather simple and not broad enough, if I may use the term, I changed them to suit my own ideas. This, of course, annoyed Mendelssohn, who, unlike Schumann or Chopin, would never take a hint from anyone. Moreover, Mendelssohn, although a refined pianist, was not a virtuoso, and never could play my compositions with any kind of effect, his technical skill being inadequate to the execution of intricate passages. So the only course laid open to him, he thought, was to vilify me as a musician.

In the early 1830s the pianistic cabal was in place, poised for greatness. Apart from Kalkbrenner, who was within range of his fiftieth birthday, and Herz who was approaching thirty, Franzi, Alkan, Hiller, Chopin and – for those four months – Mendelssohn were just leaving their teens. There was inevitably a generation gap, with the youngsters sticking together and going out on the town in groups in search of fun.

Kalkbrenner's haunt was a certain sophisticated café in the Boulevard des Italiens, the meeting place of the cream of Parisian society, in which the elegant and immaculately-mannered pianist felt very much at ease; that was until the day during Mendelssohn's Paris visit, when he was coerced into joining Chopin, Hiller and Franzi in dressing up in bohemian garb, approaching Kalkbrenner at the café like a long-lost friend and mortifying him in front of the shocked patrons by greeting him raucously and loudly and engaging him in bawdy conversation.

Kalkbrenner died of cholera at Enghien-les-Bains, a wealthy man, in 1849. His tomb, once imposing but now neglected, is in the Montmartre Cemetery.

The industrial revolution was under way, and the growth of pianism spawned peripheral industries, of which piano manufacture was in the forefront. In Paris the houses of Pape, Dietz and, above all, Erard were making enormous headway in the production of superior instruments to complement the ever-growing army of highly talented performers, who, in turn, demanded ever better instruments. The Erard double escapement action was the highest technical achievement and was considered a necessity rather than a luxury. Now a new name appeared, that of Camille Pleyel, whose pianos, gentle and sensitive, were designed for the playing of Mozart and became Chopin's favourite models. Piano makers also produced harps and an amazing array of hybrid keyboard instruments, mostly based on piano and harmonium principles and descended from the mechanical organ so loathed by Mozart. They tended to be one-off models, for which fanciful names were invented, such as the eolharmonica and the polyplectron. Chopin, in his teen years in Warsaw, went through a short 'techno' phase and became a virtuoso improviser on the choralion and the eolopantaleon. Franzi's interest in alternative keyboards came in later life, when he was looking for special effects. In the Franz Liszt Museum in Budapest there is his glass piano by Georges Bachmann, who had factories in Tours and Angers, in which little hammers strike strips of glass to produce a tinkling sound; there is also a piano-harmonium, a miniature two-in-one in which the piano part was made by Erard and the harmonium part by Jacob Alexandre. These instruments, beloved of inventors and the contemporary equivalent of 'techno-freaks', mostly second-rate keyboard players who found they could get a spectacular musical effect without too much effort or study, did not stand the test of time, and one can only speculate as to their nature.

Devices for hand position and exercise also proliferated, and did more harm than good. In 1814 one John Baptist Logier invented the chiroplast, a mechanism of brass and wood, which was clamped to the keyboard to ensure correct arm and hand position. Kalkbrenner was unenlightened enough to take this contraption seriously, and modified it into his own *guide-mains*, which ensured that the arms were perfectly horizontal and at the correct height. Franzi found Kalkbrenner's *guide-mains* a very useful teaching device. Henri Herz gave the world the dactylion, where fingers were inserted into suspended springs. Manufacturers, never slow to capitalize on marketing ideas, came up with the chirogymnaste, the manumoneon, the pocket hand-exerciser and the technicon. Home-spun techniques included placing wooden blocks between the fingers at night, a process blamed for the eventual destruction of Schumann's technique. Chopin might have suffered the same fate had his mother not discovered his ploy and put a stop to it.

Vladimir de Pachmann, on the other hand, swore by milking cows.

TWELVE

The Devil's Fiddler

1831-32

O N 20 DECEMBER 1831, Caroline Boissier, a Swiss amateur writer, pianist and composer on a long visit to Paris,
brought her daughter, eighteen-year-old Valérie, to Franzi, inquiring after piano lessons. Franzi declined and suggested Kalkbrenner,
Herz or Bertini; but Mme Boissier insisted that only Franz Liszt
would do. Franzi had been trying to cut down on his teaching,
and despite his resolve he succumbed to the implied flattery, listened to Valérie playing some piano compositions of her mother's
and an excerpt from one of Hummel's piano concertos and agreed
to take Valérie on for two hours a week on Saturdays. He gave
her some Bertini exercises to be getting along with.

Mme Boissier was an irrepressible correspondent and diarist.
Her *Liszt Pédagogue: leçons de piano données par Liszt à Mademoiselle Valérie Boissier à Paris en 1832* gives such a detailed, lesson-
by-lesson account of Franzi's three-and-a-half-month course as to
almost qualify as a piano method in its own right. It called liberally on the best teaching techniques of the time, notably those of
Czerny, Kessler and Zimmermann. Franzi's course covered all aspects
of advanced pianism, from clear fugue playing, avoiding all 'blur-
ring' of harmony among the voices, to loose hands and rapidity of
octaves, which would suggest that Valérie must have been compe-
tent enough a pianist to warrant Franzi's interest.

But Franzi's interest went even further. He asked to see Mme
Boissier's own compositions, which she humbly submitted. He found
them perfectly satisfactory, but what really excited him was her
Grand Concerto, 'La Chasse', which, she warned, was extremely
difficult. Franzi played it straight off from the manuscript, which

left Mme Boissier, who herself could not play it as it should have been played, in a daze. He then pronounced it far superior to her other compositions. 'I had the satisfaction of hearing myself and understanding my own phrases, the products of my own thoughts,' she wrote, stressing that Liszt was always honest and was not one for idle flattery. 'Nothing could have given me a more poignant pleasure. I could hardly recognize my music played so beautifully.' Mme Boissier recorded how Franzi's personality overwhelmed them both. 'Finding his love of music once again' (this after a tedious lesson with a particularly peevish pupil by the name of Consule had mercifully come to an end),

> he recovered, soared, became electrifying: he was Orpheus. He played an exercise by Bertini like no one else. . . . His fingers are in turn light, soft, velvety, then frighteningly energetic. . . . Sometimes his expression is impetuous, passionate, troubled, then melancholy, plaintive and touching, then proud and haughty, then blithe and careless. . . . He played like the god of music. . . . No one has ever felt music like this man, or ever delved so deeply into the depths of art and the mysteries of harmony. Beneath his fingers the piano yields surprising sounds. He accentuates and interprets like no other; the least phrase can move one to tears; his influence on his listeners is total. . . . This young man is surely destined to push far back the frontiers of art.

Of Franzi the teacher Mme Boissier described how he aimed to mould the complete artist and pointed out that he made all his pupils study the pieces in depth,

> so that often an entire lesson is devoted to the study of just two pages. . . . He played a duet with Valérie, then delighted us by letting us sample the finest passages of several pieces. He performed a magnificent Sonata by Czerny. . . . He made Valérie repeat thrice in succession a certain exercise by Moscheles, agitato and full of expression. He taught it to her with care and in detail, and got her to try out another exercise by Moscheles. In order to enable her to grasp his method, he introduces her to his favourite composers, and makes her play all their masterpieces. . . . To become a perfect sight-reader he explained that in his childhood he had been made to read music for three or four hours every day to achieve mastery. He claims that anyone can attain his standard. . . . He recommends many scales, not only the ordinary ones, but also in octaves and thirds, plus trills with all fingers. These are his own regular exercises.

Some of his lessons had the characteristics of a masterclass. On 19 January 1832 the lesson, which Mme Boissier called a soirée, took place at her home. The audience watched and listened as 'Liszt went though the Overture [to Weber's *Der Freischütz*] arranged for duet, which he played with Valérie, who hopped along behind him. Can one run after a hurricane? However, with perfect kindness he broke off several times to give her advice. Then we discussed the merits of Weber, Beethoven and Rossini.'

On 6 February the lesson was again at the Boissier residence. Franzi, in good spirits after a pleasant day in the Jardin des Plantes, 'played like a god'.

On 10 February the Erards gave a large-scale vocal, instrumental and orchestral concert at their showrooms. Meyerbeer, Halévy, Kalkbrenner, Herz, Pleyel, the Boissiers and Franzi were among the 800-strong audience. Adolphe Nourrit was the main singer, and the virtuoso of the evening was Ludwig Schunke, who was back in Paris, whose appearance, mannerisms and way of playing were so like those of Franzi that those with less discerning ears sometimes confused the two. Mme Boissier was not among them: Schunke's performance left her cold, although the pianistic set were eulogistic in their praise. She had eyes only for Franzi Liszt, whom she contemplated through her opera glasses.

Franzi's effect on Valérie was profound.

> Poor Valérie is overwhelmed by the power of his talent; she is dazzled and almost discouraged. He inspires awe in Valérie. She seems crushed by such musical heights, measures the distance still to be climbed and grows discouraged.... Her progress is mainly in humility; she feels reduced to nothing, and despairs of ever arriving at a tolerable level. Liszt makes her feel ill at ease; and yet, unconsciously she is progressing well.

Mme Boissier herself also felt inadequate: 'any talent of one's own is so insipid, dull and ridiculous beside these magnificent fountains of inspiration, this all-embracing memory and this creative imagination, that it could turn one against the piano for ever'.

Of Franzi the person she wrote that

> no one could be kinder or more indulgent than Liszt, who is above all petty vanity. Living alone and eschewing society, wrapped up in himself in those lofty and harmonious regions that he inhabits, he is like no one else at all.... He was so pale, this poor young man, that it saddened me. He is wasting away....

One can only marvel at a young man, scarcely out of adolescence, who has charm, perfect breeding and ease of manner, and yet has the unassuming modesty and pleasant wit of a confident man of forty.

Of Franzi's household, she wrote:

His mother watches him lovingly yet anxiously; she is ever concerned about him, and when he brightens up she raises her eyes to heaven. It could not be possible for two people to be more dissimilar, one all emotion, the other all intelligence. This tall, stout woman with her cheerful red face hardly looks as though she could have given birth to this pallid, thin young man, all soul and fire. . . . Yesterday he was practising in his room while his mother was working by the fire; the one in heaven with his harmony and his genius, the other on earth in her slippers, but both united in love, making the best household in the world.

Of Franzi the total artist, she wrote:

This sublime musician could have been a painter, an orator, a poet, for he is all these things in his wonderful playing. . . . He is a man of letters, who has read, pondered and meditated a great deal. . . . The same exquisite feeling for beauty which, in music, drives him to relish and study masterpieces, guides him in literature as well. . . . Sometimes he reads us extracts from his favourite writers, Pascal and Chateaubriand; he links music to literature, leading from one to the other.

By the second week of January she found 'a noticeable improvement already in her playing, a much broader and livelier interpretation', and by the third week Valérie was 'beginning to make perceptible progress'. Until her first lessons with Franzi Valérie played mostly light music, but 'under the guidance of such a master it was time to arrive at the classics'.

Franzi tried to stop the lessons after about three weeks but to no avail. Mme Boissier's entreaties bore fruit, and he agreed to continue until the spring. Valérie's last lesson, the twenty-eighth, was on 30 March. The relationship turned to a friendship based on mutual regard and a love of culture. Franzi often visited the Boissiers and promised to visit them at Le Rivage, their Geneva residence. Valérie later married the Comte Agénor de Gasparin, and achieved distinction as a writer of moral tales and travel books. Franzi dedicated his *Fantaisie romantique sur deux mélodies suisses* (S 157) to her.

While Franzi was teaching Valérie, Mendelssohn, after a month in Paris, had come to the conclusion that Romanticism had infected all Parisians with a predilection for plague, the gallows, the devil, childbeds and suchlike dramatics. Parisians soon had a taste of the first of these at first hand. The cholera pandemic began in India in 1830. In 1831 it was raging in Russia and Poland, where it added considerably to the death toll of the Polish insurrection, on both sides. It arrived in Vienna shortly after Chopin, who needed Austrian health certificates to enable him to travel on to Paris. All precautions were futile, and in early 1832 the first cholera casualties occurred.

On a different level, Franzi was plagued with requests for music lessons, most of which he turned down. But he did take on at some time Pierre Wolff, of Geneva. The teacher–pupil relationship turned to friendship, and Franzi paid Wolff several visits in his home city. In February, Mendelssohn, in his letter to the Berlin composer Karl Zelter, commented that there were 1,800 piano teachers in Paris, and still it was not enough to satisfy the city's insatiable demand for proficiency at the keyboard. He added that the Conservatoire orchestra, under the inspired leadership of the Opéra conductor Habeneck, was the most accomplished anywhere.

Franzi's sense of foreboding led to some intensive investigations into the human condition, and he took to visiting hospitals, lunatic asylums and prisons. On one occasion he presented a prisoner with a guitar and a self-instruction manual; after which he visited the man regularly to see how he was getting along. In the course of his interest in life's casualties he was approached by the Charitable Maternal Society which asked him to take part in a charity concert in aid of unmarried mothers in Rouen. Franzi accepted – the first time for nearly two years.

He left Paris at a quarter past seven on the morning of 28 January, and the concert took place in the Salle Saint-Ouen at the Hôtel de Ville, adjacent to the vast Gothic church of St Ouen at eight the same evening. The programme opened with a symphony by Beethoven, followed by a sung duet by Saverio Mercadante. Then Franzi played one of Hummel's piano concertos, and the first half ended with a Rossini chorus. The second half began with Weber's *Oberon* Overture, an air sung by Mlle Monsel and an unknown item from Franzi. There followed a trio and a chorus from Rossini, and Franzi finished the concert with an improvisation. It was just like old times. The *Journal de Rouen* reported that 'the whole of Rouen society was there to applaud the young master'. The concert was a spectacular success, and many people had to be turned away for lack of room. 'When', continued the *Journal de Rouen* indignantly, 'shall we have a venue big enough for our town?' The review added that of the ten items, nine were by German and Italian composers and bemoaned that 'there was not a Boieldieu, whose graceful and expressive airs should not be strangers to our family events and our musical occasions'. Every so often France expresses fears of the subjugation of her culture and language by foreign forces. The high spot was Franzi's improvisation, and *L'Écho de Rouen* pointed out that Liszt must have been chagrined that his prestos and allegros, replete with technical difficulties, evinced greater applause than his deeply felt adagios and cantabiles.

On 15 February, back in Paris, Franzi went along with Hugo, the poet Antoine Fontaney and the journalist Joseph d'Ortigue to hear Urhan performing his quintet. 'A fine figure of an enthusiastic and modest young man,' wrote Fontaney about Franzi. 'His eyes are brilliant and animated, the corners of his mouth turned down.' Despite his professed inclination to cut himself off from the world, Franzi's company was much in demand, and he paradoxically spent his evenings socializing and going to concerts; he found it very difficult to say no.

On 26 February Franzi and Mendelssohn went to support Chopin at his Paris début at the Salle Pleyel at 9 rue Cadet. Baillot and Urhan were among those playing Beethoven's Quintet Op. 29. Chopin joined Hiller, Stamaty, Sowiński, Osborne and Kalkbrenner in the latter's Introduction, March and Grande Polonaise for six pianos. He then played solo versions of his F minor Piano Concerto and his Variations on Mozart's 'Là ci darem la mano'. Franzi was among the first to own that Chopin was a pianist of the first rank. 'The most vigorous applause seemed not to suffice to our enthusiasm in the presence of this talented musician, who revealed a new phase of poetic sentiment combined with such happy innovations in the form of his art,' he recalled in later years.

On 18 March Franzi and Chopin went to hear Mendelssohn play Beethoven's G major Concerto at the Conservatoire, with Habeneck conducting. On 2 April Franzi appeared at a mostly vocal concert at the Salle Chantereine, given by M. Scavarda. Franzi's role constituted his lowest profile yet – in the top part of a piano duet with his pupil, the Belgian Louis Messemaekers, who soon afterwards returned to Brussels. The programme referred to 'M. Litz (whom we have not heard for a very long time)'. Franzi's love affair with the music of Weber continued unabated. In the middle of April he was working on the piano concertos, and during practice he dislocated his right thumb. Despite this inconvenience, on 16 April he went with Fontaney to lunch with Hugo, his wife Adèle and their four children, Léopoldine, Charles, François-Victor and Adèle, at his first- and second-floor apartment in the Place Royale. It was a 'house-warming' visit, as the Hugos had only just moved in that year. Franzi played the Funeral March from Beethoven's Piano Sonata in A flat Op. 26, his performance unaffected by his injured thumb. 'It was magnificent,' wrote Fontaney, 'what a fine picture that would make, all those corpses from the cholera marching towards Notre-Dame dressed in their shrouds.'

That evening being a Monday, Franzi was at the Austrian Embassy in rue St Dominique, overlooking Les Invalides, at the behest of the Ambassador, Count Antal Apponyi. Apponyi's wife, Countess Thérèse, was one of the most sophisticated hostesses on the Paris salon circuit, and Monday nights were her music nights. Their son, twenty-year-old Count Rudolf, was there, at the start of his own diplomatic career as Attaché. To the Apponyis Franzi represented a remarkable success story, and a certain pride that the family name was connected to that story could well be justified. According to Count Rudolf, Franzi's injured thumb did not impair his performance of the Weber Concerto. 'No one would have suspected it on hearing him,' he wrote. 'He is especially admirable in one passage, written entirely in octaves, which he plays with such speed and strength that his hands seem to multiply. It is impossible to follow them with the eye, such is the inconceivable rapidity with which they move; they fly from one end of the piano to the other.'

Two days later, Fontaney and Franzi were at Hugo's once more, and again Franzi played the Beethoven Funeral March; afterwards poet and pianist shared a fiacre home. The Swiss scholar Charles Didier was at Hugo's with Franzi on another occasion and wrote that 'before this evening I had no idea what the piano could do. When he had finished, Liszt seemed exhausted. He looks frail and feminine, which makes him more interesting still. . . . His head fully justifies phrenology.'

The Place Royale is now the Place des Vosges, and the Hugo house, at No. 6, is now the Victor Hugo Museum.

Among the popular salon activities that contrasted with the heavier expressions of Romanticism were charades, political or romantic mini-dramas and social comment monologues, many of them fore-runners of twentieth-century cabaret and satire. Poets and drama-tists wrote them for performance with friends for the amusement, enlightenment or plain outrage, of guests. Among the hostesses that specialized in this type of entertainment was Madame Zimmermann, the wife of Joseph Zimmermann, and their daugh-ters. It was a light-hearted salon to which she invited the greatest artists to take part in charades and games of forfeit. Gautier, Dumas and Musset were forced to recite their latest works, Viardot, Fal-con and García suffered penalties singing the latest arias, and Chopin – whose talents at mimicry at the piano were legendary – and Franzi had to serve sentences at the keyboard, improvising. On 21 April Franzi attended one such soirée.

With the coming of spring, the cholera epidemic took serious hold, and French Romanticism found a way of embracing it into its dramatic mythology. On a realistic note, the epidemic claimed 20,000 victims in Paris, 2,000 of them on one day, 10 April. The city ground to a standstill as the streets were jammed with carts bearing the dead. A kind of road rage prevailed, and a number of carts were involved in overturns, sometimes with the coffins – for those who could get them – or boxes split open. Heine, perhaps echoing Fontaney's vision on hearing Franzi playing Beethoven's Funeral March, conjured up the ultimate horror when he wrote of a riot of the dead. The rich had fled to the country, taking their doctors with them, and all social life stopped. Among those struck down was Mendelssohn, although he recovered to leave for Lon-don on 19 April.

In March Paganini paid his second visit to Paris, and this time his concerts were attended by Franzi, who missed his first visit, the previous year, when he was marooned in Marlioz with Adèle Laprunarède. The effect on Franzi of Paganini's performances was decisive and affected his whole attitude to his own art.

Niccolò Paganini was the first virtuoso showman of the violin. Born in Genoa in 1782, his skill at improvisation inspired awed disbelief, and his performances often evinced a hysteria never be-fore seen in a concert hall. The power that he wielded over his listeners earned him the nickname 'the Devil's Fiddler', and the more superstitious believed that, Faust-like, he had sold his soul to the Devil in exchange for his magical gift. He found it a good marketing ploy not to refute this. His attitude brought him post-humous trouble with the Church, and after his death in Nice in 1840, he was refused burial in consecrated land for five years. Franzi was fascinated by Paganini's techniques of improvisation, which he took to the absolute limits of music – and beyond into the realms of pure theatre. He achieved sounds from the violin that were not found in any textbooks, and Franzi saw in him an artist who was at one with his instrument. Although nearly fifty, Paganini further appealed to French Romanticism with his gaunt, cadaverous appearance – he was actually ill with tuberculosis – which, in a certain light, and with the fact that he dressed in black, enhanced his Mephistophelean image; the result was that there was more to his stage act than the music he played. It was a mind-bending total experience. Thenceforth Franzi, whose Romanticism also aspired to a totality of sensual experience, aimed to become the pianistic equivalent of Paganini.

The violin virtuoso gave his first concert on 25 March, followed by another on 20 April, which Franzi noted in his diary. 'What a man, what a violin, what an artist,' he wrote to his pupil Pierre Wolff in Geneva on 2 May, 'heavens, what sufferings, what misery, what tortures in those four strings.... As for his expression, his manner of phrasing, they are his very soul.' Paganini's programmes generally followed the conventional format of two halves, each beginning with an orchestral overture or symphony, with operatic arias interspersing Paganini's own concertos and improvisations, his *tour de force* being the Witches' Dance from Weber's *Der Freischütz* played on one string only. This latter was usually prefaced with some sensational theatre, in which he snipped three strings from his violin with a pair of scissors.

Franzi was overwhelmed by Paganini's showmanship and sense of theatre, which encroached beyond music into the realms of circus, and thereafter adapted these qualities in his own performances. Particularly taken by Paganini's second Violin Concerto in B minor, Franzi sketched out a *Grande Fantaisie de Bravoure sur la Clochette de Paganini* (S 420), the 'bell' theme from the last movement. This eventually evolved into *La Campanella*.

On 22 April, Paganini gave a concert in aid of victims of the cholera epidemic; he gave nine concerts in Paris before going on to London in the summer.

That spring Franzi had planned to go to Geneva again to visit Pierre Wolff, but the idea did not materialize. Instead, in the second week of May, he went to spend six weeks with M. Reidet, the receiver-general at the port of Rouen, at Écouteboeuf, near Rouen, to recuperate: Liszt in later life referred to a mysterious affliction which he endured every springtime in his youth. 'Except for three or four days when I was working on my new fantaisies,' he wrote to Valérie Boissier after his return, 'these six weeks have been pretty drab for me.'

Back in Paris in June, Franzi's relationship with Chopin grew into a very strong bond, yet they had only two things in common: both were pianists, and both were pale and fragile-looking. Franzi's magnanimous nature and generosity of spirit reached out to Chopin immediately; whereas Chopin, more reserved, was laid back in his attitude. Franzi had a great love for humanity and forgave fools, while Chopin was aloof and suffered fools badly. Franzi loved applause, while Chopin loathed giving concerts and insincere applause.

Musically it was very much a mutual admiration society, yet their respective arts were at opposite ends of the spectrum: Franzi was the ultimate Romantic, while Chopin was a classicist in the Romantic style. Franzi's music was larger than life, while Chopin's was meticulously measured, and his music was often, as in Berlioz's opinion, like putting one's ear to the piano and listening to a concert of elves. Franzi saw in Chopin an exceptional pianist and a singularly creative composer. Chopin rated Franzi's playing as the very best but had no positive views on his compositions. The fact was that Franzi's output to date had been sparse and lacked originality. Chopin had already written all his concerto works, his chamber music and a number of waltzes, rondos, mazurkas, polonaises and nocturnes, as well as a piano sonata. There was a sense of incompleteness or unoriginality about most of Franzi's early compositions; either they were preliminary sketches, albeit unconscious, for later works or they were bravura arrangements of other people's works. Franzi's only material that may have seriously interested Chopin – and then only circumstantially – were the twelve Études, possibly because Chopin had come up with exactly the same idea during his last months in Poland. Both pianists, in their teen years, had found a need for exercises for the improvement of technique and, being creative musicians, sought a way that was not tedious – as were Czerny's exercises. So both composed exercises in technique that aimed to be aesthetically satisfying.

Chopin's twelve 'Exercises en forme', started in Poland, were completed soon after his arrival in Paris. Although Franzi's twelve were written when he was fourteen, they ended up as first drafts for his later *Transcendental Studies* – themselves also revised. Chopin had no musical interest in Franzi's Études, yet Franzi took to Chopin's set with great enthusiasm and often played them. Franzi's influence on Chopin was marked, specifically in some of the fiery and passionate characteristics of Chopin's output since his arrival in Paris, which were absent from his Polish years; but it was the influence of the pianist rather than the composer that added the icing to Chopin's mature creativity.

On 20 July Hugo – who was renowned for not serving any refreshments at his soirées – organized a lunch party for his son François-Victor's birthday. Franzi came along afterwards with Fontaney. Hugo's eldest daughter, Léopoldine, then played her piece on the piano, after which Franzi took over and again added some dark dramatics over the birthday party with Beethoven's Funeral March.

Among Franzi's pupils – 'one of my good ones' – was nineteen-year-old Rose Petit, the daughter of Baron Jean-Martin Petit. That year the Baron, a distinguished veteran of Napoleon's wars, holder of the Legion of Honour and the military order of St Louis, and considered one of France's 'national glories', was appointed Lieutenant-General of the 15th military division, which broadly covered the greater swathe of central France. This included the peaceful and agrarian region of Berry, whose capital, Bourges, housed his headquarters.

That summer Rose became engaged to thirty-year-old Charles Haton de Langoupillière, presiding judge at the Bourges judiciary. The banns were read simultaneously in Paris and Bourges on 19 and 26 August, and Franzi was invited to the September wedding – and to stay on afterwards; this was partly because the Petit ladies were very fond of him and partly to act as an antidote to the expected influx of military, judiciary and official personages who would make up the bulk of the guest list.

On 26 August Franzi kept his appointment with Achille Devéria, who had arranged to make the lithograph of him which has now become one of the definitive pictures of young Liszt. Soon after this session, Franzi presented himself at the offices and stage of the Diligences Lafitte et Gaillard, at 128–30 rue St Honoré and climbed into the carriage for the twenty-five-hour run to Bourges.

The ancient city of Bourges was dominated by the twelfth-century cathedral of St Étienne, one of the finest in France. The authoress George Sand, at whose château at Nohant, some seventy kilometres to the south, she entertained, among others, Franzi and, more specifically, Chopin, wrote Bourges into one of her novels: 'The city . . . sweet for him who sleeps, dear to him who thinks; where wild oats with silken fringes and thistles with fluffy heads grow languorously in the streets; fine and rich houses hidden behind gardens of mystery, and at every step can be seen a Gothic head carved onto the blackened timber of a medieval gable, like a faded coat of arms.' The General, his wife Eugénie, their son Edmond, and Rose lived in splendour in rue Notre-Dame de Sales, where music and the ideals of Romanticism, as expressed by Mme Petit and Rose, were largely overshadowed by the military ethos as set by the General. Franzi's arrival at the Petit residence redressed the balance somewhat.

The marriage contract was signed on 8 September, and the actual wedding took place in the Archbishop's chapel in the cathedral on 10 September. The twenty-six guests included the procurator general, the King's procurator, the Archbishop of Bourges and the Colonel of the Bourges National Guard; there were eight holders of the Legion of Honour and three Chevaliers of St Louis. Even though such an eminent assembly normally held no problems for him, Franzi's hackles did rise after the ceremony, when he sat down to play the piano. After a very short while, having had no effect whatsoever on the party, he decided not to bother any more and stopped. This also evinced no reaction. Later, when everyone went for a walk, Franzi pointedly admired the beauties of nature and ignored everyone else. At one point he seized a parasol from one of Rose's friends and plunged it into a pond, ostensibly to ascertain its depth. This almost boorish act, which suggested that he was bored, caused, according to a contemporary report, a stunned silence, and the bridegroom 'took a fever and had to be put to bed'.

The incident may have outraged some, but Mme Petit, who was amused by it all, begged Franzi to stay longer. Franzi was anxious to get back to Paris but was persuaded in the end to stay. His plans to return to Paris on 24 September went awry, and he had to wait until a place on the Paris diligence became available. So Franzi joined in the continuing social life, with dinners, parties and walks.

The General asked Franzi if he would give a charity concert for the poor; Franzi agreed, and the venue was arranged for 28 September at the city theatre. A number of local amateurs were asked to take part, and the local Philharmonic Society's orchestra was enlisted; this recently formed organization showed great promise, partly because of the fertile recruiting ground of the military bands stationed in Bourges. They opened the programme with the Overture to *La Dame Blanche*. Then M. Fabri and M. de Scévole, 'an amateur', sang the duet from *Elisa et Claudio*, after which 'M. Litz' played an unidentified Adagio by Weber. A Cavatina from *Dorliska* followed, and the first half ended with Mayseder's Variations brillantes on a theme from Rossini's *Semiramide* for violin and piano, played by 'M. Litz and an amateur'. The latter was local musician J. le Goy, who, trembling with terror, was induced to play the duet with Franzi. 'My dear sir,' said Franzi later, 'I have been accompanied by artists stronger than you, but never has one given me as much pleasure.' Mr le Goy beamed with delight at this accolade from 'M. Litz' and fled.

The second half opened with Rossini's Overture to the *Barber of Seville*, followed by a duet from Rossini's *Mosè in Egitto* sung by M. Fabri and M. de Scévole; then Franzi and a 'lady amateur' played Czerny's Fantaisie for piano duet. Franzi's partner was the new Mme. Rose Haton de Langoupillière; Franzi honoured her marriage and climaxed his piano course with a concert performance together before an eminent audience in her own home city. Another 'amateur' sang an aria from the *Siege of Corinth*, and the concert closed with the chorus from Rossini's *Le Comte Ory*. A last-minute inclusion was the young professor from Orléans, the flautist M. Besseville, who played a Fantaisie by Tulou.

The reviews were, as always, eulogistic. 'The talent of this young virtuoso and the prospect of hearing the young lady, his pupil, were enough to draw the crowds,' wrote the *Gazette du Berry* the following day. The *Journal du Cher* reported that 'We need not say that every piece executed by M. Litz [*sic*] excited universal admiration and enthusiasm. Inspiration could be read on his face and in his movements.' The *Revue du Cher et de l'Indre* of 2 October wrote: 'M. Litz seems to communicate his superabundance of verve through his piano, which obeys every inspiration of his brilliant imagination. M. Litz's playing is passionate, full of expression and taste, and nuanced with art; his scale passages are executed with the utmost lightness and with a delicate freshness.'

On 6 October Franzi arrived back in Paris and was met off the diligence by his mother.

In the autumn John Field arrived in Paris from London. Although he had been one of the four great 'pre-Romantic' pianists, exactly half a century of deprivation, dissipation and debauchery had taken their toll, and he was well past his best. Chopin, who discovered his nocturnes in Warsaw, saw him as the pianist who had captured the human voice onto keyboard and had introduced 'cantabile' into piano dynamics. His delicate and even touch was legendary, and Chopin was proud to have been compared to him. Field gave three concerts in Paris, the first one on Christmas Day, when he performed his Piano Concerto No. 7 in C minor at the Conservatoire to a capacity audience psyched up to hear one of the world's greatest pianists.

The younger, trendier set, including Chopin and Franzi, were disappointed. The touch was still there, and the almost total immobility while he played – a legacy of his childhood under Clementi, who placed coins on his hands to ensure their steadiness – but the poetry was lacking. Franzi commented on the inferior piano, the complete lack of showmanship and the almost apathetic style of playing, as if he could not have cared less about his audience. In his view it was a grey and flat performance. As a composer Franzi rated Field highly and in later life edited some of his nocturnes and added an article 'John Field and His Nocturnes' to accompany the publication. Chopin said that he played like a beginner; Field's riposte was that Chopin was a sickroom pianist. In fact Field was by now a sick man and using morphine, suffering agonies from what is now believed to have been anal cancer, which was to kill him in Moscow five years later.

On the night of 6 November Berlioz returned to Paris after his enforced stay in Italy and immediately started to arrange a grand concert at the Conservatoire. The programme gave another chance to hear the *Symphonie fantastique* in the first half and his melologue – a mixture of music and speech in six parts, forming a sequel to the *Symphonie fantastique* – 'Le Retour à la Vie', in the second half. Habeneck was to conduct a 100-strong orchestra, with the actor M. Bocage as narrator. The whole concert promised to be a larger-than-life event that would enhance Berlioz's reputation – which had been on hold while he was in Italy – before his departure for Berlin. The concert took place on 9 December at one o'clock. Among the packed audience were Paganini, who was in town, Chopin, Dumas, Vigny, Heine, Deschamps, the writer and feminist Aurore Dudevant (better known as George Sand), Gautier, Janin and d'Ortigue. Franzi went with Fontaney and the Hugos. Perhaps most significantly, actress Harriet Smithson, the object of Berlioz's desires for the past five years, was there.

The concert was repeated on 30 December, with the addition of his Overtures to *Les Francs Juges* and *La Captive*. Franzi did not attend, as he was again with the Apponyis at the Austrian Embassy, along with Chopin and Kalkbrenner. Rossini was also there, with his stable of singers, part of the kind of package deal he offered for a set fee. Count Rudolf Apponyi found the whole musical event 'delicious'.

The year 1832 was not a prolific one for Franzi as a composer. The autograph of a 'Grand solo characteristique à propos d'une chansonette de Panseron' (S 153a) is in a private collection, and no editions exist. Derek Watson suggests that the central section eventually evolved into 'La Chapelle de Guillaume Tell' from *Album d'un voyageur* and its later transcription in the *Années de pèlerinage* – 'première année: Suisse'. Auguste Panseron was much admired by Franzi. Born in Paris in 1796, he studied harmony and counterpoint at the Conservatoire with Gossec and won the Prix de Rome in 1813 with his cantata *Herminie*. After touring Europe, he returned to Paris where he worked as accompanist at the Opéra Comique, taught singing and wrote a number of very successful one-act comic operas and over 200 enormously popular 'chansonettes', which he sang himself and which featured distinctive obbligato parts for a variety of different instruments – a legacy of his training in counterpoint. He often appeared in the same concerts as Franzi. Panseron died in Paris in 1859.

Among Franzi's other works there was a first draft of 'La Romanesca' (S 252a), and a Ballade (S 754b); also a coda to Exercise No. 3 by Meyer, which Mme Boissier mentioned in her *Liszt Pédagogue*. This is missing, as is an 'Introduction et Valse', which was written in the album of Comte Gustave de Reiset. As a composer, Franzi had now been left far behind by his peers. Chopin, Mendelssohn and Hiller were already in their prime, establishing works that were now in the repertoire. Franzi's sketches, drafts, experimental writings, fantaisies on other composers' works and bits and pieces – and, of course, *Don Sanche* – have survived, in manuscript, print and legend, as interesting and often attractive curiosities which point to a style which was yet to find its characteristic form.

THIRTEEN

Marie

1833

ONE OF Franzi's very few and select pupils was Charlotte
Talleyrand, who was being brought up by her elderly aunt,
the Marquise Le Vayer. She ran musical evenings which Franzi
attended – provided that the gatherings were small and family-
oriented, which was not always the case; a chance to hear and see
the reclusive M. Litz was an opportunity not to be missed, and Franzi
was too good-natured to take umbrage if too many people turned up.
'I know thirty thousand people in Paris,' he wrote that year, 'and
whether I like it or not, I have to put up with a few of them.'

Among the Marquise Le Vayer's friends was 27-year-old Comtesse
Marie d'Agoult. Born Marie Flavigny in Frankfurt-am-Main in
1805 of wealthy parents, she was educated at the Convent of the
Sacré Coeur in Paris. She came out at eighteen, in the same year
as Franzi arrived in the capital with his father. In 1827 she had a
short but torrid affair with the 30-year-old poet Alfred de Vigny,
and soon after she married the lame war veteran Comte Charles
d'Agoult. Marie continued to socialize liberally at all the most fashionable salons, where she met the leading members of the Romantic set. She was serious, well-read, played the piano and the
organ at the chapel at school and was the very soul of Romanticism. The d'Agoults – Charles, aged forty-two, Marie and their
two little girls, Louise, four, and Claire, two, and Marie's mother
– lived in an apartment overlooking the Seine on the corner of
Quai Voltaire and rue de Beaune.

Marie, her head in the clouds but stuck in a loveless if 'open'
marriage, was going through a period of boredom and depression
– the phrase 'mal de siècle' was coined to describe the despair of

ever attaining the ideals of perfection sought so passionately by Romanticism. Hoping to bring her out of herself, the Marquise invited Marie to one of her evenings to meet Franz Liszt. Marie did not want to go, fearing yet another evening of trivial conversation and listening to yet another piano virtuoso, but, reluctant to give the old Marquise offence, she forced herself to go. When she arrived there was quite a gathering, but no sign of Franz Liszt; he had gone to the next room to copy out a part for Weber's Hunting Chorus that he had been preparing for female voices. Then he entered. Marie saw him across the crowded room. 'A tall figure,' she wrote in her *Memoirs* years later,

> excessively thin, a pale face, with big, sea-green eyes [they were brown] glittering with fleeting flashes, like those on sun-spangled waves, with suffering yet powerful features, an indecisive gait that seemed to glide across the floor rather than step on it, a distracted air, restless and ghostlike, for whom a bell seemed about to toll to summon him back into the shadows; that is how this young genius appeared before me.

The Marquise introduced them, and Marie felt attracted by the power of his free spirit and inquiring mind, as he talked passionately about his beliefs, his ideas and opinions, about art, literature and music. When it was time to make music and the chorus took its place by the piano, Marie, trained in sight-reading, took a mezzo part, joined the ranks and sang the Weber chorus. Afterwards Franzi virtually ignored her as just another face in the crowd. The next day Marie asked the Marquise for Franzi's address and invited him to one of her 'at home' evenings at rue de Beaune, and Franzi accepted.

On her home ground Marie was more sure of herself, and Franzi certainly took notice. 'She was not exactly pretty,' wrote the Vicomtesse de Poillöue de Saint-Mars, under the pseudonym of Comtesse Dash, 'but her elegance, her distinction, her blonde hair, her eyes and her charm made her a beauty.' She had a very thin figure, onto which she would drape cascades of muslin and tulle, and she let her blonde curls fall over her shoulders, to give her an angelic appearance. 'Involuntarily,' concluded Comtesse Dash, 'one looked for her wings.'

Her feminine charms were not lost of Franzi, and he saw in her a serious soul-mate, with whom he could share his suffering as well as thoughts and opinions on all the literary and musical works of the time. They met and corresponded frequently, recommending to each other books to read and piano pieces to play. They had religious faith in common – she was a Protestant with a Catholic education – and an acute awareness of their mortality, of the goodness of God, and of salvation in the next world; added to this were wild fluctuations of mood, ranging from almost ecstatic exhilaration to deepest depression; but whereas Franzi's moods were tempered with his natural kindness and love of mankind, Marie's were more introverted and self-destructive. She was intelligent, artistic and spiritual but extremely unstable, and she bottled up her feelings.

Marie became the receptacle of Franzi's outpourings about the Adèle Laprunarède affair, which was not yet a closed book, although the final pages were cutting deep into Franzi's being. The details of the affair are not known, save that the break-up was prolonged and messy, and Franzi admitted soulfully that he had 'destroyed Adèle's love completely'. Marie, whether from solicitousness or intellectual voyeurism, encouraged Franzi to talk about it. He found in her a surprisingly interested and sympathetic listener.

Franzi returned to performing in public. His first appearance of 1833 was a vocal and chamber concert at the Salons Dietz on 19 January. The opening item was a Hummel septet in which Franzi was joined by, among others, Urhan and oboist Henri Brod. There followed two arias and a violin duo, and Franzi closed the first half with an unnamed work. He did not participate in the second half.

On 20 January and 3 February Field gave his last two concerts in Paris at the Salons Pape. At the latter he again played his new piano concerto, his seventh. Despite Chopin's and Franzi's reservations about his performances, Paris gave him yet another delirious ovation, although the Belgian writer, musicologist, critic and editor François-Joseph Fétis had reservations about the concerto, describing it as 'diffuse, but full of happy ideas' and added that 'M. Field's exquisite execution more than compensated'.

In February Franzi and Marie learned that the old matchmaker, the Marquise Le Vayer, had died, in the sure knowledge that her machinations had begun to bear fruit.

On 12 March there was a full orchestral charity concert at the Salle du Wauxhall, in rue Neuve Saint Nicholas – today rue du Château d'Eau – just off the Boulevard Saint Martin. Franzi's pupil, twelve-year-old singer Pauline García, gave her début with young Just Géraldy, who was also making his début, in a duet from Act

II of Rossini's *Semiramide*. Pauline, who under her married name of Viardot later gained considerable fame, was the younger sister of Maria Malibran. Franzi played two unnamed pieces, one by Weber. The rest of the items included the Overtures to *Oberon* and *Les Francs Juges*, some chamber music and an aria from Nourrit. Also in March there was a concert at the Salle Petzold in the Académie Royale in rue Grange-Batelière, at which 'M. Robbrechts, violinist, played three times instead of twice', since oboist Henri Brod was engaged at the Opéra, and 'M. Listz' was late.

On 19 March Panseron gave a concert at the Salons Dietz. Franzi and his usual coterie opened with Hummel's Septet, cellist Auguste Franchomme played the obbligato in Panseron's new Romance, *Sainte Cécile*, and also gave a solo of his own.

Franzi did not think that constantly visiting Marie, a married woman, at her home was entirely correct, nor did he want grounds for speculation among all and sundry. After the Panseron concert he wrote to her that he 'had hoped to call on you this morning with an album of Schubert'. The latter's music had been sliding into oblivion, until his championship by Urhan had reversed the trend. Franzi was among those converted, and he, in turn, introduced Schubert to Marie. In later life Liszt transcribed some fifty Schubert songs for piano. He had made a start that year with 'Die Rose', which he dedicated to his beloved Countess Thérèse Apponyi. Her musical Monday evenings were still in full swing, and Franzi wrote to Marie that he could always count on being fed his favourite steamed puddings and dumplings at her house by the Invalides.

Franzi did not deliver the Schubert album to Marie, as 'I truly did not have the courage to return to rue de Beaune'. He decided against it after 'turbulent and moral conversations with your doctors', which suggested that she was in a disturbed state. 'But may I hope, Madame,' Franzi continued, 'to see you at the Wauxhall on Saturday?' That Saturday was 23 March, when Hiller gave a full, orchestral concert at which his First Symphony was premièred. He also gave a performance, by popular demand, of Beethoven's E flat Concerto and his set of Études and Caprices. He was joined by Chopin and Franzi in the Allegro from Bach's Concerto in D minor for three claviers. This concerto, one of Franzi's favourites, became a mainstay of his repertoire. Franzi also joined Hiller in the latter's Duo for two pianos. Among the other artists were Franchomme and Moravian violinist Heinrich Ernst – who in later life was reputed to have equalled, and even surpassed, his idol, Paganini.

The Hôtel de Ville, opposite the Ile de la Cité – then called the Ile du Palais – had a small music venue. At the end of March Franzi executed an unnamed solo at a soirée given by singer M. Cambon, assisted by Panseron. Featured were more of the latter's new contrapuntal romances for two voices, with trumpet and flute obbligato parts, as well as an oboe item from Brod and a harp solo from Labarre.

Marie received a letter from Franzi, in which he told her that 'Last night I again heard Berlioz's *Symphonie fantastique* at a soirée of "L'Europe Littéraire". Never has this work seemed to me so complete, so true. If I don't kill myself between now and June, I shall arrange it for piano.' Franzi then set about this new and daunting task; it was one thing to play an operatic aria 'by ear' with pianistic embellishments and variations, but for this project he would have to be constrained to reducing a singularly panoramic orchestral score to what was possible with just ten fingers at the keyboard. Playing from a score was never a problem for him; as a teenager he sight-read Gluck operas for fun.

April was a particularly busy month. On the first day Franzi had two engagements; at one o'clock he took part in a 'grand vocal and instrumental matinée' given by M. Scavarda at the Salle Chantereine, and in the evening he was improvising between plays at the Gymnase, in Boulevard de Bonne Nouvelle. The next day there was a grand event at the Théâtre Italien for the benefit of Harriet Smithson, who had been having a lean time for several months and was deeply in debt. The event was postponed from March, as Miss Smithson had added to her misfortunes by breaking a leg while stepping down from a carriage onto the pavement just before the concert. The theatrical items were *Chacun de son côté*, a comedy by M. Mazères, a scene from *Athalie*, a vaudeville entitled *Rabelais*, given by the artists of the Théâtre du Palais Royal, and *Les Cabinets particuliers* played by artists of the Théâtre du Vaudeville. Among the instrumental performers playing entr'actes were Franzi, Chopin, Urhan, the violinist Haumann and the guitarist Huerta. The day after that Franzi took part in Henri Herz's concert at the Wauxhall, in which he again played Herz's Meyerbeer chorus with Chopin and the Herz brothers. On 5 April Franzi and Haumann played entr'actes at the Vaudeville in rue de Chartres, and on 15 April they were both involved in M. Berettoni's soirée at the Salle Petzold.

On 27 April Henri Brod's vocal and chamber concert took place at the Wauxhall. The long programme included two symphonies by Franz Krommer and Beethoven's Quintet in E flat for piano and winds Op. 16, played by Franzi, Brod, Buteux, Gallay and Barizel, and vocal items. The programme ran over time, and Mayseder's String Sextet, with Urhan in the ensemble, had to be cut short and Beethoven's Piano Trio in B flat Op. 97 – later nicknamed the 'Archduke' – with Franzi at the piano, Franchomme at the cello and M. Cuvillon at the violin, scrapped. On 2 May there was a vocal and instrumental benefit concert at the Salle Chantereine, in which Franzi, Brod and Nourrit took part.

Marie d'Agoult was wealthy in her own right, and while Franzi was busy on the concert circuit she was buying a château at Croissy, in Brie, a rural and agrarian region to the east of Paris, now famous for its cheese. There she hoped to find space and the opportunity to think, read, play the piano and enjoy the stillness of the countryside and to suffer in silence.

Franzi was also looking for solitude. 'My lifestyle is similar to yours,' he wrote to Marie. 'I am absolutely alone, although not six leagues from Paris, but in Paris itself, the very centre of Paris. Some evenings I stroll over to the church of the Petits Pères or across the Faubourg Saint-Antoine.' Franzi took his first Holy Communion at the church of the Petits Pères, today the Notre-Dame des Victoires. He often visited the parish priest, Abbé Duffriche-Desgenettes, who had been appointed in the previous year. In Faubourg Saint-Antoine there were two hospitals, the Orphelins and the Saint-Antoine, both on Franzi's visiting list of hospitals, prisons and asylums.

Franzi had also found a new spiritual mentor in Abbé Deguerry, whose sermons at the Church of St Roche, on the corner of rue Neuve Saint-Roche and rue Saint-Honoré, he listened to and assimilated. The Abbé was a man of music and letters, as well as of God, and frequented the salons. He was also spiritual mentor to Marie. He was taken hostage and executed by the Communards in 1871. Franzi was still in regular touch with Abbé Bardin, and visited him at rue Montholon. Now he had put it about that he had gone away but had actually taken a small room at Erard's in rue du Mail, 'where I shall read, work, and study from morning till night. My mother and Berlioz are the only ones in on this.'

The piano transcription of the *Symphonie fantastique* progressed throughout the spring. He recalled his creative process to Adolphe Pictet in 1837:

I have started something quite different with my transcription of the *Symphonie fantastique* by Berlioz; I have worked on this as conscientiously as if I were transcribing the Holy Scriptures, attempting to transfer to the piano not only the general structure of the music but all its separate parts, as well as its many harmonic and rhythmic combinations.

Six weeks after she had bought the Château de Croissy, Marie invited Franzi to stay. When he arrived he saw a lovely, 160-year-old house beautifully set in an extensive park thickly wooded with primeval forest, in which deer ran free. The château, some twenty-five kilometres from Paris, was built for the Marquis Charles Colbert, younger brother of Jean-Baptiste, minister to Louis XIV. It was springtime, and the greening woods and blossoms were at their freshest.

Marie welcomed him in the opulent salon, dominated by chandeliers, with little Louise and Claire clutching at her skirts. Franzi froze. He had never seen Marie in the context of mother, as his visits to rue de Beaune took place only in the evenings, after the girls' bedtime. The tangible realization that he was involved with a married woman, and a mother of two little girls, affected him deeply. Croissy was not a salon and a venue of heady debate and conversation but a family house and a splendid one at that. Marie showed him round, going from room to room, each with wood-panelling by Oudry, through interconnecting doors, till they came to the remarkable, octagonal library, set with medallions illustrating the *Fables* of La Fontaine. Franzi saw the residence of an aristocrat, a member of that master class to whom the artist was traditionally a paid servant.

Marie sensed a change in Franzi. A distinct coldness towards her replaced the passion with which he had communicated with her in the neutral and progressive atmosphere of liberal Paris. It was almost as though he resented her in these beautiful surroundings. Marie was taken aback and did not know what to make of him. 'From that day onwards,' she wrote in her *Memoirs*, 'the nature of my relationship with Franz changed. . . . During our brief, often interrupted conversations, an element introduced itself that was not us. The substance was the same, but the underlying tone was different.' In the cynical humour with which Franzi laced some of his comments and opinions, she read mockery. In his improvisations, often casual, lifeless and discordant, she found self-deprecation where she had previously heard the sounds of heaven. 'Without actually reproaching me,' she wrote, 'Franz, to whom

my presence no longer brought peace or joy, seemed to harbour
some secret resentment of me. On one occasion I was even surprised to detect a look of hate on his face.'

She might well have asked Franzi what the matter was, what
she had done to offend him, but Franzi was equally confused by
his own feelings and brushed aside her anxiety. He desired Marie
passionately, although she represented that which was anathema
to his art. Liberal or not, she was still an aristocrat, and he was
still a piano player; she lived in a château, a lifestyle closed to
piano players. 'He praised what he called my good life,' she continued, 'he congratulated me on my grand position in the world,
he said he admired my stately residence, the opulence and the
elegance of my surroundings. Was he being serious? Or was it
just idle banter . . . ?'

Marie was tied to a family, whereas Franzi was a free spirit.
She was five years older and had more experience of life, and
Franzi found himself not in control. Her upbringing left considerable subconscious residues, albeit involuntary, of 'classism', and
her progressive opinions inevitably invited accusations of guilt-
ridden patronization, of the kind that caused King Louis-Philippe
to call the man in the street 'comrade'. Circumstantially, everything pointed to Marie being on a higher social plane than Franzi,
whether either of them liked it or not. Likewise Franzi, born into
a class which touched the forelock to the d'Agoults of the world,
could not entirely shake off his humble origins. At this time he
still addressed her as 'Madame' in his letters. Social attitudes take
a long time to change, and the beginnings of true class emancipation were well over a century away, and in the meantime both
knew their places, even though these were becoming ambiguous.
So if he built a wall of cynicism around himself, it was because he
felt that if he did not laugh he would cry.

Franzi's struggle with himself amounted to having to make a
decision: to love or to hate Marie. In their complex and turbulent
relationship, this was no easy matter. The relationship was undoubtedly physical, but when it had become so is not clear, although
their attitudes during the violent Croissy spring would suggest a
passionate intimacy already established. It was not the behaviour
of a man and a woman in a platonic and intellectual relationship.
Things came to a head one day, when Franzi hurled a singularly
barbed and hurtful remark at Marie, who then burst into tears.
'Franz looked at me in consternation,' she wrote, 'but remained

silent; he seemed to be struggling with himself, rent with conflicting emotions which made his lips quiver. Suddenly, falling at my
feet and hugging my knees, he begged me in a voice that I can
still hear to this day, and with a profound and sorrowful look, to
forgive him. This forgiveness, in the burning clasp of our hands,
was an explosion of love, a vow, a mutual commitment to love
one another – with a love that was undivided, unlimited, without
end, on this earth and as long as the heavens last.' As often hap-
pens with two highly strung, sensitive individuals, Franzi admitted
to himself that he and Marie needed each other; to feed off each
other's emotions to fuel their own.

After that, the hours, days, weeks and months that followed
were pure enchantment for Marie. The young lovers made no
plans, no arrangements and let events take their course unhin-
dered. Franzi had made his commitment – perhaps, deep down,
reluctantly – and left everything to chance.

Halfway through May Franzi returned to Paris, to rue de Provence. Marie stayed at Croissy, dreaming and waiting for Franzi's
letters. 'It is an extraordinary life that I lead here,' she wrote on
20 May, 'which no one would understand; perfect solitude away
from the turbulence of the world, not a soul to confide in, not
even the need to commune with any other living being, no letters
interest me, no fond memories, just one single thought which takes
up all my strength, lifts me, depresses me, weighs down on me,
enlivens me, drives me first to despair then to hope.'

The single thought was Franzi. Her love for him was obsessive,
and she lived for his letters. 'No, I am being absurd,' she wrote,
'you are right not to write to me more often, because, you see,
sometimes I love you so stupidly, knowing that I could never be
for you the absolute ideal that you are for me.'

Their correspondence became tantalizingly cryptic, as in a secret, clandestine affair, with childish overtones. Marie gave Franzi
the name Thoughtful, and he called her Longinus or addressed
her letters to a nebulous Marquise de Gabriac at the Château de
Croissy. Franzi also gave her his 'forwarding' address as that of
his 'absolutely reliable' pupil, Mme Vial, in rue Chantereine, and
she asked him to send letters to the post hotel in rue du Petit
Musc, in case of prying eyes and scandal. Their letters, although
in French, often contained sentences in German or English: both
were fluently trilingual.

Two other leading pianists were away from Paris that summer:

Henri Herz had gone on a concert tour of London, and Hiller had gone home to Frankfurt for his father's funeral. In June Franzi and Franchomme met at Chopin's apartment at 5 rue de la Chaussée d'Antin to write a joint letter to him and to offer their condolences and support. 'I am writing to you,' Chopin added to Franzi's words, 'without knowing what my pen is scribbling, as Liszt is at the moment playing my Études and transporting me away from all suitable ideas. I wish I could steal his manner of rendering my own works.' Composer and pianist Karl Reinecke heard Franz Liszt play Chopin's E major Étude in 1848 and wrote that 'when he had finished, he said, sadly, I would give four years of my life to have written those four pages'. Józef Brzoski wrote in his diary about a soirée at which Chopin was present, and Franz Liszt played the C minor Étude – later nicknamed the 'Revolutionary', 'which under Liszt's left hand thundered like a storm, while his right hand expressed utmost pain and despair. Liszt's face radiated with flaming enthusiasm and Chopin's face turned pale under such powerful rendition.' Chopin's Études, which he dedicated to Franzi, were published that same month by Maurice Schlesinger of Paris as Op. 10.

Franzi continued to shun society, with the exception of Berlioz, the Hugos and the Apponyis, and was working assiduously on the *Symphonie fantastique* – as well as the Overture to *Les Francs Juges*. In July he was at Croissy again. Marie had also invited Chopin, but he had arranged to spend a few weeks with Franchomme at his home at Côteau in the Loire Valley. For Franzi and Marie it was a time of peace and reflection. 'He told me of his past life,' she wrote,

> of his joyless childhood, of an adolescence devoid of advice or support; he confessed to me his temptations, his faults, his regrets and the desire to escape from them in the cloister. He painted for me, in strokes of fire, a picture of his conflicting passions tearing themselves apart in his breast, his worldly ambitions and aesthetic aspirations, his pride and his greed, his sharp curiosity about forbidden things and all the carnal and spiritual stimuli, whipped up by the intoxications of frivolous fame which he held in contempt.

The corn was ripening, and during their walks in the fields and meadows Marie wrote of Franzi's delight at the peace and quiet of the countryside, of his artist's ear, which heard the cadences of the rustling fields, the elusive sounds beneath the grass and the music of insects buzzing. Anticipating the Impressionism of the second half of the century, Franzi was inspired by the silent sounds of Nature to begin sketching a piece, *Harmonies Poétiques et Religieuses* (S 154) – not to be confused with the set of that name written much later. But Marie feared that the idyll would not last. 'A false peace,' she wrote, 'a menacing silence. The threat of a storm in the clouds, approaching, that will devastate everything. . . . That storm is not far away.'

In the first week of August Franzi was again back in Paris. He continued his hospital visits and wrote to Marie that they might go to the hospital of La Salpêtrerie together. His latest interest was in the effect of music on disturbed people; a certain Dr Esquirol got him to examine a curious, completely demented sixty-year-old woman who had the strange gift of retaining in her memory every air that was sung, played or hummed to her. La Salpêtrerie stood on the left bank of the Seine on an open site to the south of where the Gare Austerlitz is situated today. 'It is beside the Jardin des Plantes,' he wrote, specifying the botanical gardens of the Natural History Museum, which he also enjoyed visiting.

Henri Herz had returned from his triumphant trip to England and had announced his return in the press. The pianist, publisher and London piano manufacturer Johann Baptist Cramer was also in town. On the last day of August Franzi went, unwillingly, to dinner at Pape's, along with Cramer, who was about to retire. Franzi and Cramer did not like each other. They had played together in 1831, at which time Cramer considered himself a superior player. Liszt later recalled that 'at the time I felt like a poisonous mushroom sitting next to an antidotal glass of milk'.

'The *Symphonie fantastique*,' he wrote to Marie, 'will be finished on Sunday [1 September]. Say three Our Fathers and three Hail Marys for it.' That autumn Franzi published the two Berlioz transcriptions, at his own expense: the *Symphonie fantastique* (S 470) and the *Francs Juges* Overture (S 471), as a gesture of support to his friend, to make his music available to a greater public. Berlioz's original vast score had to wait over a decade yet before it was published.

On 21 September Franzi again went to Croissy for a short stay and was back in time for Berlioz's wedding on 3 October. Franzi, Hiller and Heine were witnesses at his marriage to Harriet Smithson in the chapel of the British Embassy, next to the Elysée Palace at 39 rue du Faubourg Saint-Honoré – still the same today. Even though it was the marriage of the year as far as the Parisian arts scene was concerned, it was a strained affair, and many people had reservations about its future. Harriet, once the darling of the London theatre, was now so out of fashion there that the *Court Journal* commented that 'Miss Smithson was married last week, in Paris, to Derlioz [*sic*], the musical composer. We trust this marriage will insure the happiness of an amiable young woman, as well as secure us against her reappearance on the English boards.' The honeymoon was at Vincennes, just outside Paris, and Berlioz travelled into the capital every day.

He was actually arranging another benefit concert for Harriet. She still had some support as an actress in Paris – perhaps her slight Irish accent, which sometimes grated on the English stage, was lost on the French audiences. The arrangements, which included hiring 100 musicians, as well as the actors, actresses, chorus and solo singers, were fraught with hassle, and Berlioz, ever larger than life, only just managed to cope. The concert, or 'représentation extraordinaire', was fixed for Sunday 10 November, but since one of the leading participants, Mme Dorval, would be away, it was postponed to the following Sunday. Franzi wrote to Marie about it and hoped that she would come.

The concert finally took place at 7 p.m. on Sunday 24 November at the Théâtre Italien. The programme, of drama and music, was a very long one and started an hour late. It opened with a performance of Alexandre Dumas's *Antony*, with M. Fermin and Mme Dorval in the leading roles. According to the *Journal des Débats*, this play was followed by the Overture to *Démophon* by Woghel, probably inserted as an entr'acte to cover scene changes. There followed the two Ophelia mad scenes from Shakespeare's *Hamlet*, in which Harriet Smithson attempted, unsuccessfully, to recreate her legendary performances. Then, at 11.45, came the musical half, which opened with Berlioz's Overture to *Les Francs Juges*. Then Franzi played Weber's Konzertstück in F minor for piano and orchestra. He had written to Marie about preparations for this concert and had described how he was 'working diligently [on the Konzertstück] in order to "say" it with all the delirium and disdain of my twenty-two years'. Franzi increasingly 'said' or 'recited' his performances and later coined the word 'recital' for a solo concert. Alexis Dupont then sang the leading part in Berlioz's *Sardanapalus*.

After that the concert turned into a complete fiasco. Monday morning was well advanced by the time Weber's Hunting Chorus commenced. Some of the musicians had had enough and drifted out and home during the performance. Those who played the Weber to the end packed up as soon as it had finished, and the final item, the *Symphonie fantastique*, was – mercifully – scrapped. 'When I turned round to begin the Symphony I found I had an orchestra of five violins, two violas, four cellos and a trombone,' wrote Berlioz in his *Memoirs*.

On the plus side, the concert brought in a substantial sum of money, which went towards alleviating the new Mme Berlioz's debts.

On 15 December Hiller gave a concert at the Conservatoire, which included Mozart's Piano Concerto in C minor, the allegro of his own First Symphony and a complete performance of his Second, in which the orchestra was conducted by Habeneck. He was again joined by Franzi and Chopin in another performance of the Allegro from Bach's three-piano Concerto and by Franzi in his, Hiller's, Duo for two pianos. The *Revue Musicale* of 21 December, edited by Fétis, recorded that

> [Hiller's] piece for two pianos seemed less successful; there is more hesitancy in it and the composer seemed preoccupied with his fellow performer, M. Liszt, and has sacrificed his greater ease. . . . The movement for three pianos performed by Hiller, Liszt and Chopin was a real pleasure to hear; those three artists executed the work – and we are saying this loudly – with subtlety and excellent understanding of its character.

The young Polish Countess Paulina Plater was one of Chopin's first pupils. Her parents ran a regular Thursday evening salon where piano music was the main order; which prompted Paulina's mother to say, 'If I were young and pretty, my little Chopin, I would choose you for my husband, Hiller for my friend and Liszt for my lover.'

Berlioz, undaunted by the chaos of 24–25 November, organized another concert at the Conservatoire, at 2 p.m. on Sunday 22 December. His Overture to *King Lear*, and two of his vocal settings of poems by Marie and Hugo, sung by M. Boulanger, were premièred. Franzi gave another performance of the Weber Konzertstück, and Haumann played his Fantaisie for violin. The concert finished with the *Symphonie fantastique*.

This time the orchestra remained at their posts.

FOURTEEN

The Road to La Chesnaie
1834

F RANZI HAD now been making a particular name for himself in Paris for exactly a decade; and that name was Litz. French phonetics have a dyslexic tendency as to the pronunciation of his name, even today. It was usually misspelt in the press of the time, much to his annoyance. Chopin had the same problem with a French name in Poland: his spellings included Szopen, Schopen and Choppen. Italian-born Paër found his name spelt Payer. In an age when Europe was a melting pot of nationalities constantly migrating, many adapted their names to their adopted domiciles. Had Liszt and Chopin chosen to do so, posterity might have honoured them as Litz and Szopen; it would have been understandable for Franzi to have taken a spelling of convenience, as his father had done.

For Franzi, 1834 began with a streaming cold. 'Today, while the whole world is well and eating sweets, I am coughing and drinking barley water,' he wrote to Marie in Croissy. 'Cursed cold. What does this presage for 1834?' His relationship with Marie continued into the new year and was inevitably as fragmented as before; she spent most of her time in Croissy, while he stayed in Paris, even though their letters to each other were frequent and lengthy. Occasionally she would go to the capital, and Franzi visited Croissy from time to time, leaving from the post stage at rue du Petit Musc, just round the corner from Place de la Bastille. They did not publicize their relationship and kept the lowest possible profile. Only the closest, his mother, Berlioz and Chopin, were in on the truth; everyone else – including posterity – could only speculate on the true nature of their relationship.

On 5 January, music publisher Maurice Schlesinger – for whom Franzi once acted as a second in a duel – published the first issue of the *Gazette Musicale*, which he founded with, among others, Franzi; he and Berlioz became contributors of articles. The opening issue contained an article by A. Guemer comparing the pianistic ability of Liszt, Hiller, Chopin and Bertini. The battle for supremacy in the virtuoso piano stakes was fought by critics like M. Guemer, not by the pianists themselves. If Liszt, Chopin and Hiller competed, they did so for fun, in the sure knowledge that they had nothing to prove. Their styles were so varied that it was impossible to compare them, as all three transcended any recognized field of contest: Franzi was the first of his kind, Chopin could only be compared to Field, and Hiller was the definitive 'German' pianist who played the Mozart and Beethoven concertos and of whom Chopin said 'he is like Beethoven, full of poetry, fire and spirit'. In any case, Hiller was also a total musician: a conductor and an orchestral composer with two symphonies already under his belt.

The trio were friends who enjoyed each other's company, and lavished praise – or honest criticism – on each other's work, as the following extract from the joint letter of the previous year to Hiller in Frankfurt testifies: 'FRANZI: Do you know Chopin's marvellous studies? They are admirable . . . CHOPIN: . . . but they will only last till yours [Hiller's Études yet unpublished] appear . . . FRANZI: . . . a touch of author's modesty . . .' On another occasion Franzi, Chopin and Hiller were at the Platers', and the matter of nationalist interpretation – an embryonic concept at the time – arose. The purely academic question was whether Chopin's rendering of 'Jeszcze Polska nie zginęła' would be superior to those of the other two. This essentially Polish mazurka of ambiguous origins was the 'Song of the Legions' of the Polish forces under General Dąbrowski, exiled in Italy after the final partition of Poland in 1794. 'Dąbrowski's Mazurka' became the anthem of the Polish émigrés from the 1830–31 Uprising in Paris at this time and then the Polish National Anthem in 1926. Franzi the Hungarian, Hiller the German and Chopin the Pole each played it in his own way; needless to say, Chopin won to unanimous acclaim purely on ethnic grounds.

London-born of Italian parentage, Henri Bertini belonged to the previous generation of pianists; a sound professional pianist, composer and teacher of the Clementi school, he had settled in

Paris in 1821. Franzi often recommended his exercises and Études as work-outs for his pupils. He was more akin to Moscheles and Hummel rather than to Herz and Kalkbrenner and did not see eye to eye with the new Romanticism of Liszt and Chopin. With the pianists, the piano manufacturers also flourished. The new year opened with a double salvo from two of Paris's leading factories marketing their harps. On 19 January there was a soirée at Pleyel's at which the Paris-based composer Franz Stockhausen played the harp, his wife Margarethe sang arias and Swiss airs and Franzi and Hiller filled in with the latter's Duo for two pianos. On 26 January 'M. Litz' played two pieces at Erard's on a latest model at an orchestral concert, and Mlle Bertrand played her own Variations on a theme of Haydn 'on an Erard double-movement harp'. The Stockhausens were there, but only Mme Stockhausen performed; one might suspect a minor 'harp war'.

Franzi was a dedicated Erard man, while Chopin went for the gentler, more silvery-toned Pleyels and only played Erards when he was feeling lazy and wanted a piano that played itself without too much effort; it was this quality that made Erards very popular with amateurs.

Another circuit pianist was Wojciech (Albert in French) Sowiński. He was born in Łukaszówka, Poland in 1805 and studied the piano under Czerny and Gyrowetz. In 1828 he settled in Paris, where he gave concerts, taught the piano and composed numerous salon pieces. He also wrote books and articles on music; his most important work was a comprehensive dictionary of Polish musicians, the definitive work of its kind at the time, published in Paris in 1857. He contributed regularly to Fétis's *Revue Musicale*, and in 1828 had written to Chopin in Warsaw requesting an article on the Polish music scene. Chopin could not be bothered, but in Paris the two Poles met. 'An enormous, tall, magnificent, bewhiskered person enters, sits down at the piano and improvises he doesn't know what, thumps and pounds without meaning, throws himself about, crosses his hands, bangs on one key for five minutes with his enormous thumb,' wrote Chopin. 'Here you have a portrait of Sowiński, who possesses no qualities other than a good posture and a good heart.' Sowiński at first irritated Chopin just by being, but a true friendship grew with the years.

On 25 February Sowiński was to give a concert at the Salons Dietz but because of a damaged left hand could not play. It was time for his fellow pianists to rally round. Charles Schunke replaced him in the Hummel Septet and, according to the *Revue Musicale*, 'played it the way Liszt did on one of his good days'. Franzi and Chopin were also involved, as was Margarethe Stockhausen 'with her beautiful Swiss songs and pretty voice'.

No one rallied round John Field when he fell seriously ill in Naples during March and underwent a painful and unsuccessful anal fistula operation. He remained in hospital without letting anyone know, until a year later his friends the Rachmanoffs found out and took him back to Moscow to recover. He died there of anal cancer in 1837.

On 7 March Franzi and associates played the Hummel Septet at the Salle Chantereine, at a mainly vocal concert which included Manuel García, the talented but brutal father of Maria Malibran and the teenaged Pauline. The Easter break signalled the end of the opera season and the onset of the Concerts Spiritual and, to celebrate, the artists of the Théâtre Italien gave a soirée on 31 March. 'M. Litz' was one of the performers.

On 12 April Charles Schunke gave a concert at the Salons Pape, at which he played Hummel's B minor Concerto and his own Variations on an air from Rossini's *Zelmira*. Then MM. Schunke and 'Listz' played a Duo on a potpourri of Rossini airs.

That month Hector and Harriet Berlioz moved to 10 rue Saint-Denis – today 22 rue du Mont-Cenis – in Montmartre, at the time a small town on a hill outside Paris, which Franzi frequently visited. Franzi, still in rue de Provence, found Erard's a comfortable place to work, to which he effectively commuted. Franzi and Marie found themselves a secret hideaway, which they called their 'Ratzenloch', or rat-hole, just off rue Neuve des Petits Champs. 'My good mother said to me the other day,' wrote Franzi, 'I just don't know why you always call the apartment a rat-hole, as there are no rats in there. You should appreciate it more; it costs 200 francs.'

Of the Paris pianists Franzi was the most physical. He never lost the nervous energy that had worried Czerny when he first heard him. D'Ortigue wrote: 'he conquers everything except his nerves; his head, hands and whole body are in violent motion; in a word, you see a dreadfully nervous man agitatedly playing the piano'. Joseph d'Ortigue was a musicologist leaning towards mysticism and religion and an expert on plainchant. He was a critic and editor of the *Quotidienne* and admired Franzi, both the musician and the Catholic. Among d'Ortigue's circle of friends was Abbé Lamennais, to whom he introduced Franzi when they met in the street in April; by doing so he radically affected Franzi's concept of art, religion and his place in their context. This complex cleric, with his moods swinging from heights of euphoria to the depths of black depression, his frequent nervous headaches and fainting fits, and his very human spirituality, held a strong fascination for Franzi.

Hugues-Félicité Robert de Lamennais was born in 1782, the son of a Breton merchant with a house at La Chesnaie, near Dinan. As a child his overriding interest was Hell – the result of being locked in a library full of religious books, including a shelf devoted to Hell, as a punishment for refusing to do his lessons. From his browsings he developed a strong but undisciplined faith in God. He took Holy Orders and in 1816 was ordained at a time when the downfall of Napoleon had thrown France into a spiritual morass in which the traditional precepts of the Catholic church were questioned. Before the 1789 Revolution, church and state were inseparable, and everyone knew where they stood within this dual hierarchy. With these certainties gone, the church divided into factions: the revived traditionalists, with the Pope firmly in charge; those who saw their faith in personal terms, without allegiance to a state-oriented hierarchy; and atheists, both passive and active, who wanted to abolish religion altogether. In this climate the Saint-Simonists ruffled the feathers of the Establishment to the extent that they had to be persecuted. In the July Revolution anti-Catholic rioters burned the Palace of the Archbishop of Paris to the ground and sacked the Royal church of Saint-Germain-l'Auxerrois.

Lamennais realized that something must be done to save the church and spent the rest of his life, till his death in 1854, working towards the restoration of his vision of the true church in French society and separating it from state interference. Two months after the July Revolution he founded *L'Avenir*, a journal with the motto 'God and Freedom' that became a thorn in the side of the Establishment even greater than the mouthpieces of the Saint-Simonists. Among contributors were Hugo, Vigny, Lamartine and Balzac. It was even read by atheists such as Sainte-Beuve, who sympathized with its essential humanism. It attracted the now largely defunct Saint-Simonists, who saw in Lamennais the next stage to 'humanize' society, art and religion. In 1832 *L'Avenir* was condemned by the Pope and suppressed by the French government. Lamennais was down but not out. He had gained a devoted personal following, including Franzi, who came to be known as

Mennaisians. Franzi considered Lamennais 'one of the finest and noblest souls I have ever met on this earth, where they are not excessively common'. The admiration was mutual, and Lamennais was heard to say that Franzi was 'the greatest pianist I have ever heard, or who has ever existed'.

Lamennais symbolized for Franzi's turbulent inner self a glimmer of hope, with answers to questions that had been tearing him apart for seven years. Franzi's duality remains one of the mysteries of his character, which he himself tried to unravel. He said of himself that he was half gipsy and half Franciscan friar, conjuring up an image that does not fall easily on the imagination.

Three conflicting personalities were also detected within him: Henry Thode wrote of 'one third minstrel, one third chevalier, and one third Franciscan'. Another spoke of 'the convivial man of the salons, the virtuoso and the thoughtful, creative artist'. His split personality was becoming ever more confusing. The grass, for Franzi, always seemed greener on the other side of some great divide, and his tolerance span for a mood was comparatively short. He would emerge after a spell of religious fervour to embrace worldly passions, and his need for solitude would give way to a need for lively-minded company. His impatience with humanity alternated with feelings of love for his fellow man.

On 28 April King Louis-Philippe, anxious to see for himself how Parisian industry was progressing, paid a visit to Erard's, accompanied by his family. Franzi was there, and played some music for the occasion. The King then recalled how twelve-year-old Franzi had played for him when he was still the Duc d'Orléans. 'L PH [Louis-Philippe] found me very much changed,' wrote Franzi, 'and I permitted myself to reply that since then many things had changed.' But not for the better, quoted in addition Liszt's approved biographer, Lina Ramann, many years later. The King was not amused. The slight was said to have caused Franzi's name to be struck off the King's honours list.

After this incident, Franzi dined with some of the Lamennais acolytes, including Lamartine and Dubois of the *Globe*, a liberal paper which had supported *L'Avenir* before its dissolution. Also present were the Dominican preacher Henri Lacordaire, who helped to produce *L'Avenir*, and Abbé Gerbet, who eventually became the Bishop of Perpignan: both were Mennasian disciples at the time.

On 30 April Lamennais's anti-papal *Paroles d'un Croyant*, which he had written the previous year and which summed up his thoughts on the state of the church, was published and caused a furore in both church and state. For Franzi it became his definitive reading that summer; he was never without it, and sent a copy to Marie to study. The Bishop of Rennes, in whose diocese Lamennais' home of La Chesnaie was situated, stripped him of all clerical duties.

On 16 May Franzi accepted an invitation from the d'Hainevilles to spend a month at their home, the Château de Carentonne, near the sleepy little town of Bernay in Normandy. The Château was idyllically situated among wooded hills leading down to the south bank of the River Charentonne [*sic*], some five kilometres to the east of the town. 'I should find it very good here,' he wrote to Marie, 'Mme [Henriette Louise] d'Haineville and her daughter are friendly and solicitous; her son [Armand] . . . with whom I converse from morning till night, and sometimes from night till morning, is sincerely fond of me, as I am of him, he is so good, an excellent person.'

Franzi and Armand went for walks in the countryside, during which they would 'metaphysicize' – a Franzi expression, specifically describing conversations with Lamennais: 'Nous metaphysiquons'. 'Sometimes on our walks we argue like fanatics. He is a believer and a legitimist [post-1830 Bourbon supporter], but always polite and moderate. As for me, I frighten and disturb him. The other day he said to me, do you know that it has been a terrifying experience to have known you: you are destined for misfortune.'

Walking along the river bank towards Bernay they met the post-woman leading her donkey. Franzi's 'metaphysics' dissipated on discovering two letters addressed to him: one from his mother, another from Marie, one of many letters, heavy with religious and philosophical polemics and allusions to Franzi's turbulent love life, that were exchanged between them during his stay. Franzi and Marie's current nicknames for each other were M. Retrogradus and Mariotte respectively.

'All my time is spent studying and reading . . .' Franzi had brought a number of books with him: the philosophical and critical works of Pierre Bayle and Jean de la Harpe and the Bible. He also put in some serious practice, with 'lots of cadences, octaves and tremolos – which make my head split. I have here the Études of Hiller, Chopin and Kessler.'

The German-born pianist and composer Johann-Christoph Kessler used to entertain Chopin at his home in Warsaw, where he lived and ran music evenings every Friday. In the 1830–31 Uprising he fled Poland and settled in Paris. He was a refined pianist in the Field tradition, and his twenty-four Études Op. 20 were particularly admired. 'Chopin and I had a special liking for them in the thirties,' said Liszt later. Franzi was in two minds about his stay. His positive side wrote to Marie that 'the surroundings are beautiful – my room is very like the one I use in Croissy.... But how my head burns. I need your hand, there, on my brow, in my hair.' Then his negative side takes over:

> I hear nothing, I feel nothing, I no longer see the trees, the agitated people that go by, the sky, so pure without clouds. Derision. Despair. Incomprehension.... We do not know what it is to die.... But I no longer dream for myself, I forget myself, I work more and more for escape into oblivion.... Love consumes me and tortures me in my isolated existence... yet there will be some relief in the tomb.

One Sunday the d'Hainevilles showed Franzi the organ in Bernay's church of the Holy Cross. 'It was a great event in the town,' he wrote to Marie. As he played the organ, M. d'Haineville discussed with town officials the possibilities of Franzi giving a charity concert in Bernay; Franzi, in the throes of a negative mood, agreed, albeit reluctantly. 'We're going to have some kind of concert,' he wrote on 12 June. 'It will be awful, but it doesn't really matter as I hope there will be receipts of 1,000 francs for the benefit of the poor.' His stay at Carentonne was coming to an end, and he was glad. 'Let us hope,' he wrote on 18 June, 'that God in his mercy and infinite love will unite us and absorb us wholly. I feel very weak and close to death... yet we will revive and shatter our gravestones with our heads. I am overwhelmed with politeness, invitations and other boring things in this benighted castle. I scarcely have time to do a few scales.' Then his positive side immediately continued: 'Still, I do not regret this trip. My health is better, and I appear to have put on weight and to be less tired.'

The concert took place on Thursday 19 June; the venue is not known. On Saturday 21 June, at one o'clock, Franzi climbed into the diligence, which arrived in Paris at eleven o'clock the following morning. He wrote to Marie that 'The famous Bernay concert has taken place. It was really strange. I found myself sitting at the piano a dozen times... and they all found me charming, admirable, etc. A big thank-you.'

The Château de Carentonne was burnt down in 1870, although the attendant farm, now a manor house in private hands, is still there: the date 1782 is carved into one of its beams. The organ on which Franz Liszt played is still there in the fourteenth-century church of the Holy Cross in rue Thiers. The original instrument dates from the end of the sixteenth century, but it was rebuilt in 1818 after nearly three decades during which the church, commandeered during the Revolution, became a store-house. The organ was further restored in the 1840s and continued to give service until it fell silent in 1941: at the time of writing, a fund has been established for its restoration.

Franzi resumed his 'metaphysicizing' with Lamennais. The Pope had condemned his *Paroles d'un Croyant* with the Encyclical 'Singulari nos'. Lamennais, virtually stripped of religious duties and abandoned by many followers who did not wish to incur a papal condemnation, including Gerbet and Lacordaire, was preparing to return home to Brittany, but before he went he invited Franzi to stay with him. Franzi accepted, and after a week at Croissy with Marie he set out for Brittany.

Saturday 13 September was a glorious day, without a cloud in the sky. At five o'clock in the evening Franzi's diligence set off 'past rue du Mail, round the Petits Pères, the rue des Petits Champs, almost past the rat-hole, then Place Vendôme, then by the Louis XVI bridge'. As the coach trundled westward, Franzi, feeling troubled and oppressed, took out Ballanche's *Orphée* to read. At half past nine it became dark, and he settled down for the long night drive. The post road continued through Dreux and Verneuil, and on Sunday morning Franzi woke up at Saint-Maurice, twenty kilometres before Mortagne. While the horses were being changed, he went to the church, sat in the cemetery, reading *Orphée* and went for a walk before embarking for the next stage to Alençon.

No sooner had he entered the inn at Alençon than he was accosted by a policeman who demanded his passport. Franzi replied that he did not have one:

POLICEMAN: But sir, to travel you must have a passport.
THOUGHTFUL: I have been travelling in France for three years, and nobody has ever asked me for one. POLICEMAN: That's odd, so you haven't been to Alençon? THOUGHTFUL: Ah. Is the good town of Alençon so far ahead of civilization and more endowed with liberty than other towns? POLICEMAN: What is your profession? THOUGHTFUL: I have none. POLICEMAN: What

do you do, then? THOUGHTFUL: I read in the morning and go walking in the evening.

The policeman became angry and frogmarched Franzi to the superintendent's office between two colleagues. He was about to be carted off to prison when fortunately a lawyer, M. Masson, whose son happened to know Franzi and who had a portrait of him at home, came in and saved the day. M. Masson assured Franzi of a welcome at his house; Franzi declined with thanks on this occasion but said he would bear his kind invitation in mind for the return journey. A quarter of an hour later, the coach left for Laval. 'The adventure was a great talking point in the coach, where Thoughtful had already been recognized, we chatted, we laughed . . . and finally we slept.'

At Laval an anti-Mennaisian cleric got on the coach and engaged Franzi in a heated argument about Lamennais. 'I got impatient and bored, but there was no getting away from it.' Finally, totally fed up, Franzi asked to go on top, but there another misfortune lay in wait for him. 'Can you imagine, I found perched up there some type of rake, a man of songs, suppers, Champagne and good fortune – who just would not shut up. I had to go through the torture of little stories, little songs, liaisons, etc. It was impossible to think of Ballanche or Mariotte.'

Rennes was the next major halt, and it was there that Franzi sent off his long and detailed letter to Marie, written during halts and recounting his adventures on the road to La Chesnaie.

FIFTEEN

Threshold of a New Beginning
1834–35

L A CHESNAIE was a small, isolated, two-storey-plus-attic villa set in its own park, on the edge of the Forest of Coetquen. It could be seen from the gate at the end of a long, straight, tree-lined drive. To the left, as Franzi approached, was the long and narrow lake, visible among the reddening beech trees, running parallel to the drive.

The Abbé, who, Franzi discovered, always wore the same old torn grey frock-coat, the faded blue leggings of a rude peasant, enormous scuffed shoes and a tattered straw hat 'that had known eight summers', showed Franzi to his room on the first floor next to his own. A third room, a library extension 'because everywhere is stacked with books here', was occupied by a taciturn young librarian by the name of M. Bore. The drawing- and dining-rooms were on the ground floor, and there were further rooms in the attic. Franzi's room overlooked a kitchen garden about twenty metres long, and beyond it, set among pine trees, stood a simple little chapel, where another taciturn young man by the name of M. de Kertanguy lived, with two boys in their mid-teens. The liveliest inhabitant was the Abbé's frisky Newfoundland dog, who delighted everyone with his frolics around the outcrops of rock that bordered the lake.

Franzi's day usually began at about seven o'clock, when he slowly got up, 'browsed through some books, put on his cravat and tinkled a little on the piano'. At eight coffee was served. Between nine and midday Franzi practised, and the rest of the day consisted mostly of reconciling his urge to relax, read and compose with the almost manic restlessness of the Abbé, who talked while frantically pacing backwards and forwards. At noon Franzi lunched by himself, as the Abbé took only a cup of hot chocolate. After lunch he met up with the Abbé and the dog for a short walk, after which he was again left to his own devices. Dinner was at five, the only time when everyone was present. Franzi was relieved to find that MM Bore and Kertanguy hardly spoke: he was in no mood for small talk.

After dinner, the Abbé gathered up his flock and led the way into the woods for a long, energetic walk. 'This is a man in perpetual motion,' wrote Franzi, adding that he hardly ever slept. It was as much as Franzi could do to keep up with him. And all the time the Abbé held forth, and Franzi hung on to every word he uttered. 'Truly he is a marvellous man,' he wrote, 'prodigious, altogether extraordinary. So much genius, so much heart. High ideals, piety, passionate ardour, perspicacity of spirit, a deep and wide sense of judgement, the innocence of a child, sublimity of thought and a powerful soul, all of which makes one see the image of God within him. I have not yet heard him say: me.'

Franzi loved the isolation. The nearest village was St Pierre, where 'to hear mass we had to walk a good half-hour, likewise to have a drink in a tavern'. There were several other houses scattered widely throughout the neighbourhood. The nearest sizeable town, Dinan, was ten kilometres away.

One of Lamennais's favourite spots was a rock on the edge of the lake, on the far side, which he had designated to be his tomb. Students and acolytes that came to learn and worship at his feet knew this rock well; the Abbé always sat on it, with the lake and, beyond it, the house as a backdrop, when preaching and speaking of God, of faith and of the human condition. To Franzi he also spoke of his music and dismissed the concept of art for art's sake as flawed; he looked upon art as the supreme goal and the perfect expression of Man's highest moral values in God's eyes. To Franzi, trying to reconcile the flamboyance of his music with his à Kempis-inspired desire to 'be as nought', the Abbé, as the apostle of the fusion of art and faith, seemed to hold at least some of the answers.

In between 'metaphysicizing' and reading, Franzi continued with his composing. Between 1832 and 1834 he had written a Sonata for violin and piano on Chopin's Mazurka in C sharp minor Op. 6 No. 2 (S 127). During this year he had written a set of three *Apparitions* (S 155), the last of which was based on a Schubert waltz. He finished his *Harmonies Poétiques et Religieuses*, which he began the previous year, inspired by the Croissy summer, and dedicated it to the Abbé. He had also written his sparkling Grosses Konzertstück on themes from Mendelssohn's *Songs without Words*, for two pianos (S 257); at La Chesnaie he wrote a *Grande Fantaisie Symphonique* on themes from Berlioz's *Lelio* for piano and orchestra (S 120), and began work on a *De Profundis* for piano and orchestra (S 691), which he also dedicated to the Abbé.

After two weeks Franzi's concentration span had run out, he was suffering from a surfeit of moral indigestion, and he missed Marie. 'Believe it or not,' he wrote to her, 'I cannot stand this admirable life that I'm leading any longer. I would still prefer a hundred times my stupid and loathsome existence in Paris, with its miserable fatigues, tortures and empty, profound tedium, but where I can still occasionally find my poor M[arie], to this endless celebration of intelligence and soul, to these active, serious, varied and singularly fortifying days at La Chesnaie.' At the beginning of October he decided to go home.

The Abbé's lakeside rock did not become his tomb – he is buried at the Père Lachaise Cemetery in Paris – but stands as a memorial to him, surmounted with a stone cross and inlaid with a medallion and an inscription. The house is still there, almost unchanged since the Abbé's day, and is now in private hands.

Franzi wrote that 'The autumn sunsets are magnificent on the Breton coast', and he planned a circuitous route back, taking in the English Channel coast at St Malo and Mont-Saint-Michel. In the event, on Friday 3 October he set off for St Malo just for the weekend. First he went to Dinan, a fine granite town and an inland port built on two levels: the lower level consisted of the harbour on the River Rance, which at that point widened into a thirty-kilometre-long estuary flowing into the English Channel at St Malo. The upper town was situated on the cliffs above the harbour, with spectacular vistas onto the harbour and the twisting river below. Franzi took a steamer to St Malo, where he spent most of his time on the beaches 'listening to the music of the sea'.

On the evening of Sunday 5 October he was back for a brief stay at La Chesnaie before setting off for home. First stop was Laval, where his plans to visit the Trappist monastery had to be scrapped owing to 'a silly accident'. By Saturday 11 October he was in Alençon, where he took advantage of M. Masson's offer and stayed with him.

On the morning of Monday 13 October he was back in Paris

and had an emotional reunion with Marie, who had returned to rue de Beaune. At the end of October back in Croissy, Marie's older daughter, Louise, became seriously ill, so Marie brought her back to rue de Beaune and into the care of the best doctors in Paris. Marie stayed by Louise's bedside and would not see anyone, including Franzi.

This distressed Franzi, who did not know how to cope with the situation, but it led to another turning point in his relationship with Marie, and he again considered whether the affair was a good idea. Lamennais certainly did not, and had put to Franzi some good reasons for ending the relationship: an adulterous affair with an unstable, aristocratic older woman with two children was a recipe for both moral and physical disaster. Franzi himself was not in control of his own feelings, overwhelmed as they were by Marie's emotional power. Part of him yielded willingly to this power, and part of him listened to the Abbé's words, and his own deeper instincts. He found it hard to jump either way, knowing that Marie was going through a traumatic time with Louise and might need his support and love. In the final analysis, he decided to let things drift. He knew from experience how messy break-ups could be – the end of the Adèle affair was still a vivid memory, and now another break-up was looming, promising an even greater eruption of emotional turbulence – a prospect that he hoped to put off for as long as possible.

He called at rue de Beaune, asked the servants after Marie and Louise but did not go in and see them, as Marie, in a trance of despair while watching over Louise, would not see him.

By 4 November, Franzi was hankering again after La Chesnaie. 'Just imagine,' he wrote to Lamennais, 'even before my arrival I'd already been announced, my name stuck up on placards in big letters on every street corner. . . . What a change, what a contrast, what a sad compensation for my beautiful life at La Chesnaie.' As this was a thank-you letter, the sentiment may have been one of politeness rather than a mood change. The placards referred to a forthcoming vocal and instrumental concert in aid of flood victims, in which Franzi had agreed to take part. It was scheduled for 5 November at François Stoepel's Institution Musicale, where the Saint-Simonists used to hold their events and which was now a music school. Organized by Rossini, it was the brainchild of the philanthropic literary and drama critic Jules Janin, whom Franzi liked and admired and for whom he was prepared to do this favour. 'To face up to these wretched concerts I have had to spend whole days and nights writing, correcting and working at my miserable demisemiquavers.'

Also recruited to take part were the string players Baillot and Urhan and the singers Rubini, Tamburini and Damoreau. Franzi was due to play Moscheles's Duo Sonata with the pianist Honorine Lambert, but as she was indisposed, Chopin himself was asked to play; in the event the item was cancelled. But Franzi did play his demisemiquaver-rich, Paganini-inspired *La Clochette* – the first draft for his later *La Campanella*. The concert also included some young music students: it opened with an arrangement for five pianos twenty hands – those of ten of M. Stoepel's pupils – of Weber's *Oberon* Overture.

Some days later Franzi was introduced to the sensational authoress and feminist Aurore Dudevant, pen-named George Sand – estranged wife of the drunken and dissipated Baron Casimir Dudevant. When not at her Château at Nohant, in Berry, she lived on the third floor of 9 Quai Malaquais, overlooking the river. Franzi was struck by her writings, her sensual beauty and her exotic style statements: she was renowned for making masculine clothing appear alluringly feminine. Seven years older than Franzi, she was regarded as one of the sexiest women in Paris. She, in turn, was struck by Franzi's art – but no more; she made this absolutely clear when Franzi hinted at a more special 'friendship'. She even said later that had she become sexually involved with Liszt it would have been out of spite. Their relationship nevertheless became very lively and rich, replete with misunderstandings. Many suspected there was more to their long discourses than met the eye. Among these was Alfred de Musset. He had been having an on-off affair with her for some time, and her frequent tête-à-têtes with Franzi, sometimes well into the night, caused a measure of jealousy which often led to rows. It became the talk of the town that Franzi was a profligate womanizer with a penchant for the older, more mature woman. This reputation upset Franzi, who wrote quite specifically that he was not the 'Don Juan that he was made out to be'. The truth will be debated for all time.

On 23 November Berlioz gave a concert which featured a 100-strong orchestra. Among the items, all his own compositions – or variations on them – were a number of first performances: the Overture to *Waverley*, two vocal items with orchestra, a Fantaisie Romantique after Victor Hugo, *Les Ciseleurs de Florence*, and a

Romance and, taking up the whole of the second half, the symphony for viola and orchestra, *Harold in Italy*, with Chrétien Urhan as soloist. Franzi's contribution was to have been a Grande Fantaisie Fantastique on two themes of Berlioz – *Ballade du Pêcheur* and *Chanson des Brigands* – but according to one review, neither this item, nor *Les Ciseleurs de Florence*, was performed. A violin item by Heinrich Ernst was replaced – by popular request – by the 'March to the Scaffold' from the *Symphonie fantastique*, which closed the first half.

The following day, at one o'clock, Franzi and Urhan played Beethoven's 'Kreutzer' Sonata at the church of St Vincent de Paul in rue Montholon during low mass to celebrate the Feast of St Cecilia, the patron saint of music; this was postponed from the 22nd, the actual feast-day, when Urhan was involved in rehearsing *Harold* for the Berlioz concert.

In December tragedy struck at rue de Beaune. After several weeks in a near coma, little Louise d'Agoult died, aged five. Marie, barely aware of her surroundings, was taken to Croissy, where she had a nervous breakdown. Franzi kept away.

On Christmas Day Franzi and Chopin were both at Stoepel's vocal and instrumental concert; they played Moscheles' Grand Duo for four hands and Franzi's 'Mendelssohn' Konzertstück for two pianos, written earlier that year. Franzi also accompanied Ernst in his violin composition, and Mme de la Hye also gave two organ improvisations. The *Gazette Musicale* recorded that 'we need hardly say that this work [the Moscheles Duo], one of the composer's masterpieces, was performed with a rare perfection of talent by the two greatest pianoforte virtuosi of the age. . . . The thunderous applause told MM Liszt and Chopin better than any words from us might do of the pleasure they had given their audience, whom they electrified a second time when playing M. Liszt's Duo for two pianos.'

Berlioz the conductor had become a favourite subject for cartoonists, who liked to portray him posturing wildly in front of a vast orchestra containing cannons, his hair long and wild. On 28 December at the Conservatoire, his adoring audience viewed him in spectacular action, riding his vast orchestra into battle through both his symphonies. First came his now enormously popular *Symphonie fantastique*. This was followed by a chance to hear 'A Ball' and the 'March to the Scaffold' in Franzi's piano transcription version, which both Franzi and Berlioz hoped would make the work more accessible to the masses. The orchestra were given a chance to regain their breath while Franzi again played his 'Mendelssohn' Konzertstück for two pianos, this time with his pupil, Mlle Vial, before they were joined by Urhan for *Harold in Italy*.

At the beginning of 1835 Marie recovered enough to sift through her still unopened correspondence. 'I opened one at random,' she recalled many years later in her *Memoirs*. 'It was from Franz. He was not hoping to see me, he said, at such a time. He did not think his presence would bring any consolation. He was leaving for La Chesnaie.'

Franzi had told Marie that he was leaving Paris but did not say for how long. 'I understand that you have gone to Switzerland,' wrote Lamennais to Franzi's address in rue de Provence at the end of January. Marie had either forgotten where he was going or had misunderstood: Chesnaie and Genève might have sounded the same to a confused mind. Or Franzi had lied: Henry Reeve recorded that at that time Geneva was a very lively scene. Franzi had a number of friends in Geneva, including the Boissiers and Pierre Wolff – and possibly Adèle Laprunarède, for whom Geneva was the local big city. La Chesnaie would have sounded more wholesome. 'He asked me not to write to him any more,' continued Marie. 'The tone and the resolve of his letter had a coolness which should have hurt me. On the contrary, I found a sort of bitter comfort from it.'

The loss of Louise became wildly entangled with her apparently unrequited love for Franzi. Genève or La Chesnaie – she was past caring. She took out her anguish on little Claire, who bore the brunt of her mother's depression. 'Unjust, dark and bitter, I resented a four-year-old child for not understanding death. I reprimanded her for playing. I rejected her caresses. Soon her presence annoyed me so much that she had to be taken away from me.' Marie's very concerned mother, with the agreement of the Comte d'Agoult, had Claire sent to a 'pensionnat' – effectively farmed out to be fostered. Marie sank deeper into despondency. 'I had not slept for a long time; all food disgusted me; I had an aversion to doing anything; I neither spoke nor listened . . . I just continued to exist. For how long? It was in the month of May, six months since Franz had left for La Chesnaie.'

Franzi had actually been away for two months. In March he returned to Paris. Marie omitted – unbelievably – to mention in her *Memoirs* her meeting with Franzi during March, a meeting that was to have far-reaching consequences.

Franzi returned to his now habitual role as fill-in pianist at other people's concerts. On 1 April the Lambert sisters, pianist Honorine and singer Antonia, gave a concert at the Salle Chantereine. Franzi played his 'Mendelssohn' Konzertstück for two pianos, this time with Mlle Honorine, who herself played the 'Là ci darem la mano' Variations, from Mozart's *Don Giovanni*. This was a solo version of Chopin's early composition, which Anne de Belleville had been performing round Europe since 1830. Confusingly, there were two unrelated female pianists in Paris at this time named Lambert, Honorine and Camille.

On 3 April Franzi and Tamburini performed at a concert given by their pupil, Mlle Boucault, at Stoepel's; Franchomme also played the cello. On 4 April there was an orchestral concert at the Théâtre Italien in aid of Polish refugees, who were still arriving to a warm welcome in Paris from a Poland ravaged by Russian atrocities. The concert was presided over by Princess Marcelina Czartoryska – a friend and pupil of Chopin. Among the singers were Nourrit and Mlle Falcon, with songs by Schubert in the programme, one accompanied by Franzi. He and Hiller again played the latter's Duo for two pianos. Solo instrumental items were by Ernst and flautist M. Dorus. The highlight, as was fitting for such a concert, was Chopin playing one of his piano concertos. The concert closed with the Overtures to Weber's *Oberon* and Rossini's *Guillaume Tell*. The orchestra was conducted by Habeneck.

On the evening of 9 April the English journalist Henry Reeve walked with the writer and philosopher Pierre-Simon Ballanche in the moonlight along the broad quai by the Seine to the Hôtel de Ville, where Franz Liszt was due to give his own orchestral concert in aid of a poor family. 'When we arrived at the concert room [Salle Saint-Jean],' wrote Reeve in his diary, 'it was very full, and I stood the greater part of the evening.'

The first half opened with a symphony by Hiller with the orchestra conducted by M. Girard. Boulanger then sang Berlioz's setting of Goethe's *Ballade du Pêcheur*, and this was followed, appropriately, by the first performance of the work Franzi wrote at La Chesnaie, the Grande Fantaisie Symphonique for piano and orchestra on two Berlioz airs: the Ballade which preceded it and the *Chanson des Brigands*. It was a forward-thinking quirk of Franzi's programming to give the audience a taste first of the original, then the reworking, of a piece of music. The audience at the Berlioz concert sampled both the 100-piece orchestra and the solo piano

versions of the *Symphonie fantastique*; now Henry Reeve heard
Berlioz's *Ballade* sung by a male voice and then reworked in a
concertante fantasy. 'I do not know whether I ever described to
you my friend Liszt,' continued Reeve. 'His person is slight and
tall, a delicate frame, not worn or wasted by weakness and malady,
but perpetually strained by the flow of animated thoughts, by the
violence of a musical soul, for which no sound affords an adequate expression.'

There followed an Air with Variations, written and played by
Lambert Massart. This brilliant young violinist, born the same
year as Franzi in Liège, Belgium, shared with him the frustration
of having been refused admission to the Conservatoire by Cherubini
on the grounds of being a foreigner. As a pupil and protégé of
Kreutzer, he was eventually accepted, studied under Zimmermann
and made a name for himself as a performer and teacher, a name
that was to feature prominently in the Franz Liszt story of later
years. A shy performer and respected teacher, he continued working till his retirement in 1890.

The first half closed with what eventually became known as
Beethoven's 'Moonlight' Sonata, with the orchestra under M. Girard
playing the first movement, and Franzi playing the second and
third. 'After this latter piece,' continued Reeve, 'he gasped with
emotion as I took his hand and thanked him for the divine energy
he had shed forth.'

After the interval Reeve 'managed to pierce the crowd and [I]
sat in the orchestra before the Duchess de Rauzan's box'. The
Duchesse Clara de Rauzan, with whom Franzi was quite besot-
ted, had one of the most fashionable salons in the Faubourg Saint-
Germain; Franzi dedicated the first of his *Apparitions*, written in
1834, to her: 'my chair was on the same board as Liszt's piano'.
The second half opened with the Pilgrims' March from Berlioz's
Harold in Italy. Again, Urhan played the solo viola. Then a male-
voice quartet sang some *Scènes Caractèristiques* of M. Clapisson;
these were followed by Mayseder's Polonaise, which Franzi used to
feature with Karl Ebner, this time with Urhan on viola.

For the final item, Franzi mounted the stage with his pupil,
Mlle Vial, to perform his 'Mendelssohn' Konzertstück.

> It was a duet for two instruments, beginning with Mendelssohn's
> Chants sans Paroles, and proceeding to a work of Liszt's. We
> had already passed that delicious chime of the 'Song written in

a Gondola' and the gay tendril of sound in another lighter piece, which always reminded me of an Italian vine when Mrs Handley played it to us. As the closing strains began, I saw Liszt's countenance assume that agony of expression, mingled with radiant smiles of joy, which I never saw in any other human face, except in the paintings of our Saviour by some of the early masters; his hands rushed over the keys, the floor on which I sat shook like a wire, and the whole audience were wrapped in sound, when the hand and frame of the artist gave way; he fainted in the arms of a friend who was turning over for him, and we bore him out in a strong fit of hysterics. The effect of this scene was really dreadful. The whole room sat breathless with fear, till Hiller came forward and announced that Liszt was already restored to consciousness and was comparatively well again.

But not well enough to finish the piece. The shocked audience filed out into the Place de l'Hôtel de Ville. 'As I handed Mme de Circourt to her carriage,' concluded Reeve, 'we both trembled like poplar leaves, and I tremble scarcely less as I write.'

No one would have been more shocked than poor Mlle Vial. Franzi had conspired with the Vials of 21 rue Chantereine to use their address as a postbox for his correspondence with Marie. 'I am certain of Mme Vial,' Franzi had explained to her.

The Hôtel de Ville was destroyed by the Communards in 1870; it was rebuilt in its present form three years later.

The Conservatoire mounted its annual concert on 17 April – Good Friday. The orchestra and chorus were conducted by Habeneck. Among the items were Cherubini's 'O Salutaris' and the Overture to Weber's *Oberon*. Beethoven was featured with excerpts from his oratorio *Christ on the Mount of Olives* and his Fifth Symphony. Franzi, now fully recovered from his fainting fit the previous week, was the soloist in a Weber piano concerto.

On 23 April Franzi organized a concert for his thirteen-year-old pupil, Hermann Cohen, at the Salle Chantereine. Teacher and pupil opened with a Pixis Duo for four hands, followed by Tulou's two-flute Variations and a violin solo from Ernst. The concert finished with Czerny's *Potpourri* for four pianos, played by Franzi, Hermann Cohen, Sowiński, his left hand now recovered, and Alkan. The Styrian Singers were heard by way of an interlude.

On 3 May Berlioz mounted another spectacular at the Conservatoire. His forces, now augmented to 120 performers under the direction of M. Girard, gave the *Symphonie fantastique* and the sequel, 'Le Retour à la Vie', in which the narrator was M. Geffroy of the Théâtre Français. Franzi gave the performers some respite with Moscheles's Alexander March Variations as an interlude between the two items.

On 5 May Franzi took part, with a number of other singers and instrumentalists, including Charles Schunke, in a concert organized by M. L. Bamberger at the Salle Saint-Jean in the Hôtel de Ville, the scene of his fainting fit the previous month.

On 7 May Mme Duflot-Maillard gave a soirée at the Salle Pleyel. Franzi was there, as was someone from the *Gazette des Salons*:

> As soon as he appears in a salon, a soft murmuring is heard, and all the ladies get to their feet, their lorgnettes directed at him; he allows them this innocent little pleasure. With his own glasses, before sitting down, he himself scrutinizes this semicircle of luminance, which he is about to fill with admiration and charm. As soon as he sits down and his young fingers have fluttered up and down the whole length of the docile piano, everyone is silent, and no longer on this earth, having climbed to those celestial regions inhabited by angels and seraphim.

Also present at this soirée were Urhan and the brilliant young cellist Alexandre Batta, son of Pierre Batta, teacher of cello at the Conservatoire. With Franzi, they performed a Mayseder Piano Trio. Ernst and Sor also performed.

On 23 May the Gymnase Musical gave its opening orchestral concert of the season, with M. Tilman the conductor. The programme included the Overture to Rossini's *Maometto*, the Symphony 'La Naissance de la Musique' by Louis Spohr – probably No. 4 in F, published that year, today subtitled 'Die Weihe der Tone' (the Consecration of Tonality) – Weber's Second Symphony in C and the Overture to his *Euryanthe*. Alexandre Batta gave a cello solo, M. Bley played the violin, and Franzi's contribution was an unnamed 'Grand Piece' by Weber.

'It was in the month of May, six months since Franz had left for La Chesnaie' – Marie's *Memoirs* had skipped the events of the first five months of 1835. 'During this long time he has not written to me. His name has not been uttered in my presence, and in my hazy memory his face appeared only vague and distorted. A letter arrived from him. I broke the seal with an effort. It only contained a few words. He wrote that he had come to a decision.

He was going to leave France and Europe. He expressed a wish, if it was not too upsetting for me, to see me one more time.' The sight of Franzi's signature at the bottom of the page caused Marie to be 'struck as if by an electric current'. A quarter of an hour later, a messenger was bearing a note for Franzi arranging to meet at rue de Beaune the following afternoon. 'When I arrived, Franz was waiting for me on the doorstep. He seemed frightened by the sight of me.'

They spoke for a long while. Marie described the depths of depression to which she had sunk since the death of Louise. She told him of 'my injustices, my repulsions, the distress of soul and spirit, then my torpor, and the inertia of despair, and how, at the sight of [your] name, written by [your] own hand, I felt myself reborn. . . . "But what about you, Franz?" I said. "What have you been doing? What have you achieved? Are you leaving?" "We are leaving," said Franz with a strange tone of voice.' Marie was struck dumb, unable, not daring, to comprehend what she had just heard. She recounted Franzi's reply:

'From the very first day that I loved you, that I felt what this love was, and what it would need from me, I have trembled for you. I decided to leave you. Even now I was running from you, trying to put a great distance between us. Now see what I have done. Poor woman, overwhelmed, fallen, without strength or life, what has become of you away from me? No, no, I will not leave you to languish and waste away so miserably. I, too, thirst for life. It is enough to struggle under the yoke which ties us to the earth, enough to fight on and suffer in vain. Let us fight on and suffer, but let it be standing together. Our souls were not created for things that divine, for dumb resignation which always leads to tears. We are young, spirited, sincere and proud. Ours are great vices or great virtues. We must, before Heaven, confess the sanctity and destiny of our love.'

Then Franz took me, and held me, trembling, in his arms. 'Where are we going?' he repeated my question. 'What does it matter? As long as we're happy, or sad, whatever. What I do know, is that it is too late for anything else, that I love you, that I am cutting off all my ties, that in life or death, we are united for ever.'

What Marie does not record is that she was now over two months pregnant. Blandine-Rachel, registered Liszt, was conceived in March and born on 18 December 1835 – which may have affected the direction in which Franzi finally jumped. The lovers planned to leave for an indefinite trip to Switzerland as soon as arrangements could be made. Abbé Lamennais was horrified, and tried desperately to get Franzi to change his mind – but to no avail. Marie did not let anyone know of her intentions, except to leave a final farewell note to her husband at rue de Beaune. She then asked her mother and her brother-in-law to accompany her to Switzerland, omitting to tell them the reason for her trip. Her mother saw it as a promising sign that Marie was getting over her trauma.

'Eight days later we had left France,' continued Marie in her *Memoirs*. At the very end of May, the three of them set off by diligence for Basle. On 1 June Franzi, having said goodbye only to those closest to him, quietly slipped into the diligence for Basle, and again disappeared from Paris. He and Marie met in Basle a few days later, and Marie's mother, discovering that she had been misled, returned angrily to Paris.

The house on the corner of rue de Beaune and Quai Voltaire has been rebuilt, and the opposite corner is now more renowned as the house in which Voltaire died. The Château de Croissy no longer exists, and on its site now stands a commercial complex in the village of Croissy-Beaubourg. The ponds are still there, and the park is still unspoiled.

'All ties were broken off,' wrote Marie, 'rejected, kicked aside, except our love. The unknown God, the strongest God, took possession of us, and of our destiny.'

Franz Liszt, innovative composer, stood on the threshold of a new beginning.

Bibliography

D'Agoult, Countess (aka Daniel Stern) (ed. Daniel Ollivier), *Memoires 1833–1854*, Calmann-Lévy, Paris, 1877.

D'Apponyi, Rudolf, *Vingt Cinq Ans à Paris*, private pressing, Bibliothèque Nationale, Paris, 1835 (Shelf No.8 M. 1645).

Attwood, William G., *The Lioness and the Little One*, Columbia University Press, New York, 1980.

Bauer, W. A. and Deutsch, O. E., *Mozart: Briefe und Aufzeichnungen*, Bärenreiter Kassel, Basel, 1975.

Beckett, Walter, *Liszt*, J. M. Dent and Sons, London, 1956.

Bergan, Ronald, *Theatres of London*, Prion, London, 1987.

Berlioz, Hector (ed. David Cairns), *Memoirs*, Victor Gollancz, London, 1977.

Boissier, Auguste, *Liszt Pédagogue: Leçons de piano données par Liszt à Mlle Valérie Boissier en 1832*, Honore Champion, Paris, 1927.

Bory, Robert, *La Vie de Franz Liszt par l'image*, Les Editions Contemparaines, Geneva, 1936.

Branson, David, *Jhon Field and Chopin*, Barrie and Jenkins, London, 1972.

Brunner, Herbert, *Altes Residenztheater in München*, Bayerische Verwaltung, Munich, 1990.

Buchner, Alexander, *Franz Liszt in Bohemia*, Peter Nevill, London, 1962.

Burger, Ernst, *Liszt*, Paul List Verlag, Munich, 1986.

Cairns, David, *Berlioz 1803–1832*, André Deutsch, London, 1989.

Chantavoine, Jean, *Maîtres de la Musique*, Félix Alcan, Paris, 1910.

Chopin, Frederick (ed. Arthur Hedley), *Selected Correspondence*, Heinemann, London, 1962.

Chopin, Frederick (ed. Henryk

Opieński), *Letters*, Dover Publications, New York, 1988.

Chopin, Frederick (ed. Bronislaw Edward Sydów), *Korespondencja Fryderyka Chopina*, Panstwowy Instytut Wydawniczy, Warsaw, 1955.

Crowest, Frederick, *Cherubini*, Sampson Low Marston and Co., London, 1890.

Czerny, Car (ed. Walter Kolneder), *Errinerungen meinem Leben* (MS), Gesellschaft der Musikfreunde, Vienna, 1842.

Dupêchez, Charles, *Marie d'Agoult*, Polon, Paris, 1989.

Ehrlich, Cyril, *The Piano*, J. M. Dent and Sons, London, 1976.

Eigeldinger, Jean-Jacques, *Chopin Pianist and Teacher*, Cambridge University Press, Cambridge, 1986.

Elkin, Robert, *The Old Concert Rooms of London*, Edward Arnold, London, 1955.

Elliot, J. H., *Berlioz*, J. M. Dent and Sons, London, 1937.

Fontaney, Antoine, *Journal Intime 1831–36*, Les Presses Françaises, Paris, 1925.

Giraud, Victor, *La Vie Tragique de Lamennais*, Félix Alcan, Paris, 1933.

Haldane, Charlotte, *The Galley Slaves of Love*, Harvill Press, London, 1957.

Hallé, Sir Charles (ed. C. E. Hallé), *Life and Letters*, Smith, Elder and Co., London, 1896.

Harding, Rosamund, E., *The Piano-Forte*, Gresham Books, London, 1978.

Haweis, H. R., *My Musical Life*, Longman Green and Co., London, 1896.

Hervey, Arthur, *Franz Liszt and His Music*, Bodley Head, London, 1911.

Hill, Ralph, *Liszt*, Duckworth, London, 1936.

Holmes, Edward, *A Ramble Among Music and Music Professors in Germany*, Hunt and Clarke, London, 1828.

Horvath, Emmerich Karl, *Franz Liszt* (Volumes 1 and 2), Nentwich/Inh., Eisenstadt, 1980.

Hughes, Rosemary, *Haydn*, J.M. Dent and Sons, London, 1956.

Huneker, James, *Liszt*, Rosl et Cie, Munich, 1922.

Liszt, Franz, *Diary 1832* (MS), Bibliothèque Nationale, Paris.

Liszt, Franz (ed. Marie La Mara), *Letters*, H. Grevel and Co., London, 1894.

Liszt, Franz, *Chopin*, William Reeves, London, 1912.

Liszt, Franz, *The Gipsy in Music*, William Reeves, London, 1926.

Locke, Ralph P., *Music, Musicians and the Saint-Simonians*, University of Chicago Press, Chicago, 1986.

MacKenzie, Alexander, *A Musicians's Narrative*, Cassell and Co., London, 1927.

Mackenzie-Grieve, Averil, *Clara Novello*, Geoffrey Bles, London, 1963.

Michotte, Edmond, *Richard Wagner's Visit to Rossini*, University of Chicago Press, Chicago, 1968.

Morrison, Bryce, *Liszt*, Omnibus Press, London, 1989.

Moscheles, Constance, *Life of Moscheles*, Hurst and Blackett, London, 1873.

Neumann, Philipp von, *Diary*, Philip Alan and Co., London, 1928.

Niecks, Frederick, *Frédéric Chopin as Man and Musician*, Novello, London, 1888.

Normington, Susan, *Napoleon's Children*, Alan Sutton, Stroud, 1993.

Norris, Gerald, *A Musical Gazeteer*, David and Charles, London, 1981.

Novello, Vincent and Mary (ed. Rosemary Hughes), *A Mozart Pilgrimage*, Eulenburg Books, London, 1975.

Orrey, Lesley, *Bellini*, J. M. Dent and Sons, London, 1969.

Pourtalès, Guy de, *Liszt et Chopin*, Gallimard, Paris, 1926.

Perenyi, Eleanor, *Liszt*, Weidenfeld and Nicolson, London, 1974.

Radcliffe, Philip, *Mendelssohn*, J. M. Dent and Sons, London, 1976.

Reeve, Henry (ed. John Knox Laughton), *Memoirs of Life and Correspondence*, Longman Green and Co., London, 1898.

Robbins Landon, H. C. *Haydn: The Early Years*, Thames and Hudson, London, 1980.

Rosnak, Hans, *Der Wunderknabe aus Raiding*, Belvedere Verlag, Eisenstadt, 1985.

Schonberg, Harold, *The Great Pianists*, Victor Gollancz, London, 1964.

Scott, J. M., *George Sand*, Heron Books, Geneva, 1969.

Scott, Marion M., *Beethoven*, J. M. Dent and Sons, London, 1965.

Shelley, Lady Francis (ed. Richard Edgcombe), *Diary 1787–1873*, John Murray, London, 1912.

Sitwell, Sacheverell, *Liszt*, Dover Publications, New York, 1967.

Smart, Sir George, *Leaves from the Journals*, H. B. Cox and C. L. Cox, London, 1907.

Smith, Ronald, *Alkan*, Crescendo Publishing, New York, 1977.

Sokoloff, Alice Hunt, *Cosima Wagner*, MacDonald, London, 1969.

Stearns, Peter, *Lamennais: Priest and Revolutionary*, Harper and Row, London, 1967.

Strelezki, Anton, *Personal Recollections of Chats with Liszt*, E. Donajowski, London, 1893.

Sugden, John, *Niccolò Paganini*, Midas Books, Tunbridge Wells, 1980.

Taylor, Ronald, *Franz Liszt*, Grafton Books, London, 1986.

Taylor, Ronald, *Robert Schumann*, Granada, London, 1982.

Tiersot, Julien, *Les Années Romantiques*, Calmann-Lévy, Paris, 1904.

Till, Nicholas, *Rossini*, Midas Books, Tunbridge Wells, 1983.

Tomlinson, Craig, *Felix Mendelssohn*, Cassell, London, 1984.

Walker, Alan, *Franz Liszt: The Virtuoso Years*, Faber and Faber, London, 1983.

Weilgung, Hedwig and Handrick, Willy, *Franz Liszt*, Volksverlag, Weimar, 1958.

Whitehouse, H. Remsen, *A Revolutionary Princess*, T. Fisher Unwin, London, 1906.

Wilkinson, Anthony, *Liszt*, Macmillan, London, 1975.

Williams, Adrian, *Portrait of Liszt*, Clarendon Press, Oxford, 1990.

Other Sources

Durey, Philippe, *Musée des Beaux Arts, Lyon*, Réunion des musées nationaux, Paris, 1995.

Imbert, Daniel, *Saint Vincent de Paul*, Bureau des Musées, Paris, 1983.

Keeling, Geraldine, 'Liszt's Appearances in Parisian Concerts, 1824–44', *Liszt Society Journal*, Vol. 11, 1986, and Vol. 12, 1987.

Liszt, Franz, Letter to Madame Eders (1829), Rosenthal Collection, Library of Congress, Washington, DC.

Martz, Claudine, *Château de Pourtalès*, Dernières Nouvelles d'Alsace, Strasbourg, 1986.

Musée Instrumentale du Conservatoire (catalogue), Paris, 1979.

Ollivier, Daniel, *Correspondence of Liszt and Countess Marie d'Agoult*, Liszt Society, London, 1995.

Pocknell, Pauline, 'Franz Liszt à Bourges', *Cahier d'Archéologie et d'Histoire du Berry*, No. 113, 1993.

Schuster, Bernard, *Die Musik*, Vol. 19, 1905–6, and Vol. 35, 1909–10, Schuster and Loeffler, Berlin.

Wróblewska-Straus, Hanna and Eckhardt, Maria, *Chopin and Liszt Exhibition* (catalogue), Warsaw, 1995.

Various authors, *ein Genie aus dem Pannonischen Raum*, Burgenländisches Landesmuseen, Eisenstadt, 1986.

Winkler, Gerhard J., 'Franz Liszts Kinderheit' in *Landessonderaustellung 1985/6* (catalogue), Burgenlandische Landesmuseen, Eisenstadt, 1996.

Notre Dame de Lorette, Art, Culture et Foi, Paris, 1990.

Le Kaleidoscope, Volume 2,
Bordeaux, 1826.

Cowdroy's Manchester Gazette,
August 1824–December 1827,
Manchester.

Flora, October–November 1823,
Nos 162–5, 169–72, 177, 180,
Munich.

Gazette des Salons, 1835–7, Paris.

L'Indicateur, 7, 9, 11, 25 and 26
January 1826, Bordeaux.

Jounal de Dijon, 20 December
1826.

Journal du Gard, 18 March 1826,
Nîmes.

Le Mémorial Bordelais, Nos. 4817,
4834 and 4836, Bordeaux,
1826.

Morning Post, May–July 1824,
London.

Münchener Politische Zeitung,
September–October 1823,
Nos. 230, 237, 244, 245, 249,
254, Munich.

The Sun, June–August 1824,
May–June 1825, London.

Discography

Howard, Leslie, (piano), *The Young Liszt,* Hyperion, CDA66771/2.
Conductor: Pál Tamás, *Don Sanche* (complete); soloists: Hungarian
R&TV Chorus, Hungarian State Opera Orchestra, Hungaroton,
HCD 12744-45-2.

Index